TO HELEN

Preface

SEVERAL YEARS AGO, Irving H. Bartlett called my attention to the large Moses Brown manuscript collection in the Rhode Island Historical Society Library. James B. Hedges, who is writing a three-volume history of the Brown family, remarked on the presence of additional Moses Brown material in the Brown Papers in the John Carter Brown Library of Brown University and in the Moses Brown School Library of Providence. It was with Mr. Hedges' encouragement that I undertook to write a biography of Moses Brown. I am equally indebted to Edmund S. Morgan, who gave me the benefit of his valuable criticism over the years.

I would also like to acknowledge the assistance I have received from numerous other people. Lawrence C. Wroth of the John Carter Brown Library gave me access to the Brown Papers, and Miss Marion W. Adams and Miss Jeannette S. Black were always ready to assist me in my search for material. William G. Roelker, Clifford S. Monahon, and Clarkson A. Collins III of the Rhode Island Historical Society responded generously to my many requests for material and assistance. L. Ralston Thomas, Headmaster of the Moses

Brown School, secured permission for me to study the Moses Brown manuscripts in the school library and Mrs. Helen J. Paxton, the school librarian, gave cheerful and generous assistance.   David P. Jonah of the John Hay Library of Brown University, Miss Mary T. Quinn of the Rhode Island Archives in Providence, and Thomas Edward Drake of Haverford College also were very helpful.   I am indebted to Muriel D. Hicks of the Library of the Society of Friends at Friends House on Euston Road in London for the photograph of Moses Brown's house.   Mrs. Etta Soireff Onat of Brown and Henry J. Cadbury and Donald H. Fleming of Harvard read the original manuscript and gave me valuable suggestions.

Finally, I wish to thank the editorial staff of the Institute of Early American History and Culture for seeing this manuscript through the press.   I owe a special word of thanks to E. James Ferguson and James Morton Smith for their penetrating criticism and sound advice.

Mack Thompson

Riverside, California
May 1, 1962

Table of Contents

Illustrations

MOSES BROWN

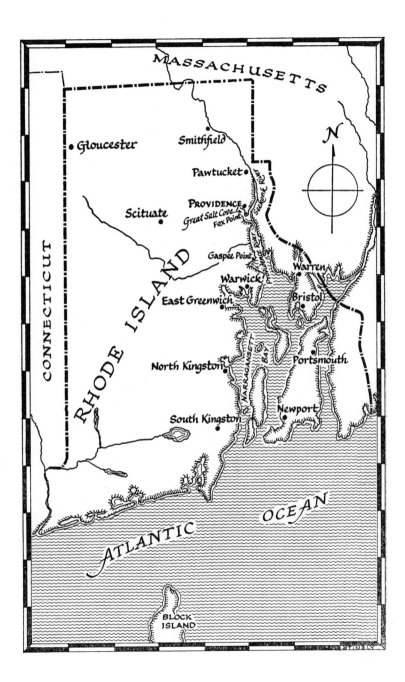

Prologue

THE HOUR was late. The candle on the high desk had burned far down; it alternately sputtered and burned bright. The old man sat reading from a sheet of paper, the last of several piled neatly before him on the desk. When he had finished he slipped it under the others, and, after a few moments' contemplation, took up his quill, dipped it, and slowly but in a firm hand wrote at the top of the first page, "TRUTH a chosen Description of Truth and Eror," and signed his name, "James Browne A servant of the Lord Jesus Christ. Advice to all men to refuse Eror and Chuse Truth."[1]

This scene is not completely imaginary. James Brown was elder of the First Baptist Church of Providence in the English colony of Rhode Island. When he wrote this sermon for delivery to his congregation in the meetinghouse on Sunday, he was in the last year of his life. He would not deliver many more sermons. This one had a special significance for him. Elder Brown had always taken an interest in the

1. *James Browne: His Writings In Prose and Verse Concerning the First Settling of the Town of Providence and a Memorandum of his Efforts to Prevent a Separation in the Baptist Congregation there in October, 1731: Together with Some Metrical Observations* (Boston, Mass., 1917), 4.

spiritual welfare of his neighbors but recently he had become greatly disturbed by what he thought was an accelerated decline of piety among the church members. This trend he attributed to events that were taking place all about him.

Providence in 1731 was no longer the small agricultural community he remembered as a young man. Then only an occasional ship from England, the West Indies, or one of the southern ports had tied up at the stick of a wharf in the Great Salt Cove below the main street. Then he had known every man, woman, and child by sight. Now there were strange faces in the town, and trading ships were no longer a rare sight in the harbor. New shops had sprung up, and there was a bustle of activity along the water front that made him knit his brow as he walked down to the meetinghouse to consult his colleague, Pardon Tillinghast, about the Sunday service. Meetings were still well attended, but too many communicants seemed to be there as a matter of habit; they were more interested in earning profits in this life than attaining salvation for the next. Now was the time for plain speaking. He would "wright something by way of description of Truth and Eror" to warn his congregation of the dangers of this new age of commercialism.

"Truth" James depicted in terms of "the man of God" who "laboreth under a promise of salvation which neither the flesh nor the devil can take from him."[2] "Eror" was associated with the "marchant man" who, although he could take great delight in seeing his shop full of customers, should not make the mistake of thinking that he was as secure as the man of God. Profits, the things the merchant labored for, were uncertain; he could never be sure when he would lose them or who would enjoy them when he was gone. When James delivered his sermon, his comparison of "the man of God" and the "marchant man," to the discredit of the latter, must have been obvious to a part of his congrega-

2. *Ibid.*, 6-7.

tion—the rising generation of businessmen in the town, who were turning from the soil to the sea, and, according to Elder Brown, from God to the Devil.

Brown's sermon had a poignancy that reflected more than a concern for the souls of his parishioners. He had not been able to bar the door of his own house against the evil, commercialism; his own son, James, Jr., was a merchant. By failing to become an elder in the Baptist Church, the boy had departed from a family tradition established nearly a century earlier by Chad Brown, the first member of the family to come to Providence. Chad had been known for his "holiness," and was the "first settled Pastor of the Baptist Church" in Providence, or so his descendants claimed with pride. Subsequent Browns followed in his footsteps, until the arrival of James Brown, Jr. This is not to say that young James was irreligious, but whereas the father certainly identified himself with "the man of God" in his sermon, the son was definitely "the marchant man." It was no accident that James recorded his children's births in his business ledger and not in the family Bible. The possibility of larger profits in commercial enterprise had caused young James to lift his eyes from the soil that had been tilled by his father and his father's father, and to gaze longingly toward the sea. Commerce was not only profitable, it was becoming highly respectable. James deserted the plow and the pulpit for the quarterdeck and the countinghouse, thus establishing a tradition that was to endure for decades.

He started his career in business at an early age. In 1721, when only twenty-three, he was commander and part owner of a sloop named the *Four Batchelors,* that he took to the Leeward Islands in the West Indies.[3] The voyage must have

3. Moses Brown Papers, Miscellaneous Papers, I, 1, Rhode Island Historical Society Library, Providence, Rhode Island, hereafter referred to as Moses Brown Papers. The basic book on the business activities of the Brown family is James B. Hedges, *The Browns of Providence Plantations: Colonial Years* (Cambridge, Mass., 1952).

been a success, for soon after his return James opened a shop on Towne Street, opposite his home, near the Wading Place in the center of town. Since in early America capital was scarce and investment risky, the businessmen did not chance everything in one venture. James did not confine himself to the shipping trade or to shopkeeping, but over the years drew within the compass of his activities a rum distillery and a slaughter house. He was a frequent moneylender, slaver on at least one occasion, and a whaler when the season was particularly good. He was also a farmer, for he owned land on the outskirts of the town, where he grew crops and grazed cows, horses, and other stock. The inventory of his estate, probably made by his younger brother Obadiah, shows that when he died on April 26, 1739, he owned four Negro slaves—the mark of a man of means.[4]

James Brown, Jr., survived his father only seven years. His early death was attributed to an injury sustained in a weight-lifting contest at a fair in Providence. Although not a big man he apparently possessed great strength and was fond of demonstrating his powers. On this occasion he over-taxed himself "and hurt his constitution and some of the internal visserary, that at times affected his nervous system."[5] In the spring of 1736 during a short illness, he wrote the following public letter: "This may sarve to notifie all my neighbours, that if it be the pleasure of the heavens to take the breath out of my mortal body before it is their pleasure to raise me up and to enable me to assist and support them again as I have done in time past, I am quite free and willing that my body may be opened, in order that my fellow cretures and neighbours may see whether my grievance hath been nothing but the spleen or not."[6] There is a prophetic

4. Probate Court Records, A 411, Probate Docket No. 1, Book W, No. 3, 355-60, City Hall, Providence.
5. Moses Brown to Nicholas Brown, Jr., Aug. 20, 1823, Moses Brown Papers, XIV, 23.
6. Moses Brown Papers, I, 1. See also Moses Brown to Nicholas Brown, Jr., Aug. 20, 1828, ibid., 22.

note here, for as if to prove that his "grievance" was not due entirely to his "spleen," James Brown died within a year of his announcement. He was forty-one, father of six children, and one of the most successful businessmen in the town.

The lives of James, the man of business, and his father, the man of God, symbolized a conflict between the flesh and the spirit that became one of the distinguishing characteristics of the Brown family. In its early manifestations the clash came between father and son; in the next generation it came between two brothers, John and Moses. And in the case of Moses it was combined within one person, although it lay dormant in his soul for thirty years while he learned the shipping trade. Moses was the youngest of James Brown's five sons.

I

The Apprenticeship

PROVIDENCE LIES in the northwestern part of Rhode
Island only a few miles from the Massachusetts border.
It stands astride the Providence or Great Salt River
at the head of the great Bay of Narragansett that stretches
down to Newport and the Atlantic. In the eighteenth century, a score of sloops, schooners, and brigantines could ride
safely at anchor in a great salt cove near the center of town
while their owners outfitted them for a new voyage to the
southern coast, the West Indies, or England. The most
important part of town lay on the eastern bank of the river.
There the land rose sharply up to a plateau that stretched
eastward to the Seekonk River. The shoreline was obscured
by a clutter of warehouses and shops. Wharfs jutted un-
evenly into the river like the broken spokes of a rimless
wheel. On the slope two streets of houses, some brightly
painted, others weathered by the salt air, ran for half a mile
from Fox Point on the bay inland parallel to the river. In
the early years of the colony the land that extended back
from the river towards the plateau had been divided among
the first settlers, and there they had built their houses and
cultivated their fields. Over the years the plateau had be-

come a patchwork of orchards, grazing fields, and gardens. From the plateau a road led down to the narrowest part of the river where a bridge connected the east side of the town to the west side.

It was on the east side that the first Browns settled. Chad Brown and his family arrived in Boston from England aboard the ship *Martin* in 1638 but quickly moved to Providence. Chad was a man of strong character and exceptional ability. He soon rose to a position of eminence in the civil and spiritual affairs of the tiny commonwealth. Two years after his arrival he was chosen one of five arbitrators to settle a serious land dispute that divided the colony. The same committee drew up a new frame of government—"the Combination"—which served for several years. He was an elder in the Baptist Church and a man of deep religious feelings. Subsequent generations of Browns followed in Chad's footsteps, adding occasionally to the family's property holdings, continuing their interest in the Baptist religion, and extending their influence by marrying into other prominent families throughout the colony.

Moses Brown was thus born into a family that had lived in Providence for a hundred years. His father recorded his birth in "James Browne's First Ledger": "Heir folloth the time of the bearth of the children born of the boddey of hope Brown wife of James. . . . Seventh and Lastly Moses September the 12 AD 1738."[1] For fifteen years Moses celebrated his birthday on that date, but in 1752 the Gregorian calendar was adopted in the British Empire and thereafter the celebration was held on September 23.

Moses' mother, Hope (Power) Brown, left no account of her life or of her son's childhood, but he undoubtedly attended the Baptist Church with other members of the family

1. James Brown: His Book of Accounts Both Debt and Credit, 1, R. I. Hist. Soc. Moses was probably born in the old Homestead House on Towne Street near what is now the junction of College and North Main Streets.

and held the conventional religious beliefs of the time and place. George Taylor, a Church of England man, kept a schoolhouse for a time near the Quaker meetinghouse in the north end of town, and Moses may have received his early education from him.[2] There is a legend—perhaps true— that Moses attended school until he was thirteen; at any rate, by the time he had reached his teens he could "read, write, and do a sum in the rule of three."

Whatever formal education he received was supplemented by informal schooling at home, in his uncle's countinghouse, and on the Providence wharfs. As a boy he was fascinated by the busy water front and often waited on his uncle's wharf for the sloop *Four Brothers* to tie up after a voyage of several months to the West Indies. As a nephew of the owner, he was undoubtedly allowed to satisfy his curiosity about the ship and cargo and to question the master and crew about their experiences in the Indies, on the Guinea Coast, or at one of the southern ports. He quickly won a reputation as an expert judge of West Indian molasses. The story is frequently told of the importer who was asked by a prospective buyer "What casks are your best?" and the reply, "Ask that little molasses-faced Moses, he will tell you."[3]

Moses' education in business really began when he moved from his home on Towne Street to his uncle's house across the lane and started his apprenticeship in the shipping business. Removal to his uncle's home was dictated by common sense. James, Moses' oldest brother who had probably assumed responsibility for Moses' education, had recently died while on a voyage to Virginia. The other brothers, Nicholas, Joseph, and John, were serving their apprenticeship with uncle Obadiah, and were still not old enough to look after

2. Petitions to the Rhode Island General Assembly, 1734-38, III, 20, Rhode Island Archives, State House, Providence, hereafter cited as R. I. Archives.
3. Hedges, *The Browns*, 14.

their young brother. Since Moses was expected to follow them into the shipping business, what could be better than close association with a man of Uncle Obadiah's proven business acumen. To a certain extent, his uncle also would fill the vacancy left by the death of his father. Moses was Obadiah's favorite nephew, and since Obadiah had no male heir, he expected Moses to become a partner in his business and attend to his personal affairs after his death. Shortly after Moses was taken into the family, these plans were formalized. In his will Obadiah assigned his adopted son the same share in his estate that he granted to each of his four daughters.[4] Moses left no record of the nine years he spent in his uncle's home, but his life there was apparently pleasant. Later he referred to Obadiah as "Father Brown," or "my dear Uncle," and named his first son after him.

Moses' years as an apprentice in his uncle's business coincided with important developments in the Rhode Island economy.[5] During the 1750's Newport rivaled Boston, New York, and Philadelphia as a shipping center, and Providence was coming on fast as a commercial center. Obadiah extended his shipping trade beyond the usual ports of call in the British, Dutch, and French islands in the West Indies to include ventures into such widely separated areas as Newfoundland and the coast of South America. When the French and Indian War began in the middle of the decade, he took advantage of the great profits to be made in the illicit trade with the foreign islands, particularly the French. And in an effort to break the dependence of Rhode Island on imports of English goods from Boston and New York, Obadiah even sent a ship directly to London.

During Moses' apprenticeship Obadiah was not only expanding his shipping interests abroad, he was diversifying

4. Probate Court Records, A 807, Book W, No. 5, 305-7, City Hall, Providence. The will is dated "March 14, 1753—26th year of Geo. II's reign."
5. Hedges, *The Browns*, 8-9.

his activities at home. He started a mill to grind into choco-
late the cocoa bean he imported, and he distributed it through
his store on the water front. He became a marine insurance
underwriter and a moneylender when he could get a good
rate of interest. By far the most significant enterprise that
Obadiah initiated, and the one that Moses participated in
most actively, was the manufacture and sale of spermaceti
candles. Unlike some of the colonies, Rhode Island had no
staple crop which her merchants could export to pay for the
goods imported from England. The development of the
candle manufacturing business was one of Obadiah's efforts
to solve the problem. In addition to the expansion of the
shipping trade and new manufacturing enterprises, Obadiah
sent at least one ship to the African coast on a slaving expedition. The slave trade did not, however, form an important
part of his business; it was not the source of his wealth. In
fact, Obadiah may have had misgivings about his involvement in the slave trade, for in his will he freed one of his
Negro servants and gave him twenty acres of land.

Moses' first duties as apprentice in his uncle's countinghouse were of a miscellaneous nature. He ran errands
around town, carried messages to the company ships at the
town wharf along the Salt River, to shops of other businessmen on Towne Street, across the bridge to the west side, or
up the river to Tockwotton where the spermaceti candle
factory was located. When he was sixteen he went on horseback to Newport on company business; later, he copied letters, kept the insurance and shipping ledger books, and at
the age of eighteen began transacting routine business in his
own name.[6]

With the construction and development of the candle
works he also kept the records of that enterprise, a task he

6. Obadiah Brown, Misc. MSS., B-814, unbound MSS., R. I. Hist. Soc.
Moses' business activities can be traced in the Brown Papers in the John
Carter Brown Library, Providence, hereafter cited as Brown Papers.

shared with his brother Joseph, who was nearing the end of his training. Moses probably learned double-entry book-keeping from his brothers and from uncle Obadiah's 1729 edition of *A Guide to Book Keepers according to the Italian Manner*.[7] As he became more familiar with the intricacies of his uncle's business, and demonstrated that he possessed common sense and the necessary discretion to be trusted with company secrets, Moses made frequent trips to Boston as well as Newport. He became acquainted with many of the leading merchants in those busy ports, and some of the rough edges of the boy from the small community on the Providence River were worn off.

Moses was too young to participate in the French and Indian War when it began in 1756. But the following year, when news reached the town that the enemy was about to break through the thin defenses English troops were maintaining in the west, he watched the militia form and march away to defend the colony against attack. They had gone only a few miles when news arrived in Providence that the enemy had been driven back and the danger had passed. Moses was dispatched on horseback to bear the glad tidings to the men. This was as close as the future Quaker ever came to participating in war. When he was an old man he looked back on the event with some amusement and recorded the details as "an historical fact worth preserving."[8]

Moses' business education was not confined to bookkeeping or carrying messages for his uncle and brothers. He also learned how to navigate ships and to transact company business in other American ports. James, his oldest brother, had owned several useful books on navigation and seamanship, including one of his own composition called *Geometrical Problems*, and another, *The English Pilot, the Fourth Book Describing the West India Navigation from Hudson's Bay*

7. Hedges, *The Browns*, 5.
8. Moses Brown Papers, Misc. MSS., B-814, Box 2.

to the River Amazones, published in London in 1745.[9] Like
his brother Joseph, Moses had a flare for mathematics, and
after he had quickly mastered the elementary material in the
family library, he ordered advanced texts from friends in
New York and New Haven. He had a chance to widen his
book knowledge after 1754 when his brothers Nicholas and
John, with several other prominent men of the town, formed
a library, purchased a collection of books, and placed them
in the council chamber of the Colony House for public use.
In December 1758, when the Colony House burned and the
library with it, Moses took an active interest in the movement to rebuild the library and replace the collection, and
he served as clerk of the meetings of the Proprietors of the
Providence Library in 1760 when they were conducting a
lottery for that purpose.[10]

Life for Moses during the years of his apprenticeship was
not all work. During the summer months there were excur-
sions with his friends down Narragansett Bay, "Turtle
frolicks" along the river, and pleasant evenings in Luke
Thurston's tavern near the Great Bridge or in Joseph Olney's
inn at the top of Stamper's Hill. And the letters Moses
wrote to friends who were attending Yale College show that
he courted the young ladies of the town frequently.[11] When
he was twenty, Moses became a Mason in St. John's Lodge
of Providence, and he spent many hours with his friends at
the meetings.[12] He served as secretary of the lodge for ten
years and discharged his responsibilities to everyone's satisfaction. When he became a Quaker in 1774, he severed his

9. Hedges, *The Browns,* 10. James' composition is in the R. I. Hist. Soc.
10. William R. Staples, *Annals of the Town of Providence, from its First
Settlement, to the organization of the City Government, in June, 1832* (Providence, 1843), 534, hereafter cited as *Annals of Providence.*
11. Moses Brown Papers, I, 10.
12. For a list of Providence members of the Lodge, see the petitions to the
Rhode Island General Assembly, 1758-61, X, 82, R. I. Archives. See also
Henry W. Rugg, *History of Freemasonry in Rhode Island* (Providence, 1895).

formal connection with the fraternity, although he maintained an interest in its activities.

By the time Moses reached the age when most apprenticeships expired, he was thoroughly familiar with all phases of his uncle's business and was known from Boston to Charleston as a trusted representative of Obadiah Brown and Company. He was particularly noted for his knowledge of the West India trade. Requests came to him from merchants in New York and Philadelphia for information about prices and trading prospects in Surinam, Antigua, Monte Cristo, or Port-au-Prince.

In 1760 Moses' apprenticeship ended, and he inherited a farm from his father's estate of 145 acres in Providence Neck, an area to the rear of the settled portion of town.[13] Moses celebrated these events with a trip, perhaps his first, to Philadelphia.[14] Boarding the *Charles Moley* in Providence, he sailed from Widow Tillinghast's wharf "on Sunday June 8th at 5 P.M. . . . On bord the sloop as passengers, John Brown, Abraham Smith, Joseph Mowry, Isaih Hawkins and Saly Smith for Newport and Widow Mary Hopkins for Philadelphia." An hour and a half underway, they ran aground on "the sunken rocks," probably the shoals that became famous shortly before the Revolution as Gaspee Point. They lay there until the tide floated them off at half-past three in the morning, when they proceeded to the Quaker City without further incident.

Moses left no account of his activities in the big city, but on his return trip he stopped off in New York and rode over to see Dr. William Barnett's hospital for smallpox inoculation in East New Jersey. The frequent appearance of that disease in New England and its dire effects had stimulated great interest in inoculation, or variolation as it was called,

13. "Brown Family Personal Letters," March 15, 1760, Brown Papers, P-B7.
14. "On Board Charles Moley Sunday June 8th at 5 p.m. 1760 to Monday 16th June," Moses Brown Papers, Misc. MSS., I, 8.

which was practiced in most of the colonies by the middle
of the eighteenth century.[15] In April, Jabez Bowen, one of
Moses' friends, had taken the cure in Windham, Connecticut, and Moses was curious to try it himself. His desire was
intensified in this instance by the fact that Boston had suffered from a particularly virulent smallpox attack in 1760;
he feared that the disease would spread to Rhode Island.
But Moses seldom ventured anything without first making a thorough investigation. He wanted to see Dr. Barnett's inoculation hospital for himself, and he prolonged
his trip to inspect the establishment. Apparently satisfied
by what he saw there, and encouraged by the recovery of
Bowen, he returned to New Jersey and was himself inoculated. He came through the ordeal without incident and
wrote to Dr. Barnett thanking him for his hospitality. Inoculation against smallpox was not only an advantage to his
health; it also qualified him to participate in the supervision
of the pest house in Providence, a task he performed for many
years. Moses' life-long interest in preventive medicine and
in the cure of disease originated at this time. Of more immediate importance was the association he made with Dr.
Barnett, which was a pleasant and lasting one. Convinced of
the value of inoculation, he served as Dr. Barnett's unofficial
agent in New England to steer prospective patients to the
hospital in New Jersey. He was largely responsible for
Barnett's coming to Massachusetts and setting up another
hospital on Point Shirley, where John Brown and many
other Rhode Islanders were inoculated.

When Moses received his inheritance, he was no longer
an errand boy in Uncle Obadiah's countinghouse or an occasional partner in a voyage to the West Indies. A serious
young man of twenty-two years, he had enough property,

15. There is a long discussion of smallpox in colonial America in John
Duffy, *Epidemics in Colonial America* (Baton Rouge, La., 1953), 16-112. His
statement that inoculation was practiced in all the colonies by 1750 appears
to be without foundation as far as Rhode Island is concerned.

business experience, and potential to take his place beside his uncle and brothers as one of the leading citizens of Providence. Both the town and the colony admitted him as a freeman with full political rights, and his uncle made him a full partner in his shipping business, Obadiah Brown and Company.[16]

He also acquired an interest in the candle works.[17] Obadiah Brown and his nephews were well on their way to becoming the largest manufacturers of candles in the colonies. Technical difficulties of refining the spermaceti oil and of manufacturing the candles had finally been ironed out and the "Works" was functioning smoothly. Obadiah served as general manager of the candle works, Joseph was production manager, Nicholas and John were concerned primarily with the marketing of the finished product, and Moses performed the duties of purchasing agent and traveling salesman. At first he shared this role with brother John, but soon he assumed the major responsibility for the job. It fell to him naturally, for his brothers had served their tour of duty in that capacity. Moses was still single and it was less of a hardship for him to be away from home than it was for his brothers. His responsibilties sent him on repeated trips to Nantucket, where he bargained with the suppliers of whale oil—the Starbucks, the Husseys, the Rotches, the Coffins, the Folgers—and bought whalebone and fish. When in Nantucket, Moses usually stayed with Sylvanus Hussey, Heziah Coffin, or Benjamin Tupper, who wrote him long chatty letters when he returned to Providence.[18]

Moses played a significant role in the negotiations leading

16. Deputies and Freemen, Providence, 1732-1778, 88, R. I. Hist. Soc.; *Rhode Island Acts and Resolves, 1758-62*, May sess., 1760 (facsimile no. 27, publ. by J. Harry Bongartz, n.d., Providence).

17. The correspondence concerning the spermaceti candle business is voluminous. Moses' activities may be followed in the Brown Papers, P-U5; in Obadiah Brown, Misc. MSS., 1742-57, 1758-62, 1759, R. I. Hist. Soc., and in Moses Brown Papers, I.

18. Moses Brown Papers, I, 48, 76, 77.

to the formation of the "United Company of Spermaceti Chandlers" in November 1761 and in the subsequent agreements that were made over the years. A complicated venture which associated the Browns with other candle manufacturers of Providence, Newport, and Boston, the United Company attempted to divide the limited supply among the manufacturers and to control the price of whale oil according to agreement.[19] As buyer for the Browns, Moses was required to honor the agreements and at the same time safeguard the interests of the company, a job requiring skill and sharp wits. As a result of the experience acquired in bargaining with the suppliers of oil on Nantucket Island, he acquired a keen knowledge of human nature and a wide reputation as an able negotiator.

For almost a decade after 1760 Moses and his brothers did not engage in the London trade, relying instead on Boston or Newport for English dry goods, hardware, and other merchandise which they sold in their store or consumed in their own households. As purchasing agent Moses often visited Boston, where he discussed business matters with Henry Lloyd, the company agent resident in the city, and with Boston members of the "Spermaceti Trust."

In the summer of 1762 Moses' role as a young partner in a large and expanding business was abruptly changed when his uncle unexpectedly died. Obadiah was riding from his business house in Providence to his summer home in Gloucester when he was taken ill "with a stopage of the surculation of the fluids and some what like a billious colick with which he continued only 48 hours, he dyed on the 17th Ultimo."[20] The attack caught John and Moses in Newport on business, and when a messenger was sent to fetch them, Moses left

19. For the history of the spermaceti candle manufacture and the "Spermaceti Trust," see Hedges, *The Browns*, 86-122.
20. Moses Brown to Walter and Samuel Franklin, July 6, 1762, Brown Papers, P-F75. The letter is unsigned but in Moses' hand. See also Nicholas Brown to Francis & Relfe, July 6, 1762, *ibid.*, P-F7, I.

immediately for the bedside of his uncle, arriving in time to speak to him before he died. John characteristically remained behind "to compleat sum business of importance which was not done when he [Moses Brown] left Newport."[21] The contrasting pictures this incident reveals of the two men are not overdrawn. John seldom allowed personal considerations to interfere with his business activities. Not that he was purposely callous—on occasion he could be indulgent and considerate of others; but he was so intent on getting rich that he was frequently oblivious to anything that distracted him from attaining that goal.

As Obadiah's adopted son and business partner, Moses naturally assumed the responsibility of looking after his uncle's affairs—settling his debts, drawing up an inventory of his estate, filing the necessary papers with the town clerk, and providing for his wife and daughters. Obadiah was one of the more well-to-do citizens of Providence. Moses' share of his property, added to the inheritance recently acquired from his father's estate, furnished him with capital to launch himself in the shipping business.

For some months, Moses was preoccupied as attorney for his uncle's estate. Settling estates in colonial America was often a long and tedious affair, and Moses discovered that Obadiah's estate was no exception. Collection of outstanding debts was the most difficult of all his duties; he engaged in this disagreeable job exclusively for several months during 1762, and intermittently for years. But Moses pursued delinquent debtors unremittingly until the estate was settled. One hard-pressed man who resisted Moses' persistent efforts to make him pay a trifling debt referred to him as "that damn little Moses."

The death of Obadiah Brown forced a reorganization of the candle works, the key to the Browns' business success. On November 18, 1762, the four brothers drew up an agree-

21. John Brown to Palmer & Belsher, June 18, 1762, *ibid.*, P-U5, I.

ment to share equally in the profits of the business and to continue its operation as in the past, with Joseph as production manager. In their other business ventures, Moses' brothers also decided to form a new family enterprise, organizing Nicholas Brown and Company for their shipping and commercial activities. For a time Moses seems to have weighed the advantages of continuing Obadiah Brown and Company under his own name. By the spring of 1763, however, he had resolved to join his brothers. As a full partner in the company Moses continued his activities much as before, with frequent trips to Nantucket to buy spermaceti oil and to Newport and Boston to negotiate with members of the "Spermaceti Trust."[22]

As business enterprises in the eighteenth century went, Nicholas Brown and Company was a fairly large, complex organization. Its success would depend upon the resourcefulness, energy, and sound business judgment of the four young brothers. Fortunately, Obadiah had trained his nephews well. Within a few years Nicholas Brown and Company had become one of the most successful businesses in the English colonies.

Nicholas, the oldest of the brothers, quickly stepped into his uncle's shoes as leader of the company. He possessed qualities that ideally suited him for such a role. A tall, well-built man, with a severe countenance that did not entirely conceal a placid personality, he was methodical in his habits and cautious in his business dealings, but he was not afraid of innovation and willingly took a plunge when there seemed to be a good chance for success. Business was risky during the 1760's, and many a trader was unable to make the adjustments demanded by war and peace, prosperity and depression. Nicholas' shrewd sense of timing permitted him to contract or expand an enterprise or to begin an entirely new line when circumstances made it the most profitable thing to

22. The agreement is in *ibid.*

do. He was the necessary balance wheel among a group of men of widely divergent interests and personalities.

John was in many respects the antithesis of his older brother. He was a big man, energetic and eager to get on in the world. He found business stimulating and tended to regard it as an end in itself. Full of schemes for expanding the activities of the company, he was never at a loss to suggest new enterprises and frequently lost patience with his more cautious or indifferent brothers. John discharged the civic obligations that were expected of a man of his position and wealth, but even at the age of twenty-eight, he was, like his father, first and foremost a businessman. In his efforts to satisfy a voracious appetite for money, he departed frequently from the accepted code of ethics in the business world and there were few years when he was not involved in disagreeable arguments with his brothers about company policy or in lawsuits with businessmen. Highly competitive and resourceful, he was probably the richest man in Providence by the time he was thirty.

Brother Joseph, described by his brothers as "a man with a speculative mind," was little concerned with money. He seemed uneasy among his more aggressive brothers, and found management of the candle works, located far from the center of town, more pleasant than the busy countinghouse, the docks at Newport, or the great wholesale houses in Boston. He left the formulation of company policy pretty much to his partners and confined his activities to things that interested him: the technology of candle manufacturing, the operation of the iron furnace when it was built in 1765, and in his leisure hours, the study of mechanics, electricity, and astronomy. Often ignoring the world of business and politics which his brothers John and Nicholas found so stimulating, Joseph built his own world of intellectual pursuits. As the years passed, Joseph drew closer to his younger brother Moses.

At twenty-five, Moses was a short, slight man, with bright eyes and a prominent nose that turned down toward a slightly jutting chin. Like Joseph he was somewhat withdrawn and given to introspection, a characteristic that became more pronounced as he grew older. Unlike John, who was a voluble talker, Moses was reticent in conversation. Just what effect being the youngest of four successful brothers had on his development, it is impossible to say. Perhaps his reticence was partly defensive. Thrust into a position of responsibility at an early age and forced to associate with men older and more experienced than himself, he developed the habit of remaining silent until he was sure of his ground. When he did speak, therefore, people usually listened, for his remarks reflected careful thought. This must have pleased him immensely, for in one of his rare unguarded moments he confessed to John a weakness for "popular approbation," which he added, was "a snare I am not unacquainted with."[23] He also had a suspicious streak in his nature that often led him to question others' motives, and he was just as quick to defend himself against the slightest imputation of wrong doing. Thus, he did not make friends easily, although he had a wide circle of acquaintances who respected him.

Shortly after Moses joined Nicholas Brown and Company, the brothers, in conjunction with Governor Stephen Hopkins and a number of other Providence businessmen, bought a recently discovered iron ore deposit near the town and established an iron manufacturing business.[24] The scheme may well have originated with Moses, who had already attempted to introduce the stocking weaving industry into Providence and to encourage the cultivation of mulberry trees for the growth of silkworms.[25] In any case, the brothers were un-

23. Moses Brown to John Brown, Providence, March 24, 1797, Moses Brown Papers, Misc. MSS., K-AB.

24. For the definitive account of the origin and operation of the Hope Furnace see Hedges, *The Browns,* chap. 6.

25. Moses Brown to Hezekiah Sabine, July 16, 1764, and Ephraim Bowen to Moses Brown, Sept. 2, 1764, Moses Brown Papers, I, 60.

doubtedly attracted to iron manufacturing because they thought it would provide them with another exportable item of domestic manufacture to help pay for imports. Their candle factory had turned out to be a great success; perhaps a similar venture would prove equally profitable. Cautious Nicholas had made a careful investigation of iron manufacturing in other colonies and concluded that the risk was worth taking.

By early summer 1765, the partners started construction of their furnace, and by the next summer they were ready to begin producing iron.[26] During these months, Moses and his brothers extended themselves to accumulate enough specie to finance the iron works. Moses spent long hours traveling to Newport to outfit ships for the West Indies trade and to Nantucket to buy supplies for the sake of increasing production at the candle factory. With his brothers he put in late hours in the company office going over the books trying to devise ways to cut costs and increase profits. During the summer and fall, Moses, Joseph, and John spent several weeks in Newport on a special project, fitting out the brig *Sally* for a slaving voyage which they hoped would net them large and quick profits. Moses had qualms about dealing in human lives, but because he himself owned slaves and because his brother John urged him to suppress his misgivings, he finally gave in—a decision he was later to regret.

Moses' role in the building and operation of the Hope Furnace was extensive. He made frequent trips to supervise its construction and operation and exerted a strong influence on the formulation of general policies in regard to production and distribution.[27] Stephen Hopkins, defeated in his bid for re-election as governor, joined Moses in directing the tests of the ores at a nearby furnace and in overseeing the

26. *Vox Populi, Vox Dei; A Providence Gazette Extraordinary*, Aug. 24, 1765.

27. Nicholas Brown & Co. to Job Hawkins, Dec. 5, 1765, and Job Hawkins to Moses Brown, June 27, 1765, Moses Brown Papers, I, 64.

construction of their own works. Perhaps Moses' most important service in the building of the iron works was to induce the Rhode Island Assembly to enact legislation necessary to the success of the project. The location of the furnace was of crucial importance; it had to be situated so that water power would be available, and it had to be near the ore beds. Moses and Governor Hopkins decided on a place called Salmon Hole in Scituate as the ideal location. The river would have to be dammed before its power could be utilized, but an old law specified that all dams on the river and its tributaries had to be kept open from April 10 to May 20 to allow fish to come up the river.[28] In August 1765, the owners of the furnace petitioned the General Assembly to invalidate the old law or exempt the furnace company from its provisions on the grounds that the Pawtuxet River was the only suitable place to build a furnace.[29] They observed that, unless their petition was granted, they would have to abandon a project of great benefit to the welfare of the people of Rhode Island and the neighboring colonies. Moses, when he was a deputy in the General Assembly from Providence, was charged by his partners with guiding the petition through the lower house, and it was because of his skill and persistence that it finally passed.

Moses did not devote all of his time during these busy years to business. In the course of his many visits to Newport and Boston, New York and Philadelphia, he enjoyed the amusements of the larger cities and acquired a new circle of friends. When acquaintances visited Providence he entertained them, introduced them to his family and friends, and inducted them into the social life of the town. For a while he carried on a flirtation with Polly Olney in competition with William Palfrey, grandson of one of the first

28. Journal House of Deputies, 1735, R. I. Archives; *Acts and Laws of Rhode Island, 1730-1736*, Aug. sess., 1735, 271 (facsimile no. 8, publ. by J. Harry Bongartz, n.d., Providence).

29. Journal House of Deputies, 1765-66, Sept. sess., 1765, R. I. Archives.

historians of New England.[30]   Alternately he courted his
cousin Anna "Nancy" Brown, Betty Kinnicutt, and Susannah
Crawford, escorting Susannah to his brother John's wedding.
By the summer of 1763 his feeling for his nineteen-year-old
cousin, daughter of Uncle Obadiah, had developed into
something more than the usual fondness one might expect.
Moses' brothers and friends were all married and raising
families; he too was apparently ready to settle down.   On
November 13, 1763, in a letter to his good friend Heziah
Coffin on Nantucket, he casually mentioned the important
step he was about to take: "My mother, sisters and the friend
whom I have chosen and intend for a partner before long for
my life, Anna Brown, join with me in our saying to you and
all the Coffins, if I can do you any service at anytime please
to command freely."[31]

John's wedding in 1760 had been the occasion for a turn-
out of all the ladies and gentlemen of the town.[32]   Carriages
and chairs had been borrowed to carry friends to the ceremony and the gala celebration that followed.   Such a lavish
spectacle was typical of John, who did things on a grand
scale, but Moses was not like his brother, and his wedding
was a modest affair.   The Reverend Samuel Winson, elder
of the First Baptist Church, who had married Moses' brothers,
now performed the ceremony for Moses and Anna.   The
Providence Gazette announced the union in the January 7
issue: "Last evening Mr. Moses Brown, of this Place, Merchant, was married to Miss Nancy Brown, (Daughter of the

30. Some of the correspondence dealing with this episode has been printed in the *Course of True Love in Colonial Times Being the Confessions of William Palfrey of Boston and the Friendly Advice of Moses Brown of Providence Concerning Polly Olney* (Boston, 1905). See also Moses Brown Papers, I, 33, 35, 38.
31. Moses Brown Papers, I, 56, and Coffin's reply, Sept. 13, 1764, *ibid.*, 61.
32. "List of Sundry persons who attended John Brown's wedding," Brown Papers, P-B7; Obadiah Brown & Co. to Walter & Samuel Franklin, Oct. 10, 1760, Moses Brown Papers, Austin MSS., pkg. XX, 1-11, Moses Brown School Library, Providence.

late Obadiah Brown, Esq;) an agreeable young lady, with a handsome Fortune."

During the early years of his marriage Moses was often absent from home transacting business for Nicholas Brown and Company or, after 1764, performing his duties as a deputy in the General Assembly, and in his letters to his brothers he made only passing reference to his wife. Anna was a small, frail woman, with a delicate constitution, and did not bear up well under the hardship of childbirth. She and Moses had three children, Sarah, in 1764, a second daughter who died soon after birth in 1767, and a son, Obadiah, in 1771. There are hints in Moses' letters that she had several miscarriages between the second and third child. At any rate, she was almost constantly ill and a source of concern for Moses, although their early years together were aparently pleasant, with trips to Newport and Nantucket during good weather, and occasional journeys to Plymouth and to the seaside near Boston to escape the heat in Providence.

2

Countinghouse and General Assembly

URING THE TEN YEARS that Moses was actively engaged in business with his brothers, he was also deeply involved in political affairs. Experience in business and politics shaped his thought and character, defined his interests, and developed his capabilities. His later conversion to Quakerism surely had a profound influence on his life, but his lifelong interest in education, in science and technology, in preventive medicine, in philanthropic and humanitarian projects, and his deepening concern for the general welfare of his community clearly originated during the decade of the 1760's before he apparently gave any thought to becoming a Quaker. The tradition of public responsibility had been firmly established by the first member of the family in America, Chad Brown, and it now found expression in Moses Brown and his brothers.

When Moses became a full partner in his uncle's business, Providence was a town in transition. Still an agricultural community in many respects, it was well on its way to becoming a commercial center of first importance. After the middle of the century communities in the northern part of the colony began to regard Providence rather than Newport

as their natural market. In some respects the town was situated in a more advantageous position geographically than Newport. It possessed a protected outlet to the sea, and its merchants could draw on the areas to the south and west for their lumber, horses, and other supplies that went into their cargoes for the West Indies trade. Obadiah Brown had bought many of these items in Kent County in the central part of the colony, and when his nephews launched their shipping business, their purchases of local products, particularly of horses, tobacco, and dairy products, became even more extensive. The Browns and other businessmen in Providence began to serve as middlemen for the Newport merchants who could not find in the south the supplies their expanding commerce needed.[1]

Providence's economic expansion was complemented by civic projects carried out by men acutely aware that the advancement of their self-interest was intimately connected with the advancement of the town in which they lived. Leadership came largely from the merchants who held the important posts on the town council and in the courts, the militia, and the churches; as a group, businessmen set the tone for the entire community. Although the merchants were rapidly becoming a homogeneous economic class, and some of them were undoubtedly intent to a large degree on personal self-aggrandizement, they were able to take a broad view of the welfare of their town and colony. Their awareness of the possible contradictions between their interests and those of other groups—farmers and artisans—was as yet only slightly felt; the co-operation of these different groups

---

1. This analysis is based on a study of the business activities of the Browns and other merchants in Providence, and on an examination of the newspapers of the period and of the election returns. For a more extensive treatment, see my article "The Ward-Hopkins Controversy and the American Revolution in Rhode Island: An Interpretation," *William and Mary Quarterly*, 3d Ser., 16 (1959), 363-75. See also David S. Lovejoy, *Rhode Island Politics and the American Revolution, 1760-1776* (Providence, 1958).

in politics was not made impossible by extreme economic differences.

Moses was active in many of these projects for civic improvements.[2] He joined with other energetic citizens in rebuilding the Colony House where the Assembly met, which had burned in 1758, and in efforts to collect books to replace the library which was also destroyed; he was a leader in the paving of Providence streets and served on town committees to examine suspected smallpox cases, vigorously supporting a plan to build an inoculation hospital on one of the islands in Narragansett Bay.

The most important of Moses' civic activities during this period was that of deputy in the General Assembly, a position he held for nine years. He learned firsthand the game of politics from his close friends, Stephen Hopkins and Daniel Jenckes, and from his uncle Obadiah and his brother Nicholas. Members of the Brown family had frequently held political office and Moses had no difficulty getting elected to the Assembly in April 1764; endorsement by Stephen Hopkins and the Providence party leaders guaranteed his success. When he entered the Assembly at twenty-six, he held strong opinions about the main political issues confronting the colony. His debut as a deputy coincided with a vigorous contest between Providence and Newport for the economic and political leadership in the colony. Over the years two groups of men, one in the north and the other in the south, tried to create political machines to control the government and to use its power to achieve ascendancy in the colony. The leaders of these two groups, Samuel Ward in the south and Stephen Hopkins in the north, each

2. Providence Town Papers, 1642-1761, I, 153, R. I. Hist. Soc.; Rhode Island MSS., 1677-1806, VIII, *ibid.*; *Rhode Island Acts and Resolves, 1758-62,* Sept. sess., 1761, 39-40; William Hunt to John Brown, Aug. 3, 1761, Brown Papers, P-H75; Town Council meeting, Nov. 3, 1762, Town Council Records, IV, 207, City Hall, Providence; Petitions to the Rhode Island General Assembly, II, 71, R. I. Archives.

became a symbol of his party's cause, about whom the less obtrusive leaders, like the Browns, could rally the freemen; they also served as convenient targets at which criticism and abuse could be directed by the opposition. On the important issues of the time Moses naturally took the side of Governor Hopkins and Providence.[3]

Rhode Island politics in the 1760's were chaotic. Political parties in the modern sense did not exist. Annual elections found public officials devoting more of their time to cultivating private interests in order to get re-elected than to studying public issues to improve the general welfare. For a decade and a half Rhode Island was the scene of a continuous election campaign. In such circumstances political life was dominated by personal relationships.

As a member of a prosperous, well-established family, Moses had valuable personal and business connections with most of the northern political leaders and was warmly welcomed into the Providence delegation to the Assembly. Stephen Hopkins, frequent governor during the period, dominated the Providence group by virtue of his political skill and his connections. He frequently participated in business and community enterprises with Moses and his brothers. A similar relationship existed between Moses and Esek Hopkins, the governor's brother, who was a successful merchant, shipper, and civic leader. Another important member of the delegation, Daniel Jenckes, a prosperous merchant, book dealer, and shrewd politician, was related by marriage to Moses—his daughter Rhoda became the wife of Nicholas Brown in 1762. The combination of social, family, and economic ties existing among the Providence members was typical of the bonds that held politicians from the northern part of the colony together in a working coalition, which

3. The only biography of Stephen Hopkins is William E. Foster's *Stephen Hopkins, A Rhode Island Statesman: A Study in the Political History of the Eighteenth Century* (Providence, 1884).

Providence dominated. With few exceptions, the failure of assemblymen from other northern towns to co-operate with the Providence delegation meant defeat in the election by a Hopkins man.

Moses' activities as a freshman deputy were extensive. Characteristically, he was careful to attend all the sessions of the lower house during the first year—his attendance in subsequent years was also extraordinarily good—and he conscientiously discharged the routine duties of a deputy from the second largest town in the colony. He considered himself a representative of the people in general and of the Providence merchants in particular—there was never any doubt in his mind that the interests of the two groups were not identical.

From the outset, Moses' legislative interests reflected his concerns as a businessman. On the primary issues of currency regulation and tax apportionment, he continually supported a hard money policy and a more favorable tax apportionment for Providence and the northern towns. In his first session he also tried to get the Assembly to appropriate money to restore the washed-out Weybosset Bridge in Providence and to repair the lighthouse on Beavertail Island in Narragansett Bay, both of value to the Browns' shipping interests. At a subsequent session he protested an act establishing a new table of fees which the colony officers could charge for their services, and he must have got some satisfaction when the act was repealed in the fall.

If Moses' entrance into politics was partly to promote private interest it could not have been more propitious, for it was about this time that he and his brothers, along with Governor Hopkins and some others, began to consider widening their business activities by entering the iron manufacturing industry; success depended upon a General Assembly responsive to their interests. And here Moses performed an

important service, for he was successful in securing legislative approval for measures that made the furnace possible.

In the long struggle for supremacy between Providence
and Newport, between the north and the south, the climax
came in the campaign of 1767, when the Hopkins party inflicted an overwhelming defeat on Samuel Ward and the
southerners. Moses and the leaders of the Hopkins party
machine achieved their political triumph through efficient
organization, practical leadership, and consistent campaign-
ing. Their victory coincided with another development in
the colony that went a long way toward ending the vicious
intramural political campaigns between Ward and Hopkins.
By 1767 most thinking people recognized the necessity of
a strong and united front against Parliament's attempts to
tax Americans. Leaders of the two factions realized that a
continuation of the annual election battles would be detrimental to their own immediate private interests and to the
interests of the entire colony. Some suspected that the home
government might use domestic discord as an excuse to
rescind the charter and institute a royal governor, a fate that
all but a few Rhode Islanders hoped to avoid. By 1768 these
pressures forced the leadership of the two parties to establish
a coalition government, which would put an end to party
strife.

Although this agreement reduced the bitterness of election contests in the colony, political partisanship did not
immediately cease with the election of 1768. Within a year
the coalition had dissolved, and for a short time it looked
as though the Ward-Hopkins fight would be resumed. Determined to prevent a revival of ancient animosities, Moses
and the northern faction put Joseph Wanton from Newport
at the head of its ticket in 1769; with northern and southern
support the coalition candidate won easily over the old Ward
party nominee, Josiah Lyndon.

Samuel and Henry Ward, William Ellery, and a few

other men in Newport and the southern part of the colony continued to oppose the reorganized and revitalized northern-southern coalition, now under the leadership of Moses, John, and Nicholas Brown, and Darius Sessions in the north, and Joseph Wanton and his son in Newport.[4] But the Ward party never regained its power in the political life of the colony. Joseph Wanton served as governor from 1769 to 1775 and his re-election was never seriously challenged.

During the pre-Revolutionary period more and more political leaders in Rhode Island began to realize that if they continued to devote most of their time and energy, and an increasing amount of their money, to domestic party squabbling, they would not be able to resist Parliamentary laws. The wisest course to follow was for the two factions to unite against the common enemy, and united action was possible because they were in fundamental agreement in their opposition to British policy.[5] As long as the Hopkins-Wanton coalition did not go too far in advancing the interests of the north to the detriment of the south, Samuel Ward and his few remaining friends who wanted to renew the domestic struggle for power had little chance of success in gaining popular support.

The conflict with England that induced Moses and other Rhode Islanders to bury the political hatchet had been building up for a number of years. Rhode Islanders had always been touchy about interference in their domestic affairs by the Board of Trade and other royal agencies, but they had learned to live with these annoyances. They were greatly alarmed in 1763, however, when George Grenville, Chancellor of the Exchequer and the King's chief minister, proposed an overhaul of the creaking British colonial system

4. The political in-fighting that went on from 1768 until 1772, the last year Moses sat in the lower house, may be followed in Moses Brown Papers, I-II, and in the Brown Papers, P-W2, P-P6.

5. Thompson, "The Ward-Hopkins Controversy," *Wm. and Mary Qtly.,* 3d Ser., 16 (1959), 370-71.

to balance the budget that had been strained by heavy military expenditures during the war with France and Spain.

News of the specific measures he proposed—strict enforcement of the existing laws of trade, and revision and renewal of the old Molasses Act—reached Rhode Island in the early fall of 1763.[6] As a businessman engaged in trade that would be affected by these measures, Moses opposed them without a second thought. Like most other merchants he felt that restrictions on trade were already too severe; only lax enforcement made them bearable at all.[7] Extension of the Molasses Act under these circumstances was particularly alarming to the Browns, for they imported large quantities of molasses and sugar, little of which they obtained legally. This forbidding news reached Rhode Island at the end of the war when merchants were looking forward to a return to normal business conditions. Moses and his brothers had just launched the shipping firm of Nicholas Brown and Company and they were anxious for it to succeed.

There was probably not much connection between the proposed extension of the Molasses Act and the subsequent decline in business prosperity in Rhode Island, but the break in prices shortly after Grenville announced his policy of reform convinced the merchants of Providence that there was. Certainly, as Grenville's policy unfolded, business grew worse. The merchants drew the obvious conclusion: cut out the nonsense about enforcing the Molasses Act, return to conditions existing before the war, and everything would be all right. It was as simple as that.

In Providence, the merchants furnished the leadership in the movement to resist Grenville's policies, not only because

6. *Providence Gazette; and Country Journal,* Sept. 3, 1763. See also the issues for Sept. 24 and Oct. 1, and the *Newport Mercury,* Sept. 26.

7. Nicholas Brown & Co. to Tench Francis, Oct. 10, 1763, Brown Papers, P-F7, II. Hedges, *The Browns,* 200-214, contains a discussion of the reaction of the Browns to the American resistance to British attempts to tax the colonies.

their economic interests were the first to be seriously affected but also because for at least a decade they had controlled the political as well as the economic life of the town virtually unchallenged. Since Moses was one of the leading members of the business community and an important political figure, he was, from the beginning of the imperial conflict, involved in the resistance movement. Actually, there was little need for vigorous leadership. Public opinion almost unanimously supported decisions taken by the merchants against the trade act. Resistance arose and developed under its own momentum—leadership was collective rather than individual. Moses was in the thick of things, serving on committees in Providence and in the General Assembly to study problems, draft petitions to King and Parliament, and organize resistance.[8]

The dire predictions of Rhode Island merchants that their trade would be ruined if the Molasses Act was extended proved to be somewhat exaggerated. Notwithstanding frequent skirmishes with His Majesty's officers, shippers were able to arrive at a rough working agreement with customs officials about the procedure of entering and clearing vessels, and there seems to have been a tacit understanding that the other provisions of the new law would not be enforced. Despite a general dip in business activity, Brown and Company prospered; the brothers formed and executed plans to branch into the manufacture of iron, and even began to think about entering the English import trade. These were not the acts of men who felt that the world was coming to an end.

But the crisis had just begun. During the winter and spring, ships bore the news that Parliament was considering

8. The Providence "State of the Trade of this Colony especially so much thereof as relates to the County of Providence with the Several Remarks and observations Subjoined, . . ." is in Moses Brown Papers, Misc. MSS., I, 12-13, 19. For the details, see the Journal House of Deputies, 1763-64, Jan. sess., 1764, 961-63, and Journal of the Senate, 1761-67, 49, R. I. Archives. For the "Rhode Island Remonstrance," see John R. Bartlett, ed., *Records of the Colony of Rhode Island and Providence Plantations in New England*, 10 vols. (Providence, 1856-65), VI, 556-67, hereafter cited as *R. I. Col. Recs.*

a bill to saddle the colonists with a stamp duty, and, in April, Rhode Islanders learned that the bill had actually passed. The next month they read that the Virginia House of Burgesses had denounced the act in a set of determined resolutions, which the *Newport Mercury* soon printed, spreading ideas of defiance among New Englanders.[9] There was not the slightest doubt, of course, where Rhode Islanders stood. The politics of the colony might be of a pretty low order, but the leaders of both parties stood shoulder to shoulder against any extension of Parliamentary authority to America, and the people of the colony stood directly behind them.

In Providence a town meeting instructed Moses and the other deputies to support vigorously "the plan—now general in all of the colonies—of sending commissioners to New York to represent the colony in a united protest against the tyrannical measures of Parliament."[10] They were likewise instructed to do everything in their power "towards postponing the Introduction of the Stamp Act into this Colony, until the Colonies may have opportunity to be heard in Defence of such just Rights, as they will be deprived of by an Execution of it."[11] The Virginia Resolves were approved and, with some changes and additions, put into the instructions.

Rhode Islanders also registered their opposition to the Stamp Act in more emphatic ways. In Newport, an effigy of the stamp distributor was hanged from a specially erected gallows in front of the courthouse, then cut down and burned in a public bonfire. The next night a raging mob forced the distributor to flee to a waiting man-of-war. Deprived of the pleasure of his company, they carted off part of his pos-

9. Aug. 19, 1765.
10. *Vox Populi, Vox Dei; A Providence Gazette Extraordinary*, Aug. 24, 1765.
11. *Rhode Island Acts and Resolves, 1765-69*, Sept. sess., 1765, 56 (facsimile no. 27, publ. by J. Harry Bongartz, n.d., Providence).

sessions, then sacked the homes of two royalist ring leaders for good measure.[12]

So general was the spirit of opposition that Moses and his fellow legislators in the General Assembly passed a resolution ordering Rhode Island officials to ignore the Stamp Act.[13] When a justice of the peace in Providence threatened to defy this recommendation, Moses Brown intervened to prevent a re-enactment of the Newport riot. The case originated when John Foster, clerk of the Inferior Court of Common Pleas in Providence County, declared that he would not issue writs nor carry on the customary proceedings contrary to the Stamp Act.[14] On December 12 a large crowd surrounded his house at the north end of town and threatened physical harm if he did not conduct the business of the court, but Foster refused to be intimidated.

Fortunately for Foster, there were a few cool heads in the crowd who thought that private conversation with the clerk would be more effective than public riot. Someone asked Moses, who was in the back of the crowd watching the spectacle, to speak to him. He had known Foster for years and had been partially responsible for his election as clerk of the court and as justice of the peace. Moses considered him to be a reasonable man, except for a tendency to be legalistic and bullheaded. At any rate, he thought no harm could come from talking to him.

Quieting the crowd, Moses pushed his way into the clerk's modest home. Foster quickly confessed that he had been sufficiently intimidated to be willing to yield and asked for protection from the mob. Moses promised that he would "defend him harmless" if he would agree to "act and transact all kinds of Bussiness in the same manner as usual before the

12. For a sketch of the Newport riots, see Edmund S. Morgan, *The Stamp Act Crisis: Prologue to Revolution* (Chapel Hill, 1953), 145-50.
13. Bartlett, ed., *R. I. Col. Recs.*, VI, 452.
14. Affidavit, Dec. 12, 1765, by John Foster with a note added by Moses Brown, Moses Brown Papers, Misc. MSS., B-615, Box 1.

first Day of November last," the day the Stamp Act had gone
into effect. Foster, no doubt looking at the threatening
crowd and reflecting upon the coat of tar and feathers and
the cold wet walk out of town that would surely be his fate
if he refused, promptly signed the statement. "The people,"
Moses recorded, "quietly went hom[e] sattisfyed."[15]

Following the repeal of the Stamp Act early in 1766 there
was a lull in the running fight between England and her
colonies in America. But trouble flared again in 1767 when
Parliament adopted a series of new trade regulations, the
Townshend Acts, which were designed to achieve the same
end as the Stamp Act, the raising of a revenue in America.
While they remained in force Moses was one of the colony's
most active organizers of resistance. As corresponding secretary for Providence's nonimportation committee, he wrote
lengthy letters to Boston, Philadelphia, New York, and
Charleston in an effort to unite the colonists.[16] In the General Assembly he was active on committees to draw up petitions to the King; he corresponded with the Secretary of the
American Department, the Earl of Hillsborough, and with
the colony's agent, Joseph Sherwood, concerning American
affairs. When Hillsborough ordered the governor to reject
Massachusetts' famous "Circular Letter" urging Americans
to unite in defense of their rights, Moses took the position
that "this Assembly instead of treating that letter with any
degree of contempt think themselves obliged, in duty to
themselves and to their country, to approve the sentiments
contained in it."[17]

In March 1770, Parliament repealed the Townshend
duties except for a token tax on tea. For two or three

15. *Newport Mercury*, Dec. 23, 1765; *Rhode Island Acts and Resolves, 1765-69*, May sess., 1766, 5.

16. Moses Brown to the Committee of Merchants in Boston, May 23, 1770, Moses Brown Papers, I, 108. See also Committee of Merchants in Providence [Moses Brown] to Committee of Merchants in Boston, June 1, 1770, Rhode Island MSS., VI, 36, R. I. Hist. Soc.

17. Bartlett, ed., *R. I. Col. Recs.*, VI, 541, 556-67.

months there was some uncertainty whether the nonimportation agreements should be continued until the remaining duty on tea was taken off or whether they should be confined solely to that article.[18] In July, Moses informed the colony's agent in London that the colonies had resolved to continue their boycott until the tea duty was repealed. Americans understood that the tax on tea was to be a test of Parliament's right to tax the colonists. They were aware that tea was cheaper than it had been, he told agent Sherwood, but "we are not thereby to be induced to receive the bate."

Once the Townshend duties had been taken off, however, the temptation to import goods was too great for Rhode Island businessmen to resist. News that merchants in New York had ordered or actually imported fresh merchandise from England gave merchants in Rhode Island the excuse they needed to do likewise.[19] Once the nonimportation agreements broke down, Moses worked hard to restore Rhode Island's trade with the other colonies and with England.

Resumption of trade ushered in a new era of peaceful association between the colonies and the mother country. But the seeds of distrust planted in the minds of the Americans by years of wrangling and near conflict could not be easily wiped out. Who could tell what would happen if Parliament chose to reassert its supremacy over the colonies? Moses Brown was well aware of the danger. He wrote to friends in England that some satisfactory solution must be found, because people in America were very "jealous" of their rights, "even to the lowest peasant."[20]

The new direction of Rhode Island politics after 1768 coincided with events in Moses' life that foreshadowed mo-

18. Arthur M. Schlesinger, *The Colonial Merchants and the American Revolution, 1763-1776* (N. Y., 1918), 214-15.

19. Nicholas Brown & Co., to David Van Horne, July 3, Aug. 8, 1770, Brown Papers, OL 59-02 M.

20. Moses Brown to Joseph Sherwood, July 3, 1770, Moses Brown Papers, I, 111.

mentous changes in his attitude and interests. Up to this point, Moses seems to have been representative of a group of men who were perhaps only slightly above average in aspirations and abilities. Like his associates, he seemed to think in local terms; his interests, like theirs, were confined largely to his business and the community in which he lived. But in 1768 his locus of interest began to broaden and deepen, first slowly, then swiftly, infused with a zeal and energy characteristic of many nineteenth-century reformers.

His behavior in the spring of 1768 gave evidence of approaching changes. While his partners began feverish preparation for the rush of business that would come with the return of good weather, Moses' interest flagged, and his attendance at the furnace and the countinghouse virtually ceased. He developed an acute case of insomnia, had difficulty eating, and felt inert and depressed. This was the ominous beginning of the debilitating fevers and prostrations that were to become more serious within a few years. When neither his doctor nor apothecary could help him, he prescribed for himself a six months' vacation. He informed his brothers of the decision in a long and carefully written letter: "I think it necessary to inform the company that my health is so impaired as to be much injured by a close attention to any kind of business," he wrote, "and I have concluded to leave the care and charge of my part of the business of the company this summer and fall among you." He added that if he did not find relief during the summer and was not an invalid by the fall, he would take a trip to New York to consult doctors.[21]

It is impossible, at this distance, to state categorically the causes of Moses' melancholia, but his letters suggest that it was aggravated, if not caused, by the shock of a number of deaths in the family. Late in 1766 John's daughter Abigail, or Naby as Moses affectionately called her, died suddenly

21. Moses Brown to brothers, July 6, 1768, ibid., 85.

from causes unknown.[22] Brother John was out of town and the responsibility of looking after his grief-stricken wife, Sarah, fell on Moses. Scarcely six months later, Nicholas' daughter Hope "fell in the water at the head of the wharf where the tide runs swift and was drowned," despite heroic efforts by John to save her.[23] In February 1768, Anna, Moses' wife, gave birth to a second child, a daughter, who "expired after just two hours."[24] The young couple had looked forward to the arrival of their second child with keen anticipation, and her death was a blow to them both. Although Anna Brown eventually regained her strength and seemed to recover from her ordeal, she remained for many months in a state of lassitude that resisted the collective efforts of local physicians and Boston specialists. Moses was very sensitive about illness and death. He worried a great deal about the meaning of these events. He worried so much, in fact, that he himself became ill; at least he thought he was ill.[25]

His illness led to his decision to quit his business activities for a while. In his leisure he could pause, take stock of his affairs, and give some serious thought to the meaning of life. Heretofore he had followed pretty much without question the code of conduct of relatives, friends, and business associates; now, he began to have reservations about that code. After prolonged meditation he concluded that his and his brothers' misfortunes had been caused by too close an attention to business and by too gross an indifference to the spiritual welfare of themselves and their families. Feeling

22. Moses Brown to Jabez Bowen, Oct. 15, 1766, Brown Papers, P-37.

23. Nicholas Brown & Co. [probably John] to William Wiley, July 30-31, and Nicholas Brown to Elder Samuel Winsor, July 31, 1767, Brown Papers, Misc. Letters, 1767, I.

24. Joseph Wanton, Jr., to Moses Brown, Jan. 13, 1768, Moses Brown Papers, I, 80; Records of Births and Marriages, II, 6, in the City Clerk's Office, Providence City Hall.

25. Thomas Robinson to Moses Brown, Aug. 4, 1768, Moses Brown Papers, I, 86.

that he must make adjustments in his life, he decided to devote more time to his personal and public affairs and less attention to business and politics. Although he was not a wealthy man he had acquired a large estate through inheritances and business profits and was relatively independent financially.

During this period of enforced leisure, Moses turned his attention to a number of subjects that he had long neglected: he dabbled in mathematics and astronomy, developed the farm he had inherited from his father, and began a systematic study of plants and animals. He found a willing companion for his activities in his brother Joseph, who spent a large part of his time studying mechanics, surveying, and computing the elevation of local hills. He also spent many hours with Benjamin West, who operated a bookshop in the north end of town, published an almanac, wrote pieces on the weather and allied subjects for the *Providence Gazette; and Country Journal,* and was the outstanding scientist in the town, if not in the colony.[26] From his brother and his friend Benjamin West, as well as from private study, Moses extended his knowledge of mathematics, astronomy, and surveying. Like most people in America, he was acquainted with Benjamin Franklin's experiments on electricity, and he had probably heard the lectures given in Providence in March 1764 on that fascinating subject by William Johnston.[27] He had an inquiring and speculative mind, and the intellectual climate of his day was favorable for experimental inquiry.

During his illness, therefore, Moses asked his friend Joseph Harrison, former resident of Newport but now customs collector in Boston, to order a microscope and other scientific instruments from England. He planned to amuse himself during the spring and summer "in some observations of other animals and vegetable produce" and wanted a microscope to

26. See Raymond Clare Archibald in *DAB* s.v. "West, Benjamin."
27. *Providence Gazette; and Country Journal,* Mar. 3, 1764.

which "a micrometre may be easily fixed to it if it has none already. If it should not be such I should decline having it as I want one that with the solar one belonging to our library will be compleat for making all the various microscopic observations with ease." After numerous inquiries Harrison found what Moses wanted in Boston, although the price, Harrison wrote, was too high. But microscopes of any kind were scarce in America, and Moses told his friend to buy it. Harrison had the instrument repaired and sent it to Moses along with a copy of Baker's *Employment for the Microscope made Easy* as a gift.[28]

Moses' scientific interests were also reflected in his library purchases. He probably acquired James Ferguson's *Astronomy*, and *A new and Complete Dictionary of Arts and Sciences* at this time, along with Stephen Hale's *Husbandry* and *Vegetable Staticks* and Holme's *Principles of Vegetation*.[29] Scientific farming attracted his attention increasingly and he devoted considerable attention to it following his illness. He started a nursery and experimented with black and white mulberry bushes, read the pieces on their cultivation that appeared from time to time in the newspapers, and sent some of the slips of the white variety to his friend James Warren in Plymouth, advising him that "from a small tree you might soon raise a large nursery."[30] His interest stemmed from his attempt in 1764 to introduce the silk industry to Providence during the initial enthusiasm in America for developing domestic manufacturing. At that time he had realized that the obstacle to the growth of silk worms was their food supply, and from 1768 on he made efforts to develop a mulberry bush that would grow in New England.

28. See Harrison to Moses Brown, Jan. 15, Feb. 23, Mar. 2, and Moses Brown to Harrison, Feb. 20, Feb. 27, Mar. 14, 1769, Moses Brown Papers, I, 90-91.

29. See Moses' "A Catalogue of Books belonging to Moses Brown's Library," in Moses Brown Papers, Austin MSS., II, "Republic of Letters," Moses Brown School Lib.

30. Oct. 28, 1768, Moses Brown Papers, I, 88.

Brown's experiments with grape vines, millet, apple trees, and evergreen flowering shrubs must have been successful, for he received repeated requests for seeds and plants from friends and strangers, not only in Providence but in Newport and Boston. His interest in agriculture was not confined to increasing the productivity of his farm; he hoped that others would follow his example and thereby contribute to the wealth of the colony. Moses maintained an interest in agricultural experimentation all of his life and was a member, many years later, of some of the earliest agricultural organizations in America.

In the spring of 1769, Moses and his brother Joseph participated in the preparations in Providence for the observation of the transit of Venus, an enterprise which "goes far," as one commentator has observed, "to dispel the notion that Americans were scientific illiterates" in the colonial period. In North America alone there were no less than sixteen attempts to determine the sun's parallax, and several colonial governments gave encouragement to the enterprise.[31]   In Philadelphia the American Philosophical Society applied to the Pennsylvania legislature for funds to purchase the equipment to conduct the experiment, and Joseph got the idea for the observation from a newspaper notice about this action. Instead of applying to the General Assembly for funds to purchase the equipment, however, they put up the money themselves.   Joseph had a few instruments and agreed to pay for additional equipment from London at a cost of £100.[32]   When Moses attempted to borrow the colony's astronomical quadrant from the Redwood Library in New-

31. Albert E. Lownes, "The 1769 Transit of Venus and its relation to early American Astronomy," *Sky and Telescope*, 2 (1943), 3-5. See also Brooke Hindle, *The Pursuit of Science in Revolutionary America, 1735-1789* (Chapel Hill, 1956), 154-55; and Harry Woolf, *The Transit of Venus: A Study of Eighteenth-Century Science* (Princeton, 1959), 150-97.

32. Benjamin West, *An Account of the Observation of Venus Upon the Sun, The Third Day of June, at Providence, in New England with some Account of the Use of those Observations* (Providence, 1769).

port, his request got mixed up in local politics; only after haggling with the librarian, the Reverend Ezra Stiles of the Second Congregational Church in Newport, and securing an order from Governor Wanton, was he able to get the instrument. It was brought to Providence aboard one of the ships of Nicholas Brown and Company.[33]

Preparations for this exciting scientific enterprise got underway a month before the eclipse. A sturdy platform was built for the instruments, they were thoroughly tested, and the most learned and well-to-do men in the town were recruited to lend a hand. The apparatus when assembled consisted of a three-foot reflecting telescope "with horizontal and vertical wires for taking differences of altitudes and azmuths, adjusted with spirit-levels at right angles," a "divided arch for taking altitudes; a curious helioscope," and a micrometer "of a new and elegant construction, with rack motions and fitted to the telescope." The astronomical quadrant from the Redwood Library was also available along with two excellent clocks; one, a local product, was the work of Edward Spalding,[34] and another, a wonderfully accurate piece made in London, belonged to Governor Hopkins. This equipment was set up in what is now known as Transit Street, and for two days the participants could be seen testing each piece and rehearsing procedure. On July 3, shortly before the time for the experiment to begin, a public notice was circulated asking the people to mark meridian lines on their windows at a signal from a cannon. Benjamin West and Joseph Brown supervised the operations.

Characteristically, Moses made very careful notes of the proceedings. "Mr. West was to view the first external con-

33. Nicholas Brown & Co. to Ezra Stiles or Henry Marchant, May 22, 1769, Brown Papers, Misc. Letters, 1769, I. See Donald H. Fleming's concise discussion in *Science and Technology in Providence, 1760-1914: An Essay in the History of Brown University in the Metropolitan Community* (Providence, 1952), 14-15.

34. West, *An Account of the Observation of Venus Upon the Sun*, 11.

tact of Venus in [the] tiliscope and with Joseph Brown at the
instrument the whole time." Governor Hopkins was detailed "to keep the telliscope section level," and Jabez Bowen,
Jr., to "count the clock." John Burroughs was to observe
the progress of Venus across the sun while Nicholas Brown
would "write the observations." Besides taking notes, Moses
was "to observe in the section." David Howell and Joseph
Nash were also on hand to lend assistance when necessary.
Clearly the project was a co-operative one and the entire
community participated in it.[35]

Considering their limited experience and primitive
equipment, the Providence scientists achieved a remarkable
degree of success. Not satisfied to have completed the difficult task, the participants moved to make their conclusions
available to the public. "It required not only Mr. Browns
money but Mr. Wests brains to do this work," Moses observed. To verify their findings, Joseph took West's calculations to Boston to check them with Joseph Harrison, who
was considered something of an expert in scientific subjects
and probably had information about the observation of
Venus that had taken place in Boston.[36] The Providence
account of this momentous scientific achievement was published by John Carter in his shop at Shakespeare's Head, and
Moses probably assisted West and Joseph in seeing it through
the press.

Moses' participation in the observation of Venus no doubt
whetted his appetite for "amusing" pastimes. He developed
his skill as a surveyor by helping Joseph measure "the rise or
fall of rodes or streets" in Providence,[37] and when they found
that their surveying instruments were neither very accurate
nor easy to handle, he ordered "one pocket case of surveyors

35. June 1769, Moses Brown Papers, Austin MSS., XII, "Personal," Moses
Brown School Lib.
36. Moses Brown to Harrison, Aug. 15, 1769, Brown Papers, Misc. Letters,
1769, II.
37. Joseph Brown's memorandum of a Journal, Jan. 19, 1770, *ibid.*, 1770, I.

instruments with 6 inch brass scale, protractor etc.," from London. He also asked Captain Shand, master of the *Tristam*, to buy him in London "one thermometer graduated from 15° below o up to boiling water in a plate fitted to a mahogany case to have a slider in front, of the plainest sort but good."[38]

When the scientific instruments then available seemed unsatisfactory, Moses made improvisations to suit his purpose. Nor was he reluctant to challenge the authorities as to what could be built. In 1770 he ordered a theodolite from a Mr. Wright through the Nicholas Brown and Company agent in London, Hayley and Hopkins, with a reflector attached, "fitted with cross wires or hares, at right angles." Moses observed to the manufacturer that if his own instructions were followed, the instrument "will certainly be more accurate in taking distant objects to determine there elevation etc. the objects will not appear inverted which to me is a considerable objection to a refraction." In reply to a letter from Mr. Wright, in which he was told that a reflector had never been fitted to a theodolite, Moses replied that, "though it may be true; it is not sattisfactory to me that there never may."[39]

But Moses was no Benjamin Franklin; indeed, it is doubtful whether he can be referred to with accuracy as a scientist at this time of his life, but he resembled America's greatest scientist in his curiosity about the natural and physical world, his willingness to test ideas by experiment, and his passion for accuracy. Like Franklin he was interested in scientific inquiry for its own sake, but he also placed great emphasis on turning his scientific investigation to "useful purposes in the interests of the community."

In the months following his illness, Moses' scientific experiments formed a part of his conspicuous services as a man

38. Dec. 16, 1769, *ibid.*, 1769, II.
39. Moses Brown to Captain Shand, Dec. 10, 1770, *ibid.*, 1770, II.

of public responsibility. During this period he began to consider public service as his primary occupation rather than as a mere avocation. By 1770 he could no longer conceal his growing aversion to the highly competitive business world which his brother John found so congenial. As he saw it, devotion to public good gave meaning to his life because it served as a unifying force, a principle by which he could judge the value of his private and public activities. In a letter prompted by proposals from John to expand the operations of the shipping business and to continue the blasts at the furnace the year around, Moses defended his past delinquency in the business, rejected John's proposals for it, and at the same time formulated a full, maturely developed statement of his thoughts on the businessman's role in society.

The purpose of trade, he reminded John, was to accumulate an estate large enough to make one independent of the "various scenes of fortune incident to trade." Admitting that the amount "to lay by" would vary depending on the trader, he thought it "most rational that the laws of society or of injoyment of ourselves by no means will extend any man's business beyond what he can attend with due care and leave time to injoy his family and connections." Some people, he pointedly remarked, live only for business and enjoy it whether their activities were profitable or not. When a man has business enough to earn reasonable security for the present and the future, then he has an obligation "to lay by all his profits where it will be most advantageous to society." If a man would not donate his excess business profits, then he most certainly should donate "part of his time in the business of the community without profit so soon as his business brings him in any overplus more than to supply his family." In an obvious slap at John's extravagant style of living, he noticed that "prudence directs that no man in trade [should] live upon his hole profits but lay up something in a surer place, and this he may do even if his business does not half

employ his time providing the profits are so large as he can afford it." In view of these considerations, Moses informed his brothers that "I would be understood by no means to expect to enlarge [the business] hereafter should we be so fortunate as still to thrive."[40]

Moses did not confine himself to theoretical statements about the responsibilities the citizen owed to the community; he tried to apply his theories to the practical problems of his town and colony. Quick to lend money to the government when the regular moneylenders refused, he also contributed money towards public improvements in Providence when there was a good chance that he might not get it back. And it is significant that later, when his conversion to Quakerism led him to sever his connections with company business and to discontinue his political activities altogether, he never withdrew entirely from community affairs.

Following his illness in 1768, whether of the mind or the body, Moses reflected about his life and began the transition from secularism to spiritualism which would culminate six years later in conversion to Quakerism. Slowly he abandoned the easy acceptance of his friends' code of conduct; hesitantly he began to hammer out his own ethical principles, a heightened sense of moral responsibility which increasingly governed his career as a man of public affairs, and to a great extent, set him apart from his contemporaries.

Prior to 1768 Moses' letters do not mention his religious thoughts. From youth to early maturity, he belonged to the Baptist Church in Providence and worshiped alongside other members of the family in the meetinghouse in the north end of town. Not until his early thirties, when he began to worry about his health, did he show any marked interest in religion. On the surface his interest lasted just as long as his illness and no longer, but the experience seems

40. Memorial from Moses Brown to Nicholas Brown & Co., Oct. 27, 1764, Brown Papers, V-misc., Misc. Ship's Papers, Calendared, I.

to have left a more indelible mark on his mind. He later remembered that at this time he had been in "a lingering state of health . . . , in which state I was favored to see my unfaithfulness and convenanted and engaged to greater obedience when restored to health." But after he had recovered, he admitted, his "mind was drawn off with the cares of the world and a flush of new spirits," and he "relapsed into a lukewarm state."[41]

Moses' description of his religious experience tallies closely with the picture that emerges from the record. Although he borrowed books on religion from Thomas Robinson, a Newport Quaker,[42] and purchased sets of Philip Doddridge's *The Family Expositor* (the New Testament) and Isaac Penington's *Works,* his letters, even to close Quaker friends, failed to reveal any significant attachment to Quakerism at this time. For a while his correspondence took on a religious tone, but it soon disappeared entirely. Except for this brief interval, his religious feeling was lukewarm, or at least submerged, during the first thirty-four years of his life. Later, however, when he had suffered a much more severe emotional disturbance and had begun to embrace Quakerism, this early experience was to assume a premonitory significance in his own mind.

41. Moses Brown to brothers, Sunday morning [probably early in October 1770, from Boston], *ibid.,* Misc. Letters, 1770, I.
42. Moses Brown to William Wilson, Mar. 22, 1774, Moses Brown Papers, Misc. MSS., K-AB.

3

Rhode Island College

L ONG BEFORE the "cares of the world and a flush of
new spirits" caused Moses' relapse "into a lukewarm
state," he was caught up in an educational reform
which transformed the Providence schools. For most Providence children education began in the home and all too often
ended there. Sometime before 1752 the town had erected
a school building near the Colony House, but the schoolmaster had to depend on tuition fees for his salary, a very
uncertain source of income. After a few years the master
left, and the schoolhouse was put up for sale.

A second effort had to wait until a new generation of
leaders recognized the value of education and decided to
support it. The rise of Providence as an important port
partly explains the renewed interest in the late 1760's. The
proliferation of trading companies, shops, and light manufacturing establishments created a growing need for apprentices who could read, write, and figure.[1] The demand coincided with a growing awareness that the town's educational
facilities had not kept pace with the rapid growth of popula-

1. "Memorandum for School House," May 20, 1767, Moses Brown Papers,
Misc. MSS., III, 153.

tion nor with advances in other cities, particularly with Newport. After the establishment of the *Providence Gazette;
and Country Journal* in 1762, essays and editorials stressed
the desirability of education in foreign languages and classi-
cal literature and applauded the century-old publicly supported educational system in Massachusetts.[2] By the spring
of 1767 the public was engaged in a vigorous discussion of
ways and means of raising funds for a new school.

In the course of the debate the town divided between
those who wanted publicly supported schools open to all
children regardless of their parents' ability to pay and those
who preferred privately financed schools, open only to the
children of those who contributed to the costs of construction
and operation. At a town meeting on December 2, big John
Brown in his characteristically blunt and forceful language
pointed to the absence of public education and urged establishment of a school "so publick that every inhabitant of said
town may have liberty of sending his children to it." There
had been much talk recently, he told his audience, about
building a large public school and the job would have been
done except that "sum gentlemen in town . . . had, considering the grait disadvantage their children laboured under
for want of proper schooling had on their own expence and
for their private use, built two considerable houses for that
purpose." These people now objected to paying taxes to
support a public school, even though the lack of one distressed the poorer people of the town. To remedy the situation, he proposed that the town take over the schools already
built, that the proprietors of the private schools be excused
from the tax levy necessary to build the new public school,
and that the owners have the "same right in said public
schools as though they was absolutely taxed for the same."
John insisted that education was a public, not a private, re-

2. See for example, *Providence Gazette; and Country Journal*, Feb. 26,
1763.

sponsibility. It would be an easy matter, he observed, for a few well-to-do citizens to raise money to build a school-house, as others had already done, "but as that would not be a servis to hundreds their is in this town who is not able to build a house to school their children in I think it much better to incorage a town school as that will certinly be the most serviceable to the publick." John anticipated strong opposition to this plan, and he lamented that "so grand an attempt to searve the publick" should be "apposed by aney gentlemen of learning," particularly by "gentlemen from whose station of authority the publick have reasons to expect the graitest incoragement."[3]

But opposition soon materialized. On New Year's Day, 1768, a majority of freemen rejected a public school plan presented to them by a committee headed by Moses and John Brown. The greatest opposition, Moses discovered, came from two sources: the poorer people generally, who were "strangely led away not to see their own as well as the public interest," and the inhabitants on the west side of the Great Salt Cove, who expected to be separated from the main part of the town and therefore opposed paying taxes to build schools on the east, which within a short time their children would not be able to attend.[4]

Supporters of the public school idea now launched a plan to raise money for a small private schoolhouse on the old Colony House lot. Moses, Nicholas, and Joseph each sub-scribed £500, but John, probably piqued by the rejection of the original scheme, promised only £300. The Browns, including John, were not the kind to brood about a setback, however, and they immediately set to work to make the best of a bad situation. Moses acted as moderator and clerk, simultaneously, of several of the meetings held on the new project. And as a deputy from Providence he presented the

3. Brown Papers, P-P6.
4. Quoted in Staples, *Annals of Providence*, 500.

petition to the General Assembly requesting authorization to establish a schoolhouse. Moses contributed generously of both time and money to the "New Brick School House" that was finally built, and for years served as one of the overseers of the project.[5] It was decades, however, before his fellow citizens recognized the wisdom of publicly supported education.

Despite their failure in efforts to initiate a public school system in Providence, Moses and his friends soon became involved in a more important educational undertaking, the permanent location of Rhode Island College at Providence. The initial impulse for establishing a college in the colony came from the Philadelphia Association of Baptist Churches. Other religious sects—Presbyterians, Anglicans, Congregationalists—had founded colleges to train ministers and educate the children of the faithful, and the Baptists followed suit in 1762. The Baptist Association chose Rhode Island as the home of the college because of the numerous Baptists in the colony and because of the colony's reputation for religious toleration.[6] To take charge of the enterprise the ministers selected young James Manning, who had graduated

5. The proprietors of a private schoolhouse built in the north end of town called themselves "The Whipple Hall Society," and the school was named "Whipple Hall." The proprietors petitioned the Assembly for full authority to manage the affairs of the society; the petition was granted. See *Rhode Island Acts and Resolves, 1765-69*, Oct. sess., 1768, 57-58.

6. The standard works on the founding and history of the college are Reuben Aldridge Guild, *History of Brown University, with Illustrative Documents* (Providence, 1867), and Walter C. Bronson, *The History of Brown University* (Providence, 1914). See also William Green Roelker, "The Browns and Brown University," *Brown Alumni Monthly*, 49 (Dec. 1948), 3-7, and Hedges, *The Browns*, 194-98. All of these accounts of the locating of the college at Providence are based on the manuscripts preserved by Moses Brown. On May 25, 1833, at the request of President Francis Wayland, Moses sent him "a file of papers containing copys of originals I preserved at the time of their Transactions respecting the Removal of the College from Warren. . . . I had them Copied soon after we conversed." These papers, with others, are now in the John Hay Library, Providence. Most of the originals, however, are in the Moses Brown Papers, Misc. MSS., B-814, Box 2, folder marked "College Papers."

from the College of New Jersey in 1762 and had been or-
dained a pastor the following year.[7]

In July, on a religious visit to Halifax, Manning stopped
off in Newport where he approached a number of influential
Rhode Islanders who seemed to be interested in a college
for the colony. Once the seed was planted it was not long
in sprouting. In less than a year the men Manning talked
to had produced a charter for a Baptist college. For a time
there was dispute over the charter, but in June 1764 the
General Assembly approved it, and Rhode Island College
was established the next year in the small town of Warren,
several miles southeast of Providence. Although the govern-
ing body was dominated by Baptists, representation was
provided for Congregationalists, Quakers, and Anglicans.
Among the officers of the infant institution were Governor
Hopkins as chancellor, and Daniel Jenckes, John Cole, and
Nicholas Brown as fellows. James Manning returned to
Rhode Island the same year to settle in Warren, where he
opened a Latin school and became the first pastor of the
Baptist Church. Well thought of by all denominations, he
was the corporation's choice for president of the college.

Before the first class graduated, the members of the corporation faced critical questions: the college needed new
buildings and it also needed money. Since the institution
in Warren had neither an endowment nor the necessary facilities to attract students, the Baptists in 1767 began to
consider the question of another location that would offer
more in the way of patronage and community support. Newport leaders hoped to move the college there. The town was
the largest in the colony; it possessed a class of well-educated
gentlemen financially able to support a college; and it boasted
the Redwood Library, the largest in the colony, as well as

7. See Reuben Aldridge Guild, *Life, Times, and Correspondence of James
Manning* . . . (N. Y., 1864), 71, and Harris Elwood Starr in *DAB* s.v. "Manning, James."

a number of very good private libraries. In addition, over
the years Newport had been the cultural capital of the colony,
and its citizens quite naturally expected northern towns to
recognize Newport's superior claim to the college.

But the people in the north no longer agreed. Since the
middle of the century Providence had been successfully chal-
lenging the pre-eminence of Newport in the political and
economic spheres. By the late sixties, it extended the contest to the cultural realm. In September 1767 Moses, who
was attending the Assembly in Newport, wrote that he "had
great encouragement that the college not be located on
Rhode Island," meaning at Warren or Newport.[8] But as
late as the anniversary meeting of the college corporation
on September 7, 1768, it appeared that the corporation had
decided to remain at Warren and construct more buildings
there.[9]

Within a short time, however, a group of enterprising
men in Kent County decided that East Greenwich would be
a more suitable location, and they asked President Manning
to call a meeting of the corporation to consider their proposal.[10] About the same time, Moses Brown decided to acquire the college for Providence. On October 23, 1769, he
rode down to Newport. On the way he met Darius Sessions,
deputy-governor of the colony and a Providence man, and
there astride horses in the middle of the road, they discussed the location of the college.[11] When Moses suggested
that Providence should have it, Sessions agreed and promised to advance $100 and use his influence to secure students.
Although he had previously declined appointment to the

8. Brown Papers, P-P6.
9. Minutes of Proceedings of Corporation Meeting, Sept. 7, 1768, Rhode
Island College Misc. Papers, 1763-82, I, 31, 43, John Hay Lib.
10. *Ibid.*, 49; Guild, *History of Brown University*, 177.
11. For Moses' discussions with Sessions and his subsequent activities, see
Moses Brown to Nicholas Brown & Co., Oct. 23, 1769, Moses Brown Papers,
Misc. MSS., B-814, Box 2.

corporation, he said he would accept if asked again, and work hard to make the college a success.

Moses had been mulling the matter over for some time and was encouraged by his discussion with Deputy-Governor Sessions. In Newport he made discreet inquiries among his friends about moving the college to Providence and was pleased to find them enthusiastic about the plan, particularly Governor Wanton. The Governor cautioned, however, that unless Providence could raise a building fund of at least £1,600, the plan would fail. A few days later when subscriptions had produced considerably more than that amount, Moses observed: "I see already the observation of small causes producing great effect in this case as when I went from home there was little talk about it, and no expectation of it."

When Moses returned to Providence he called together his brothers and a small group of friends—Governor Hopkins, John Cole, Silas Downer, and a few others—to read them a memorandum he had written on the location of the college. He argued that eventually Newport and Providence would so outdistance the other towns in population and wealth that the General Assembly would meet only in those places. Whichever town got the college would eventually become the sole capital of the colony. If Providence acquired the college, it would be of assistance in the town's effort to secure a customs house, "other officers and indeed every other publick emolument," and would certainly advance private economic interests. If Providence missed its opportunity and East Greenwich got the college, that town would become a rival of Providence instead of an ally. Moses' arguments convinced his audience that they should exert every effort in a bid for the college. By the time the corporation met, on November 4, the Providence subscription amounted to over £2,600, about a third of it pledged for a college building regardless of its eventual location.

The all-important meeting of the college corporation to decide the location of the college, and in a sense its fate, was held in the Newport courthouse. After a day of preliminaries, the committee from Kent County proposed to repeal the previous vote locating the college in Bristol County, which included the town of Warren. A committee from Warren replied by presenting the amount of the subscription it had raised to support the college, and the Warren Baptist Church, in an effort to strengthen the town's claim, agreed to place its meetinghouse at the disposal of the college and to allow it to be used for commencement exercises, "provided that the college edifice be founded and built in the County of Bristol."[12]

Moses then presented the subscription from Providence County amounting to £1,878 "besides £800 before subscribed in Providence without any conditions where the edifice should be erected." Thus, while there were people in Providence who eagerly sought the college for their town, there were also those who were willing to support the institution regardless of its location. This manifestation of public spirit proved to be of considerable importance in the ensuing struggle, and in the end may have been the decisive factor in Providence's victory.

In the "Minute of Proceedings" that Moses kept, there is no mention of a memorial's being presented by Newport at the meeting in November. A subscription had not yet been raised, and no one spoke for that county. Nevertheless, the leaders of Newport soon made clear their determination that Providence would not get the college. When spokesmen for Kent County requested that the vote locating the college in Bristol County be rescinded, Henry Ward of Newport, secretary of the colony and one of the fellows of

12. Minutes of Proceedings of Corporation Meeting, Nov. 14-15, 1769, *ibid.* There is a copy in Rhode Island College Miscellaneous Papers, I, 55, John Hay Lib. The events of the meeting are reconstructed from this "Copy of the Minutes made at the time by MB," a detailed and valuable document.

the corporation, observed that the charter required the two bodies of the corporation—the trustees and fellows—to vote as separate and distinct bodies. Ward had apparently noted that if the trustees and fellows voted as a unit the decision might be in favor of Providence, whereas if the two bodies voted separately the vote would end in a stalemate since three of the fellows were from Newport and were known to favor Warren over either East Greenwich or Providence.

A long, involved, and heated debate followed. Someone tried to brush aside Ward's objections by pointing out that the previous meetings of the corporation had never been conducted in that way. Ward made his motion again, this time being seconded by his brother Samuel, the former governor. Upon examining the charter, everyone agreed that Ward's interpretation was correct, but they also agreed that to adopt his motion would result in the invalidation of "4 years of proceedings"; "if the fellows had a negative," moreover, "the vote of three against 2 fellows would compel the whole 22 of the corporation to agree or there could be no building erected." The vote ended in a tie. As Moses recorded, "nothing could be done in this dillima." But his pessimism was premature; a procedure was finally agreed upon. The corporation agreed that the fellows and trustees would vote by head on the original motion to recede from the previous decision to locate the college in Bristol County; the matter of voting in the future would be settled at the next meeting.[13]

The corporation agreed to abandon the Warren location "by a majority, if I mistake not," Moses remembered, "of about 8 or 10," and he promptly made a motion for an immediate discussion of the new location of the college. The committees from East Greenwich and Warren, and Henry Ward and his friends from Newport, countered with a pro-

13. Today the fellows and trustees meet together as prescribed by the charter.

posal to put off the question until the next meeting in May.
These delaying tactics failed, however, and Moses' resolution passed, although he had to accept a reservation allowing
Newport or any other town the right to call another meeting
at any time before January 1 if it raised a larger subscription
than those already before the corporation.

Providence then made its bid. Since Moses had been
chiefly responsible for the committee's memorial, he presented the claim.[14] The first and principal reason why the
college should be located in Providence, he argued, was that
the people had unconditionally subscribed the large sum of
£800 "upon principals of regard and esteem of so useful
and necessary an institution"; but finding this sum plus the
other unconditional subscriptions insufficient to erect the
college building, and the conditional subscriptions in the
other counties also too small, the people of Providence
County had generously increased their contribution. When
added to the unconditional subscription of £800, the total
would surely be adequate to the needs of the college
buildings.

From this very persuasive argument, Moses went on to
enumerate the advantages that would accrue to the institution, students, and faculty if the college were moved to Providence. Since Providence was more centrally located than
either Warren or East Greenwich (Newport was not mentioned, since it was not an open contender), communication
with other towns in New England would be facilitated;
moreover, the town had an abundance of cheap food, clothing, and fuel, sufficient libraries to serve the intellectual
needs of the students, plus a suitable number of physicians

14. For what follows, see Moses Brown's memorial "To the Chancellor,
President, and other gentlemen of the Corporation for founding and En-
dowing a College within the Colony of Rhode Island and Providence Plantations, convened at Newport, the 14th of November, 1769," Moses Brown
Papers, Misc. MSS., B-814, Box 2. The memorial is printed in Guild, *History
of Brown University*, 181-84. Moses used information provided him by
Darius Sessions, John Cole, and Stephen Hopkins.

to take care of their physical illnesses. Commenting on the charter provision that the college should be founded upon "the most catholick and free principles," he contended that the number of students attracted to the college would be greater in Providence than at Warren or East Greenwich because there was a greater diversity of religious institutions at Providence: a college there would be more apt to attract students from all localities and religious denominations in the province. Such religious diversity would help prevent the college, including teachers as well as students, from representing a narrow sectarianism. In his view the future usefulness and prosperity of the college depended upon maintaining its nonsectarian character. Although the control of the college was in the hands of the Baptists, he insisted that the atmosphere of the institution should not be tailored to one denomination; the faculty should be made up of men of various religious faiths.

By emphasizing the religious diversity of Providence and stressing the need for "the preservation of the freedom of the institution" to be established there, Moses turned what might have been a defect into an asset. Providence was the Baptist stronghold in the colony, and people of different religion might have feared that locating the college in that town would place it under too strict control of one sect. When the college had been chartered in 1764, Congregationalists in Newport had charged that the Providence Baptists had deserted them in a plan for a liberal institution free from control of any one religious denomination; the Baptists countered by accusing the Congregationalists of resorting to underhanded methods to gain the controlling voice in the corporation. By playing down the Baptist influence and emphasizing the advantages of religious heterogeneity for maintaining a college free from domination by one sect, Moses made a clever appeal for the widest possible support for the college. Many years later he recalled that the very

existence of the college in its infancy depended upon the support of all religious groups because, at the time, there was no single faith strong enough to support a college. He was right.

Moses concluded his argument by stressing the financial performance of Providence supporters. "It is necessary in the execution of all matters of a publick nature that the undertakers have a zeal for promoting it. This qualification so requisite for the perfecting the college institution we are conscious we have, as has been made manifest by the town of Providence from the very beginning [of the contest] to this time not only by their liberal subscriptions amounting to more than all the money that had been subscribed within the colony, but every other mark of respect for the institution and the favours of it." In his opinion the necessary "zeal for promoting" the college existed only in Providence. To settle it in any of the other proposed locations would be a serious mistake because the people there would not give a college the support that would make it a success.

When the meeting resumed the next day, Providence obviously was the frontrunner; before voting on the question, however, the corporation decided that "in case any subscription be raised in the county of Newport or any other county equal or superior to any now offered . . . then the vote fixing the edifice shall not be esteemed binding in case they [the fellows and trustees] shall think proper."

There were twenty-two trustees and five fellows present, with the Chancellor, Stephen Hopkins, presiding. When the vote was counted, Providence had thirteen; East Greenwich, seven; and Warren, six. Hopkins voted for Providence, giving it a majority of one. Moses, sensing that some of the members of the corporation might feel uneasy at so small a majority and desiring to alleviate their apprehensions, proposed another vote, this time between Providence and East Greenwich, the vote to be secret. When the ballots were

counted this time Providence received nineteen and East
Greenwich seven. It was evident that victory lay with Providence, and that unless Newport or one of the other counties
acted quickly and raised a large subscription, Providence
had a college.

As leader of the Providence forces, Moses undoubtedly
felt some satisfaction over his success. Riding home through
the snow the next day, however, he probably realized that the
fight had not ended, but had merely moved from the pre-
liminary into the decisive stage. From the actions of the
Ward brothers, William Ellery, Dr. Thomas Eyres, and
others from Newport and King's County, he knew now that
they intended to make an effort to reverse the corporation's
decision. He was surprised, not that they had come forward,
but that they had delayed so long. Newport possessed certain advantages for a college over Providence—a greater
variety of churches, more and better libraries, numerous
citizens of superior education—and the town was better able
financially to support a college. During the three-day meeting he had heard rumors that Newporters were already being
approached about contributing money to have the college
built on the island. Fortunately he had friends there who
would keep him informed of any further developments along
that line.

Shortly after Moses returned home, a Newport friend,
James Clarke, informed him that the town government was
holding meetings to raise a college subscription, lest Newport lose its position of leadership in the colony.[15] The fund
drive was headed by those unfriendly to Governor Wanton's
administration and to his supporters in the north. "I wish
a regard for the Seminary was their motive," he concluded.
"Mr. Secretary [Henry Ward] and Mr. Sam Carr are very

15. Nov. 22, 1769, Brown Papers, Misc. Letters, 1769, II. For an account
of the Newport subscription, see Sarah K. Birkhead to Walter C. Bronson,
Mar. 10, 1914, Archives, John Hay Lib.

zealous; I shall endeavor to obtain the best information from time to time of every proceeding and acquaint you therewith."

Spurred by the news from the camp of the enemy, Moses and the Providence group adopted a new strategy, writing to friends in Warren, Scituate, Gloucester, and other towns in the north asking for support and additional subscriptions to the fund raised by Providence.[16]   A college located in Providence, they pointed out, would bring in great quantities of money and consequently increase the markets for all kinds of the country's produce; it would also raise the value of real estate.   Of no small importance, they argued, was the fact that the college would do much to increase the influence of the northern part of the colony in the government.

On New Year's Eve, next to the final day for Newport to submit its subscription, Moses and other members of the Providence committee added up all their subscriptions and found that they amounted to £3,424.[17] On the same day, they learned that Henry Ward and Dr. Thomas Eyres, fellows of the college, had written to President Manning requesting a meeting of the corporation for January 23, to reconsider the location, because, they claimed, Newport now had a larger subscription than Providence.   But the president, acting on the advice of men from both Newport and Providence, did not call the meeting because the request had been signed by only two fellows when three were required, the subscription had not been verified, and the deadline for the meeting was January 1.[18]

The building committee in Providence now assumed that

16. Copy of a letter sent to the town council of Scituate, about the college, Dec. 8, 1769, Moses Brown Papers, Misc. MSS., B-814, Box 2.   Moses received an anonymous offer of help from "one of the Judges of the County of Kent, Dec. 30, 1769," *ibid.*

17. Nicholas Brown & Co. to Joseph Brown, Dec. 30, 1769, *ibid.*

18. Nicholas Brown & Co., to Joseph Wanton, Jr., Dec. 26, 1769, *ibid.*; Rhode Island College Misc. Papers, I, 73, John Hay Lib.   Henry Ward and Thomas Eyres signed the request for the meeting.

the matter was settled and got busy with plans, and the directors of the college fund instructed Moses Brown and eleven others to lay the subscription before the corporation.[19] A few days later Moses and John were detailed to select the site upon which to erect the "College edifice." They chose the home lot of their great-great-grandfather, Chad Brown.[20] They pushed ahead with the building plans, collecting materials and men to begin construction as soon as the weather would permit.

Despite these preparations, President Manning could not resist the pressure for a meeting to consider the Newport subscription. Henry Ward and Dr. Eyres finally prevailed upon Joshua Babcock, a third fellow, to join them in signing a request for a meeting;[21] although Manning was satisfied that the college should be placed in Providence, he was now obliged to call the meeting which was held February 7 at Warren. The issue was not simply one of where the college should be built, but whether Providence or Newport should gain the political and cultural supremacy of the colony. William Ellery, Dr. Babcock, Henry Ward, his brother Samuel, who still aspired to be governor, and others had tried to inject the college contest into the general election in April, attacking Governor Wanton and his supporters in the north for their support of Manning's bias in favor of Providence and his refusal to call a meeting of the corporation. A few of the old Ward party people had never given up hopes of regaining political supremacy in the colony, and they made the most of what they thought was an excellent opportunity.

Although confident that they would have the larger sub-

19. Minutes of Meeting, Jan. 5, 1770, Rhode Island College Misc. Papers, I, 75, John Hay Lib.; *Providence Gazette; and Country Journal,* Jan. 13, 1770. The notice, dated Jan. 12, 1770, was signed by John Brown and Stephen Hopkins.

20. Hedges, *The Browns,* 197.

21. See the notice in the *Providence Gazette; and Country Journal,* Jan. 27, 1770.

scription, the Providence committee made careful preparations for the meeting.[22] John Brown visited Warren and
reported that Manning was so upset by the attacks on his
character from Newport that he requested the attendance
of those who had advised him not to call the earlier meeting.[23] Moses and the Providence committee were not only
willing to back Manning's conduct; they also saw that they
might be able to thwart attempts by Henry Ward and his
friends to make location of the college a political issue. If
the corporation voted "to exculpate" Manning, it would
place Ward and his party in a bad light and perhaps it might
"settle the grand point and probably . . . prevent another
vote."

In calling the corporation to meet in Warren, Manning
used good judgment, for the Providence committee would
not only have the full support of a large delegation from the
north, but of the members of the faculty as well, who were
all for Providence. Although the faculty did not have a vote
on the corporation, they could exert some influence outside
the meeting. The corporation convened on February 7 and
spent the entire day swearing in new trustees and listening to
the committee from Warren and East Greenwich present
their arguments. It was "after candle light" when the Newport committee presented its subscription, and the discussion
dragged on until ten o'clock.

22. Copy of a printed handbill, Monday, Feb. 5, 1770, Rhode Island College Misc. Papers, I, 77, John Hay Lib. In the Moses Brown Papers, Misc.
MSS., B-814, Box 2, there is an anonymous, undated letter to Nicholas Brown,
which contains several suggestions as to the best arguments that could be
advanced by the Providence committee at the approaching meeting; many
years later Moses speculated that the author was President Manning. For
Moses' exhaustive study of comparative construction costs at Newport and
Providence, see Hedges, *The Browns*, 196; Moses Brown to Jon Gibbs, Feb. 6,
1770, and "An Account of what the College will cost more if Built in Newport than in Providence," Moses Brown Papers, Misc. MSS., B-814, Box 2.
For James Manning's account of the struggle for the college, see his letter to
Hezekiah Smith, printed in Guild, *History of Brown University*, 196.
23. Nicholas Brown to Joseph Wanton, Jr., Jan. 29, 1770, Rhode Island
College Misc. Papers, I, 77, John Hay Lib.

Debate continued all the next day. After the Newport committee had presented its subscriptions, Henry Ward, the leader, told Moses that all the Newport subscriptions were in and proposed that no more subscriptions be presented. Moses and his friends agreed. When the chairman added up the contributions he found that Providence had subscribed £4,175 and Newport £3,950. Through adroit delaying tactics, however, Ward and Ellery blocked attempts by Moses and his committee to bring the issue to a vote. Finally, an adjournment was called for dinner. When the tired participants reconvened, both sides had mysteriously gathered more subscriptions, Newport forging ahead with £4,558:14 to Providence's £4,399:13.

Moses now demonstrated his command of dilatory techniques in an effort to delay a vote until his committee could gather its resources and play its last card. Using the detailed calculations that he and John had made during January, he demonstrated that the college could be established in Providence for £574 cheaper than at Newport, an amount which he insisted "should be added to ours, leaving a balance in our favor of £415."[24] Prolonged and bitter debate followed, punctuated by reassertions of the claims of East Greenwich and Warren committees, each hoping to be selected as a compromise candidate if the leading contenders deadlocked. When the contestants began to repeat themselves, Moses put the motion: should the vote locating the college at Providence be repealed? By a twenty-one-to-fourteen vote, Providence acquired the college.[25]

The "great noise and high tumulto" which disrupted the colony during the argument over the location of the college

24. For Moses' preparation in presenting Providence's case, see his "Notes of H. Ward's arguments and some answers," "Essay on Memorial to the Corporation 7th of February 1770," and "Miscellaneous Notes," Moses Brown Papers, Misc. MSS., B-814, Box 2.
25. The much corrected motion is in Moses' hand, *ibid.*

soon subsided somewhat,[26] but it was revived in the general
election in April, when Samuel Ward once again tried to
win the governor's office. After he was decisively defeated
by the north-south coalition candidate, Joseph Wanton, the
Reverend Ezra Stiles, and some other disappointed gentlemen attempted to get the General Assembly to charter another college, to be built in Newport. In his diary on June 11,
a dejected Dr. Stiles noted that "the charter [was] read first
time in the Assembly, and opposed by Mr. Moses Brown of
Providence a Baptist." Indeed, Moses directed the campaign
to block the Newport bill, and with the assistance of Stephen
Hopkins, the Providence deputies, President Manning, and
the corporation, his group defeated it decisively.[27]

    After their victory at Warren, the Providence building
committee once again went to work to erect a "college edifice." On March 26, they decided to build the college on
the land that John and Moses had bought in January; the
price was $330.30.[28] This stirred a momentary reappearance
of divisive forces which had split the town between the east
and west sides in 1767, when it destroyed the efforts to
establish a public school system. Citizens on the Weybosset
side of the Great Bridge promptly presented a memorial,
along with a generous subscription, asking that the college
be built on the west side of town, but their petition was not
acted upon and the next day work on the foundation of the
"college edifice" began.[29] Had building contracts been as

    26. Theodore Foster to Jedediah Foster, Cambridge, Apr. 7, 1770, Archives,
John Hay Lib.
    27. Moses Brown's notes in preparation for his speech against the second
charter are in Moses Brown Papers, Misc. MSS., B-814, Box 2. For Ezra
Stiles's comments on the contest, see Franklin B. Dexter, ed., *The Literary
Diary of Ezra Stiles, DD., LL.D., President of Yale College* (N. Y., 1901), I,
46, 108, 109; see also Bronson, *History of Brown University*, 50.
    28. See the deed signed by John, Moses, Sarah, and Anna Brown, Aug. 1,
1770, Archives, John Hay Lib. The deed was sworn to before Stephen
Hopkins, Chief Justice, on Jan. 3, 1771.
    29. Roelker, "The Browns and Brown University," *Brown Alumni Monthly*,
49 (Dec. 1948), 8.

formal then as they are now, there would be a document
showing that Nicholas Brown and Company agreed to take
charge of constructing the first building of Rhode Island College, and that the three partners, Nicholas, Joseph, and
Moses, with the addition of John—he had withdrawn from
the company some months previously—supervised the work
throughout, contributing both time and money.[30]   On May
19, 1770, the *Providence Gazette* notified its readers: "Monday last [May 14] the first Foundation Stone of the College
about to be erected here was laid by Mr. John Brown, of this
Place, Merchant, in Presence of a Number of Gentlemen,
Friends to the Institution,—About twenty Workmen have
since been employed on the Foundation, which Number will
be increased, and the Building be compleated with all possible Dispatch."   Nothing was said about Moses Brown, the
man who had done more than any other to bring the college
to Providence.   He was probably content to watch the ceremony from the edge of the crowd.

30. Bronson, *History of Brown University*, 56-57.

4

Journey Through the Wilderness

WHEN MOSES rejected John's proposals to expand the business in 1770, John decided to go it alone as far as the shipping trade was concerned. Moses joined Nicholas and Joseph in the reorganization of Nicholas Brown and Company, and, whether despite John's absence or because of it, during the next three years the company enjoyed a state of stability and prosperity that made it one of New England's largest and most influential trading firms.[1]

In addition to continued concern for his business interests, Moses as usual devoted part of his time to routine affairs of government in the General Assembly. In colony politics he was involved for a few weeks each spring in the campaigns preceding the general elections. Politics were tame, however, compared to what they had been in the sixties; most of the earlier issues had been solved and economic prosperity made the remaining ones less pressing. This domestic tranquillity mirrored the improved relations that existed between America and the mother country. In the winter of 1770 Moses wrote to Joseph Sherwood, the provincial agent in London, that "we are now very quiet in

1. See Hedges, *The Browns*, 18-19, for the reorganization of the business.

the colony with respect to general as well as our own colony polliticks and indeed since the non-importation agreement is dissolved the colonys seem very easy." Referring to the disturbances in Boston on March 5, 1770 (later to become famous as the Boston Massacre), he observed that "Captain Preston and six of the soldiers are acquitted two found guilty. Should there be a repeal of the tea duty etc this sessions of parliament a compleat reconsilation will immediately take place."[2]

Moses' life during the two years following repeal of the Townshend Acts and the reorganization of the business was pleasant. For a time he assumed chief responsibility for company affairs, while his brothers either repaired their homes or built new ones. He continued to improve his farm, to develop his nursery, and to amuse himself with his growing collection of scientific instruments. He had fully recovered from his illness and his wife enjoyed relatively good health. She frequently accompanied him to Boston or Newport where she bought items for their home and visited friends while Moses transacted company business. In the summer of 1771 Moses moved his wife and family out to the farmhouse he had built two years before. Anna was expecting a baby and was more comfortable in the country during the hot summer. She had had "an ill turn of the plurisy," which, added to her difficult pregnancy, "made her case very afflicting." But, Moses wrote to Joseph Wanton, Jr., she soon recovered from "those pains and is now as comfortable and reconciled to receive what further must soon come upon her."[3] He apologized for not attending to business matters for Wanton by explaining that he was worried about his wife and wanted to remain close to home.

The child, a boy, was born at the farmhouse on Monday,

2. Dec. 10, 1770, Moses Brown Papers, II, 3.
3. July 8, 1771, *ibid.*

July 15.[4] He was named Obadiah after Anna's father and
Moses' uncle. To Moses' great relief Anna, despite her
delicate constitution, suffered no ill effects. She was up and
around in a short while and by early fall was able to accompany Moses to Boston. Before cold weather set in, Moses
moved his family back into the town house.

His household was now quite large. Besides his own
family he had living with him Mother Brown, his widowed
sister Mary Vanderlight, and Anna's sister Mary, who had
moved in from the farm at Gloucester. In addition there were
a number of Negro servants, five men and one girl of his
own plus several belonging to other members of the family.
Although most of the servants did not live in the main
house—they had quarters in one of the smaller buildings to
the rear near the barn—Uncle Obadiah's old house was bulging with occupants. It had been built many decades before,
probably some time after the destruction of the town by the
Indians during King Philip's War, and although a lean-to
had been added and frequent repairs made, it was old,
drafty, and uncomfortable, besides being crowded. The
house was not favorably located either; in the heart of the
rapidly developing business district, it was slowly being
hemmed in by new buildings. Moses was anxious to move
his family away from the heavy traffic of wagons passing the
front door to the hayward to weigh their loads or to cross
over the Great Bridge to the west side, and he worried about
the children falling off the wharf and drowning as John's
daughter had done some years before. Several families who
had lived for years on Towne Street were moving up the hill
to Benefit Street or to the outskirts of town.

Moses could have moved out to his Aunt Mary's farm in
Gloucester or to his own farmhouse on the Neck, but the first

4. Records of Births and Marriages, II, 6, City Hall, Providence. See also
the letter of congratulation sent to Moses by Joseph Wanton, Jr., Mar. 28,
1771, Moses Brown Papers, II, 7.

MOSES BROWN'S ELMGROVE ESTATE

The Greek-style mansion overlooking the Seekonk River, Providence, R. I., is part of the Elmgrove estate that Moses

was too far away from town and the second was not quite suitable for year-around living. Moses had, over the years, been enlarging the small farm that he inherited from his father by buying up small parcels of adjoining land, and he had long had his eye on a piece of property bordering his own land owned by John Merritt, who had built a large Greek-style mansion and improved the grounds during the fifteen years he had lived there. In 1772 Merritt died and the estate was put up at auction. Moses put in a bid and got the place, lock, stock, and barrel.[5] By early summer he and his family were comfortably installed in their new home.

Situated on the top of the hill that sloped gently toward the Seekonk, flanked on the north by Richard Brown's farm and the Cat Swamp, on the south by Knight Dexter's farm and the road leading to the Narrow Passage Ferry, the mansion house commanded a view of the wide expanses of the river and caught the gentle breeze that came off the water, even on the hottest summer day. The location was ideal— within convenient distance of the countinghouse and shop, yet out of sight and earshot of the busy commercial center of town. It was far enough away, so that on the still evening of July 9, 1772, Moses did not even hear the beating of the drums summoning the menfolk to Sabin's tavern to prepare for the destruction of His Majesty's ship, the *Gaspee*,[6] whose captain had made a nuisance of himself trying to enforce the custom laws.

Unfortunately Moses and his family did not have much opportunity to enjoy their home. In September 1772 the first of a series of tragic events occurred that radically altered his life. He and his wife were in Boston on a combination business and pleasure trip when Anna suddenly collapsed. Moses

---

5. Moses Brown Papers, Austin MSS., IV, "Deeds and Platts," Moses Brown School Lib. Moses paid £1250 sterling for Merritt's estate, which contained a "Mansion House," several other buildings, and "about Two Hundred and thirteen acres."

6. Hedges, *The Browns*, 208-10.

anxiously consulted Doctors Perkins and Lloyd, but they
candidly admitted that they were at a loss to account for her
condition and told him that medicine and treatment would
probably be ineffectual.[7] Moses was greatly alarmed. Convinced that his wife's condition was extremely serious, perhaps fatal, he wrote to his brothers: "Nature must be dissolved and all our joys come to an end! Providence un-
erring Providence determines these events, not only to be
sinsible to this but be prepared by the kind preminitions is
our best comfort."[8] After Moses moved her from Boston
to Providence, he sat throughout the fall and winter by his
wife's bedside and watched her die. Anna knew that she
was dying and as her time approached she turned more and
more to God for comfort; Moses turned with her. In search
for some explanation for his wife's affliction, and no doubt
in an attempt to find some comfort for his grief, he began to
attend religious services at the Quaker meetinghouse in
Providence. Anna could not, of course, accompany him, but
he brought Friends to visit her and silent meetings were held
by her bedside; together they moved away from the Baptist
Church and toward acceptance of Friends' doctrines.

Anna died in February. "She went to sleep the 5th of
the 2d month last," Moses wrote to William Wilson, one of
the Quakers he met during the winter, "and I have no doubt
in the favour of her dear Lord and Saviour."[9] Anna's death
was a severe shock to Moses. He identified himself with his
wife to a remarkable degree; her death was, in a sense, also
his death. He became obsessed with a sense of guilt for the

7. Dr. James Lloyd was a well-known physician in Boston, skilled in surgery and midwifery. Nathaniel Perkins was less known than his colleague.
James Thacher, *American Medical Biography or, Memoirs of Eminent Physicians Who Have Flourished in America* . . . (Boston, 1828), 24, and Henry
R. Viets in *DAB* s.v. "Lloyd, James."

8. Sept. 1772, Brown Papers, Misc. Letters, 1772.

9. July 20, 1773, Moses Brown Papers, Misc. MSS., K-AB. Moses began to
date his letters after the Quaker custom in the winter of 1772-73. For Anna's
death see Records of Births, Marriages and Deaths, V, 430, City Hall, Providence.

tragedy and plunged into the depths of despair. Like John Bunyan, he was a man with "a great burden upon his back" who "wept and trembled," and cried out "What shall I do." His health suffered. For a time he complained of indigestion and of severe headaches and a general depression. He went on long horseback rides and spent prolonged periods in seclusion frantically searching for an answer to his troubles.

For about six months after his wife died, Moses was unable to come to any decision about his future. During this period he ceased to attend to business at the countinghouse, and, since he had not stood for re-election to the General Assembly in April, he did not attend the sessions. Although he continued to perform some of his duties in the local community—he gave assistance to the construction of the college buildings and the Market House—the only thing that really interested him was Quakerism. He undertook an extensive course of study of the New Testament and the important works of Quakers that were available to him, such as William Penn's *Works,* Isaac Penington's *Works,* which he had bought some years before, and William Sewel's *History of the Rise, Increase, and Progress of the Christian People Called Quakers.* Many of his surviving letters are "Ruff Copies," and they show the intensity of his religious education and the pains he took to acquire a knowledge of Quakerism. Along the margin of a copy of a letter to Mary Dexter, written in May 1773, Moses made twenty-nine biblical references, and he undoubtedly had the Bible by his side while he wrote. He took great care in composition, and, as was his custom, made many interlineations before making a clean copy. His letters, in which he tried to express his emotional state, are filled with long religious metaphors and direct quotations from the Bible. During the summer of 1773 Moses presents a pathetic picture of a man whose world had been utterly destroyed, struggling to find a new one. His

mind tells him to embrace Quakerism, but his heart is reluctant to respond.

His spiritual journey was slow and tortuous. Many months passed before he could write to a friend that he was able "clearly to distinguish between the leaven of the Pharises from that of the Kingdom, and the transformations of the spirit of truth which alone can make us free." Moses had attended Quaker meetings regularly and had envisioned Quaker principles before his wife died, but he delayed a formal application for admission to a monthly meeting while he debated whether he should break with his family and the Baptist Church.

The crucial period in his efforts to withdraw from his older environment came in the winter of 1772-73. He all but stopped corresponding with his former circle of friends. Except for attendance at Friends' services at the Providence branch (the Lower House) of the Smithfield Monthly Meeting, he lived a hermit-like existence. Then he began to cultivate an entirely new group of friends, to use the word in a double sense. At the June New England Yearly Meeting at Newport he met many Friends from New York, New Jersey, and Pennsylvania. Some of these men had come to Quakerism in much the same way as Moses, and he no doubt found them very sympathetic with his sufferings. They were devoted to the work of the Society, particularly its humanitarian aspects, and it was to them that he turned. To John Sleeper, a Friend he had met during the winter, he wrote that:

the all supporting arm has been underneath to bear up and support me through the see and at the moveing of the cloud and appearance of the light I have moved forward as I hope and trust toward the promiced land. But it is but a little and the wilderness still surrounds and at times [I] feel the with drawings of the leader, but have heither to been graciously presarved from murmering or desiring any other, though have been solicitus to

enquire after the return of my beloved whose mannifest presence though ever so short more than recompences for any length
of absence.[10]

In another letter a few days later, he wrote to Friend Samuel
Emlen of Philadelphia that he desired "a continuance of thy
correspondence on all ocations, . . . as I have need of every
aid in my intended travel through the wilderness." He
literally begged Emlen for "advice or adminition," and said
that "indeed I have need of much pruning." At times he
seemed to be "willing and desirous" to surrender his heart
to God and "to stand collected from every object that can
grattifye and delight the sensual part." He was prepared
"to labour after an assembly of all the powers and facultys
of the soul that they may be sanctifyd by him who gave them
and to be devoted to the divine will and presarved from
doing any thing against the truth." "If I have at times," he
lamented, "unworthly partook of the extended branch of the
divine fountain, alas how often are they absorbed in the dry
and barren hearth."[11] Peace of mind did not come easily.

Why Moses turned to Quakerism for spiritual comfort
rather than to the family church is difficult to determine.
Undoubtedly he was influenced by his wife who became a
spiritual Quaker before she died, and by her sisters, Mary
and Phebe, and John's wife, Sarah, who were attending
Friends' meetings as early as the winter of 1773, and perhaps
earlier. Even that old rascal Uncle Elisha had "got religion,"
and was attending Friends' meetings. Perhaps Moses followed their lead. At any rate, Anna's illness and death produced in him a desire to make a complete break with the
past, to carry out a total revolution in his life. He seems to
have held himself responsible for her death. Earlier he had
attributed business misfortunes, illnesses, and death to a
"luke warm" religious attitude. Now he felt that God had

10. July 29, 1773, Moses Brown Papers, Misc. MSS., K-AB.
11. Aug. 3, 1773, *ibid.*

78

punished him for unfaithfulness by taking his wife. Moses became convinced that his capacity to do good had been severely limited by his political, business, and social commitments. He interpreted the death of his wife as a divine injunction to free himself from these commitments; his withdrawal from public affairs and his acceptance of Quakerism were attempts to comply with that injunction.[12]

By mid-summer Moses had recovered sufficiently from his melancholia to come to grips with the problem of his continued relation with his brothers in Nicholas Brown and Company and their other businesses. The desire to withdraw from business was an attitude shared by many converts to Quakerism. After much thought Moses decided on this course of action, although carrying out the decision was slow and painful.

On August 27 he wrote, but did not send, a letter to his brothers in which he told them that for some time he had been thinking of retiring from business, although because of an unsettled state of mind he had not said anything to them on the subject.[13] "But after the most deliberate consideration and waiting what I hope and trust is the best council, I virily believe my business and ingagements in the world has been a principal means of preventing my injoying an increase of that better part that has foundations and will induce when all things here below will vannish and be no more." He would, he wrote, be very happy if his brothers would "find a freedom to take the whole business and estate of vessels, furnace, and candle works" into their hands upon any terms they thought reasonable. To allay any suspicion that he acted because of dissatisfaction with the conduct of his partners, he told them that he had "no other motive for this proposal than a desire to pursue such a course of remaining life as will afford the most true peace of mind hear and

12. Moses Brown to Francis Wayland, May 25, 1833, *ibid.*, B-814, Box 2.
13. Moses Brown Papers, II, 18. See also Hedges, *The Browns*, 17-18.

prepare for its future injoyments in a better country for I seek one to come." He concluded: "Dear Brothers, this looks to me and feels like separating the joint from the marrow . . . but that brother love may continue and more abound among us accompanied with that charity that is not easily provoked nor think it no evil but rejoyces with truth and never faileth, is the desire of your affectionate brother."

Moses was never one to reveal his thinking on a subject before he was ready to act. After deliberating on the matter, he decided to withhold the letter until he returned from "a little journey southward," probably to Newport, Long Island, and New York. By the time he had returned, which was about the middle of September, he had made up his mind. He sent the letter to his brothers with the observation that "the foregoing I wrote at the date but finding the cross so close I put it off then for further time to contemplation upon a matter of so great consequences."[14]

His brothers reluctantly accepted his decision to retire from the company. They asked him to continue in the business until the spring importation of goods from England, when they would reorganize their affairs. He consented and wrote in an apologetic vein to William Wilson in December, explaining that retirement was complicated and that "doubtless some proper attention will be required on my part to bring it rightly about." He was sorry he could not sever his business connections immediately, but he did not want to "make any uneasiness" for his brothers by putting them to a great deal of trouble.[15]

One of the difficulties was that Moses' religious activities interfered with the negotiations to close his accounts. Early in November he was visited by John Pemberton from Philadelphia and a number of other Friends who were escorting

14. Sept. 15, 1773, Moses Brown Papers, II, 18.
15. Dec. 2, 1773, Moses Brown Papers, Austin MSS., V, "Abolition," Moses Brown School Lib.

Mary Leaver, from England, on a religious tour of America.
When they asked him to continue the trip with them, he
readily agreed, even though his decision left his brothers
and the projected meetings about the division of the business
stranded. Apologizing for his conduct, he observed that
"when Friends come 3000 miles on religious visits alone, and
are infirm and weakly they need every assistance and incouragement to make their journeying comfortable, as deep
and trying times often attend them."[16] He urged his partners to continue the business without regard to his interests,
for their affairs should not suffer on his account.

Although Moses wanted to dispose of his interest in the
candle works, as well as in the other businesses, circumstances
beyond his control prevented his doing so. His strong in-
clination to follow the example of so many other Quakers
and withdraw completely from normal intercourse with the
other elements of society was frustrated. His movement
away from his past environment was gradual, and never complete. By the time he was in a position to retire completely
from business he no longer felt the need to isolate himself.
Forced participation was not without its beneficial results;
it meant that he was not completely removed from the larger
society in which the Quaker society existed and that he never
lost sight of the non-Quaker point of view.

Moses' conversion to Quakerism and his partial retirement from business did not mean that he led the life of a
recluse on his farm on the outskirts of town, although at first
this was certainly his intention. Actually, he felt the need
for people, particularly the companionship of Friends who
would, he hoped, confirm and steady him in the principles
of truth. He often expressed disappointment because he did
not feel that closeness to God he expected to follow as a re-

16. Moses Brown to Nicholas Brown, Nov. [6], 1774, Brown Papers, Misc.
Letters, 1774. His sister-in-law, Mary Brown, Mary Olney, and Jonathan
Arnold, a local druggist, accompanied him.

sult of his conversion. He therefore kept his house bulging with Friends, perhaps in the hope that they would communicate some of their spirituality to him.

There were few months out of the year that did not find Moses entertaining traveling Friends. Those on religious visits to New England usually came to Newport by water from Philadelphia or Long Island, and after attending meetings in that area came up the river to Providence, where they invariably stayed at Moses' place. In June at the time of the New England Yearly Meeting, which was held at Newport as a rule, Moses could always count on numerous visitors. In addition to traveling Friends, people in need could always find a bed and food at the farm, as well as spiritual guidance. Moses dispensed both with generosity and kindness, and his many acts were long remembered by those who benefited from them.

One of the chief effects of Moses' gradual conversion to Quakerism was that it led him to free his slaves and become an ardent abolitionist.[17] Before his entry into the Society of Friends, there is little evidence that he opposed slavery. The only suggestion is his appointment in 1770, while still a member of the Assembly, to a committee to draw up a bill prohibiting the importation of slaves.[18] Since rejected bills were not generally retained by the colony secretary, its precise provisions are not known, but the incident constitutes the single bit of direct evidence that Moses was concerned about slavery before 1773.

17. Moses Brown Papers, Austin MSS., V, "Abolition," Moses Brown School Lib. The deed of manumission shows that Moses freed six slaves "wholely" and gave up a quarter interest in four more.

18. Journal House of Deputies, 1769-70, Sept. sess., 110, June sess., 1771, 258, and Journals of the Senate, 1771-77, June sess., 1771, Oct. sess., 1771, R. I. Archives. There is no evidence to support Thomas Edward Drake's statement in *Quakers and Slavery in America* (New Haven, 1950), 88, that the bill to tax slaves imported into the colony was supported by the Quakers and Samuel Hopkins. We can safely assume, however, that they would have supported it had they had the opportunity.

His decision to free his own slaves was not arrived at suddenly, nor without difficulty. Apparently it was made as a result of earnest conversations within his family. His wife's sister Mary, the youngest of Uncle Obadiah's daughters, who was living in Moses' house, freed her slaves six days before Moses freed his. Mary had also abandoned the Baptist faith for Quakerism. Like her sister Anna, she was a small frail girl, very emotional and sensitive to injustice and suffering. For many years she was Moses' constant companion on his visits to meetings throughout New England and the middle colonies, and served as his hostess when Friends stopped at his home to visit and rest. In her deed of manumission she gave as her reasons that "the holding of Negros in slavery however kindly used by their masters and mistresses had a tendency to incourage the iniquitous practice of importing them from their native country, and is contrary to that justice, mercy and humility required of every christian." She freed two slaves: "Eve an Negro woman with her child Eve being all I possessed of of that nation and colour."[19] In conformance to Quaker practice, Mary provided for their support and directed her heirs to see that the child received "a sober and religious education."

On November 10, Moses followed her example. It was a dramatic event in his life and performed with appropriate ceremony. He assembled his entire family and a number of Friends who were visiting him at the time in the large main hall of the house. There were fifteen or twenty people in all—Mary Brown, his mother-in-law (Elizabeth Brown), his daughter Sarah, Audrey Greene (housekeeper and nurse), John Collins and Levi Arnold, two friends from Narragansett country, a number of other unidentified friends, and ten slaves. Moses recorded that when they were all assembled

19. Mary Brown's deed of manumission, Nov. 4, 1773, Moses Brown Papers, Misc. MSS., B-814, Box 2. The deed was recorded in Council Book No. 6, Folio 75, on Nov. 16, 1773, by James Angell, clerk, City Hall, Providence.

they were "favored, providentialy favored," while they sat in silent prayer, "waiting together on our great Master." Then Moses turned to the slaves and read the articles of manumission he had so carefully drawn up:

Whereas I am clearly convinced that the buying and selling of men of what colour soever as slaves is contrary to the Divine Mind manifest in the consciences of all men however some may smother and neglect its reprovings, and being also made sensible that the holding of negroes in slavery however kindly treated by their masters has a tendency to encourage the iniquitious practice of importing them from their native country and is contrary to that justice, mercy, and humanity enjoined as the duty of every christian, I do therefore by these presents for myself, my heirs etc manumit and set free the following negroes being all I am possessed of or any ways interested in.[20]

Moses provided for the education and care of the young Negroes and in the event of his death bound his family to look after them as if they were white children. Since he thought everyone should put aside part of his earnings for emergencies and old age, he strongly urged his ex-slaves to deposit with him any surplus funds they might accumulate. He would give them a receipt for the money and pay interest. The money could be used for the welfare of their children, either to educate them if they were free, or to purchase their freedom if they were still in slavery. To encourage "sober prudence and industry" he gave to the men the use of an acre of land from his farm as long as they cultivated it. He told them to consider him no longer as master, but as friend, who would always assist them as long as they used their liberty wisely. He realized that they would encounter many temptations—"stealing, lying, swearing, drinking, lusting after women, frolicking and the like"—but if they read the

20. Moses' deed of manumission is in Moses Brown Papers, II, 18. The witnesses were Mary Brown and Levi Arnold. See Probate Court Records, Probate Wills, Book VI, 73, City Hall, Providence. The deed was recorded on Nov. 12, 1773.

advice of God in the Scriptures and heeded the "book in you
that is not confined to the English, or any language," they
would be able to resist them.

When Moses had finished reading his deed of manumission, John Collins "bore a liveing testimony to the Truth
and we had a blessed time of refreshment and confirmation.
Our Gracious Father being present a sense of which at that
time fills my mind with inexpressible grattitude and love."
The deed was done. Moses felt great relief that he had
finally taken the step that had troubled him so long. He no
doubt considered his act an atonement for his part in the
slaving venture of the *Sally* eight years before.

The chief practical consequence of his act, aside from
giving freedom to his slaves, was that it made Moses the hero
of Negroes in Rhode Island. Frequently during his lifetime,
Negroes, slave and free, called on him for aid and advice
because they had heard of his generous and humane deed.
Quakers and non-Quakers alike considered him a sincere and
devoted worker in the cause of abolition, and they brought
their problems to him.

Moses adhered strictly to his promises of friendship and
assistance to his former slaves.[21] One of them, Yarrow, was
an experienced candlemaker, and for years continued to work
at the candle works. Moses also employed him at his farm,
and when he started a salt works in 1777, he employed
him there. Tom was a cooper and had no trouble finding
employment from one of the Browns or other merchants in
the town. In 1779, Nicholas Brown, who owned one quarter
of Tom, gave him his freedom, "which freedom is to be full
force on the day that the news comes of the settlement of
the dispute between this country and grait Britain."[22]

Moses acted as a banker for all the Negroes he freed in

21. For Moses' relations with his freed slaves, see Moses Brown Papers,
Austin MSS., V, "Abolition," Moses Brown School Lib.

22. Article setting free "The Negro Man (cooper) called Tom," Brown
Papers, Misc., 1777-80.

1773. "Received of Cudg sixteene dollars cash to be put to interest for him agreeable to my advice at my freeing of him, for which and the interest received I promice to be accountable. Moses Brown," is one of many such notes in Moses' papers. In 1778 he was called on to act as referee in a dispute between Cudge and Bonno. "Having this day had Cudge and Bonnos accounts laid before me," wrote Moses, "and heard their several storys do settle all matters in dispute between them and concluded for Bonno to have the how [hoe], ax, and chopping-knife, and Cudge to have the old wheel and deliver up Bonno the head of the great wheal, his is allso the garden howe and eal spear and his is to pay as a balance due to Bonno for the cow and all other matters ninety pounds lawful money sixty pounds of which Cudge haveing lodged in my hand I deliver to Bonno in part." Frequently, Moses provided medical aid for his former slaves, and he also acted as their spiritual advisor.

Although Moses had not yet formally joined the Friends, he had been acting much like one for nearly two years. He also persuaded Audrey Greene, the nurse who had been hired to take care of Anna during her illness and had been kept on to look after little Obadiah, to stop attending Anglican services and enter the Society. For John Holden, a young tailor to whom he had given books, "a sober tender Friend . . . being straitend in his mind respecting his working in the fashions of the world," Moses arranged work that would ease his conscience, ordering some religious books from London for him to sell.[23] Sometime during the winter he also took into his household Job Scott, a young and inexperienced school teacher, who had only recently joined the Smithfield Meeting. During the winter months Scott tutored Moses' daughter Sarah at the monthly meeting school that he kept in Providence.[24] Moses said he was a

23. Moses Brown to William Wilson, Mar. 22, 1774, Moses Brown Papers, Misc. MSS., K-AB.
24. Feb. 12, 1774, *ibid.*, II, 19.

"valuable Friend and bids fare to be as indeed he is already a very useful man. His advantages for a schoolmaster has not been great but he has an improving capacity in the best things, he still lives with me and I find his company very agreeable."[25] Scott later became a famous Quaker preacher and writer. During the Revolution he lived with Moses, taught school, acted as Moses' business agent when he was out of town, and worked in his store.

On March 22, 1774, Moses wrote to William Wilson that "I am not yet formally joined to Friends. The Consideration of this step has been sometime on my mind but a sense of unfitness with other reasonings have prevented heither to my requesting." He went on to say that if he were not discouraged "with low times and having my way blocked up," he might make the attempt soon, although he considered it "an undertaking too great for such a poor thing as I am."[26] A few days later Moses appeared at the Lower House Preparatory Meeting and requested to be taken under the care of Friends. On the thirty-first, he attended the Smithfield Monthly Meeting and made his request again. Elisha Thornton and Moses Farnum were appointed "to take a solid opportunity with him concerning the motive of said request—and make a report to next monthly meeting." On April 24, 1774, the two men reported that they had talked with him, and thought that it safe to grant his request. "Therefore he is received under the care of this meeting."[27]

Conversion to Quakerism for most people was the result, not of sudden, but of a gradual change; thus it was for Moses. During a period that extended over a year, he had moved slowly but steadily toward Quakerism. At the end of that period he had surrendered completely to the "Divine

25. Moses Brown to William Wilson, May 21, 1774, Moses Brown Papers, Austin MSS., XII, "Personal," Moses Brown School Lib.
26. Moses Brown Papers, Misc. MSS., K-AB.
27. New England Yearly Meeting of Friends, Smithfield Monthly Meeting Records, 1763-80, V, 90, R. I. Hist. Soc.

THE SMITHFIELD LOWER MEETINGHOUSE

It was here that Moses Brown became a Quaker in 1774. He served as an elder from 1783 until his death in 1836. Courtesy of Old Sturbridge Village, Sturbridge, Mass.

Saviour." But conversion did not have precisely the results he desired or expected.

Moses eventually achieved peace of mind, but he was never able to attain his goal of withdrawal from the world. Even during the height of his emotional crisis—the vigil at his wife's bedside in 1772 and 1773—he performed his duties as moderator and, later, clerk of the meetings of the Proprietors of the New Brick School House; he assisted the work on the new Market House, and after much soul searching contributed to the fund that was being raised to erect the new Baptist meetinghouse, "since the building of this house, where its proposed," he admitted, "is generally agreed to promote the general interest so called, of the town."[28] And

28. Moses Brown to William Wilson, Aug. 18, 1773, Moses Brown Papers, Misc. MSS., K-AB.

shortly after his conversion in 1774 he was quickly drawn back into public affairs, first by the Quaker determination to rid the Society of slavery and to abolish the slave trade, then by the American Revolution, which caused great suffering and hardship throughout America.

Moses' relatively pleasant and tranquil domestic life on his spacious estate on the hill was marred by the fact that Obadiah was not healthy during his childhood. Moses wrote to William Wilson in August of 1774 that his son was "poorly and through a lameness by a contraction of the cords and an enlargement of the bones of his left knee cant walk—am apprehensive its of the rickety kind."[29] For two or three years Obadiah hobbled about on crutches, and he always favored his leg, but like his father he was patient and uncomplaining. Moses found him "a pleasant plant who I have dedicated to the Lord." Because of Obadiah's lame leg and delicate health, Moses did not send his son to any of the schools in the town, not even the Friends' school that Job Scott kept for a time during the Revolution. Obadiah acquired his early education from his father, or from one of the young men who lived in the house. The boy's later life indicates that he received excellent training at home.

As a result of the continued illness of his son, and the fact that it was common in the eighteenth century for the head of the house to be a doctor of sorts, Moses began to collect prescriptions for any and all physical and mental disorders, to accumulate a wide assortment of apothecary supplies, and to teach himself how to prepare and administer them. He rapidly acquired a wide reputation as a poor man's physician, and many people came to him for advice and treatment. From reading the latest books on medicine and surgery,[30] he developed an interest in diseases and a keen desire to alleviate suffering whenever and wherever he could.

29. Moses Brown to William Wilson, Aug. 22, 1774, *ibid.*
30. Moses Brown to Robert Willis, June 20, 1776, *ibid.*

No matter how heavily he leaned on God he never abandoned the notion that men could do much to better themselves.

For a time following his wife's death, Moses paid little attention to his scientific instruments and his garden, but by 1775 he was again amusing himself with them. He began to buy numbers of books for his personal use. Most of them were works on religion, for his intention was to have a "full Library of all our friends writings, that is worth preserving"; but many were on gardening, law, medicine, and science. He became keenly aware of his lack of formal education and resolutely set about trying to remedy that defect. Indeed, he read so much that he soon had to use glasses.

Shortly after he was received into the Smithfield Monthly Meeting, Moses went into the book business.[31] "This is a new and distinct concern from my other business," he explained to his agent in London, "proceeding from a desire to sarve the cause of Truth we having been pretty distitute of Friends Books." Moses wanted a number of books listed in his "Catalogue" bound in calf and lettered, "especially those marked (x) in the margin which being for my own Library," "the others for sale is not so material." He inquired about the library of Samuel Fothergill, who had recently died, which was for sale, and said that "what thou hast not [already bought] may be made up out of it which would be very acceptable to me that I might while reading them have him [Fothergill] before me as a most worthy example for though he be deceased he yet speaketh often very pleasantly to me."

When the Revolution cut off regular communication between America and England, books had to be reprinted in America, and Moses was often consulted by Friends in

31. Moses Brown to [Mary Hind, London], May 25, 1774, "A Catalogue of . . . Sundry Books . . . by the Ship Charlott John Rogers, Master," *ibid.*, II, 20.

Philadelphia and New York about such important matters. He carried on an extensive correspondence with Joseph Crukshank of Philadelphia, who did most of the printing for Friends in America. Moses was the chief distributor in New England of Friends' books. Most of those that were sold in the area during the next thirty years passed through his hands, or he made arrangements for their publication, distribution, and sale.[32] He was also instrumental in setting up the library in the meetinghouse at Woonsocket in 1775. The first librarian was Thomas Arnold, one of Moses' "companions" at the farm.[33]

The most satisfactory explanation for his failure to withdraw from the world was the persistence of the strong sense of public responsibility inherited from his family and the world in which he lived. He stated his continuing commitment to that idea when he said: "that religion that prevents public spiritedness must be a delusive and bad one."[34] He soon found that there was a side to Quakerism, which far from being antagonistic toward "public spiritedness," actually reinforced it by giving it a religious significance. He slowly came to understand and accept the Quaker belief that since the spirit of God was in everyone, it was everyone's responsibility to awaken that spirit in others to enable them to lead a more Christian life. Moses realized that there were stubborn obstacles to an individual's spiritual development, such as lack of education and material insecurity. Thus he labored to remove those obstacles. Unlike many Quakers of this period, he did not confine his reforming activities to the Quaker community, but continued to make important contributions to the welfare of the larger communities of

32. See for example Mott & Brown to Moses Brown, New York, Nov. 20, 1775, *ibid.*, 45; Smithfield Monthly Meeting Records, V, 304, Moses Brown School Lib.

33. Smithfield Monthly Meeting Records, V, 340, Moses Brown School Lib.

34. Moses Brown to William Wilson, Aug. 18, 1773, Moses Brown Papers, Misc. MSS., K-AB.

Rhode Island, New England, and America. The high repute in which he was held by his fellow townsmen was in no small measure due to his application of this philosophy to the practical problems of his day. Thus the pattern for his remaining life was set during his first few years as a Friend. Thereafter he led the life of a reformer, although a reluctant one.

5

Anti-Slavery Crusade:
First Phase

W HEN MOSES became convinced of the truth of Friends' principles and freed his slaves, the Society's testimony against slavery was in the final stages of a development begun by George Fox in the seventeenth century. In 1671, Fox had said: "Then as to their blacks or negroes, I desired them [the Friends in Barbados] to endeavor to train them up in the fear of God, as well those that were bought with their money as those that were born in their families. . . . I desired also that they would cause their overseers to deal mildly and gently with their Negroes, and not use cruelty toward them, as the manner of some hath been and is, and *that after certain years of servitude they should set them free.*"[1] For half a century Friends did not go much beyond Fox's advice, but in 1727 the Society of Friends in England spoke out clearly against the slave trade and in 1761 forced out of the Society those who continued to engage in the traffic. In the next decade— the 1760's—English Friends attacked the institution of slavery itself, not only within but without the Society. Their attack

1. Quoted in Frank J. Klingberg, *The Anti-slavery Movement in England; A Study in English Humanitarianism* (New Haven, 1926), 31.

was strengthened by the emergence of a humanitarian spirit—
"the widespreading growth of the people's mood in the care
of the aged, debtor, orphan, prisoner, the sailor, the ship-
wrecked, and the native in Asia, Africa, and America."
Under the leadership of Granville Sharp, slavery was abolished in England in 1772.[2]

In America progress toward implementation of Fox's injunction to Friends was similar to that in England. During
the first half of the eighteenth century, only a few Friends
spoke out against the traffic in humans and condemned the
institution of slavery. Toward the middle of the century,
American Friends were affected by the reforming spirit in
England, and by 1760 the anti-slavery movement within the
Society had gained headway. Within a few years, Quaker
leaders in Pennsylvania came out strongly against the slave
trade and were prepared to carry the message to meetings
in other colonies.[3]

In New England the impetus for the anti-slavery movement was provided by John Woolman of Philadelphia, who
toured the northern colonies in 1760 preaching against the
evil practice of buying, selling, and possessing Negroes.[4]
The New England Yearly Meeting responded to Woolman's
plea by admonishing Friends who imported or purchased
slaves; it remained strangely silent, however, on the subject
of ownership. This compromise with evil endured until the
Rhode Island Quarterly Meeting on June 8, 1769, recommended to the Yearly Meeting that the testimony be revised
to eliminate the implication that slavery was consistent with
the discipline. Many Friends thought that on such an important subject plain speaking was now necessary. But
Friends always moved slowly and deliberately in serious

2. Frank J. Klingberg, "The Evolution of the Humanitarian Spirit in
Eighteenth-Century England," *Pennsylvania Magazine of History and Biography*, 66 (1942), 265, 268.
3. Drake, *Quakers and Slavery*, 66.
4. *Ibid.*, 62.

matters, and a year passed before the crucial question was asked: "Are Friends clear of importing or buying or otherwise disposing of negroes as slaves and do they use those well that are under their care, not in circumstances through non-age or incapacity to be set at liberty, and do they give [those] that are young such an education as becomes Christians, and are the others encouraged in a virtuous life, and are all set at liberty that are of age, capacity, and ability suitable for reform."[5]

This became the "Tenth Query" in the New England testimony. Friends had now taken an important step along the road to abolition, although they still had some distance to go before reaching the final destination. Most Friends had become reconciled to the economic losses involved in freeing their slaves, but some were still torn between the desire to free all slaves and a sense of responsibility toward those who were not capable of looking after themselves. Between 1769 and 1773, sentiment for total abolition gained ground; Quaker meetings in Rhode Island, particularly the Smithfield Monthly Meeting, worked to get the New England Yearly Meeting to adopt a query categorically outlawing slavery among Friends. Local meetings also emphasized that part of the query concerned with freeing slaves. In October, the Smithfield Monthly Meeting appointed "the Committee to Labor for Freedom of Slaves," and its members visited and revisited slave owners belonging to the meeting, with considerable success.[6] It was this committee which expelled Stephen Hopkins from the Society for refusing to free his old Negro woman servant.[7]

The aggressiveness of the Rhode Island Quarterly Meet-

5. Yearly Meeting Minute, June 1770, Rhode Island MSS., XII, 85, R. I. Hist. Soc.

6. Minute for Oct. 29, 1772, from Smithfield Monthly Meeting Records, in Moses Brown Papers, Austin MSS., Misc., XXX, Moses Brown School Lib.

7. The committee's dealings with Stephen Hopkins may be followed in Smithfield Monthly Meeting Records, V, *ibid.* See also Drake, *Quakers and Slavery*, 79-80.

ing was reflected in the action of the New England Yearly Meeting of 1774 which revised the Tenth Query to close all loopholes; proscription against Friends holding slaves became absolute. New England Friends were called upon to free all slaves regardless of their status. Furthermore, those who were "aged and impotent, also infants and those in their nonage" were to be "provided for, brought up and instructed" as required by the Tenth Query.[8] A traditional characteristic of the Quaker position on slavery was that owners were strictly responsible for the material welfare of their slaves, and when they set them free they did not abandon them to the world but assisted them to become adjusted to their new freedom and the responsibilities that it entailed. Unhappily, not all Friends complied with this part of the testimony, although the numbers who did were surprisingly large.

The cultivation of the Friends' "inner plantation" in Rhode Island was now almost complete as far as slavery was concerned. Many Friends still owned slaves, but the Society had ways of bringing them into line. If they failed, the Society had the weapon of disownment to uphold its position on slavery. Throughout the Revolution the process of visitation and persuasion went on, and Moses was an active participant. With other Friends he made the rounds of Quakers under the jurisdiction of the New England Monthly Meeting to encourage them to manumit their slaves. Speaking of their progress in a letter to Dr. John Fothergill in London, on November 15, 1776, he wrote that "our Testimony against slavery is greatly advanced there by the manumission of several hundred Negroes last year, and the meetings uniting in agreement that such members as do not restore to freedom those they hold as slaves shall (after due labour is

8. Records of the Yearly Meeting of New England from 1683 to 1787 inclusive being 105 Years, 300, Moses Brown School Lib., hereafter cited as New England Yearly Meeting Records.

bestowed to convince and reclaim them) be disowned."[9] The real work of the Quakers in bringing their actions into line with their testimony had been completed by 1776; after that date all that remained was a mopping-up operation.[10] By 1782, the New England Yearly Meeting could write to London: "We know not but all the members of this meeting are clear of that iniquitious practice of holding or dealing with mankind as slaves."[11]

The proscription of slavery in the New England Yearly Meeting in June 1774, and in the quarterly and monthly meetings shortly thereafter, was followed almost immediately by an attack on slavery outside the Society. In this movement Moses rapidly assumed a leading position. His acquaintance with all the important men of the colony, his familiarity with the government, and his financial resources (by no means a negligible consideration), eminently qualified him for the task. Of more importance than any one of these qualifications, however, was his zeal; his unrelenting attack on slavery was his personal fight against an evil he had once condoned. The sense of guilt he felt as a result of his participation in slavery and the slave trade, particularly the voyage of the *Sally* in 1765-66, was deeply imbedded in his memory. Allusions to it appear frequently in his correspondence, and he undoubtedly considered his anti-slavery work an atonement. No one, not even defenders of the slave trade and slavery, ever doubted his sincerity. He became the conscience of New England on the issue of slavery.

The first blow against legalized slavery in Rhode Island was struck in Providence. Ironically, the political revolution against English rule that many Quakers abhorred produced a move to stop the slave trade, a move they approved. In a

9. Moses Brown Papers, Austin MSS., Misc., XXX, Moses Brown School Lib.; Yearly Meeting at Newport, June 14, 1776, New England Yearly Meeting Records, 314.

10. Moses Brown reviews this phase in a letter to Peter Morrill (or Morris), Nov. 22, 1777, Moses Brown Papers, Misc. MSS., K-AB.

11. Quoted in Drake, *Quakers and Slavery*, 79.

town meeting on May 17, 1774, the freemen passed a resolution to stop all trade between England, Ireland, Africa, and the West Indies, which incidentally would put an end to the importation of slaves. Quakers who were opposed to the slave trade on religious grounds also got the town meeting to adopt a resolution instructing the town's deputies to introduce an act into the General Assembly prohibiting the importation of slaves into the colony, and freeing all Negroes born in the colony after a certain age. To show that they meant what they said, the townspeople voted to free two adult Negroes and their children who had become town property when their owners died intestate. It was, they reasoned eloquently, "unbecoming the character of freemen to enslave the said negroes."[12]

Moses Brown and Stephen Hopkins, who was one of the Providence deputies in the General Assembly, were behind the anti-slavery resolution, and they quickly drafted a bill to be introduced into the General Assembly in the June session, calling for an end to the slave trade.[13] Hopkins and Henry Ward took the resolution to Newport where they were joined by an anti-slavery committee from the New England Yearly Meeting. No copy of the bill has been found, but abolition of the slave trade and eventual freedom for all slaves born in the colony were undoubtedly the main points. Whatever the exact provisions, they were too radical for a majority of the deputies, who amended the bill out of all recognition.[14] Moved by the petitions of Newport mer-

12. See Staples, *Annals of Providence*, 235, 237.

13. For Moses' earlier interest in abolishing slavery, see his letter to William Wilson, Mar. 22, 1774, Moses Brown Papers, Misc. MSS., K-AB; for his part in drafting the bill, see his letter to Judge Theodore Foster, Sept. 3, 1778, *ibid.*, II, 93.

14. The act finally adopted is in Acts and Resolves of the General Assembly, 1774-75, XII, 26, R. I. Archives, and is dated June 18, 1774. The act is not in the handwriting of Moses, Hopkins, or Ward. It has been printed in Bartlett, ed., *R. I. Col. Recs.*, VII, 251-53. The act was approved by the lower house on June 17, and by the upper house the next day. See Journal House of Deputies, 1774-75, June sess., 1774, 397, and Journal of the Senate, 1771-77, June sess., 1774, 397, R. I. Archives.

chants trading with Guinea and the West Indies, the representatives put self-interest before principles of justice and
humanity, and provided that Rhode Island shipowners who
offered slaves for sale in the West Indies unsuccessfully might
import them into the colony for one year.[15] The owners had
to post a bond guaranteeing that slaves would be taken out
of the colony after expiration of that time. Passed by the
lower house on June 17, the legislation won approval by the
upper house the next day. But it attracted little attention;
the *Providence Gazette* noted laconically that "an Act prohibiting the future Importation of Negroes was passed at the
present Session."[16]

The amendment, which virtually nullified the intent of
the original bill, reflected the General Assembly's chief concern; the legislators were more concerned with injuring
British commerce than with abolishing the slave trade. By
capitalizing on these circumstances, however, Moses Brown,
Stephen Hopkins, and the Quakers were astute enough to
push through a bill against the slave trade. However in-
effective, it at least brought the subject to the public's attention, and smoothed the way for the next step.

Moses immediately set out to force the Assembly to take
that step. In a vigorous one-man campaign, he tried to educate the public in the evils of slavery and to persuade public
leaders to speak out against it. To his friend President
Manning at the college, he sent an address on slavery written
by Thomas Arnold and suggested that it be included in the
September commencement exercises. When Manning re-

15. Moses Brown to Judge Theodore Foster, Sept. 3, 1778, Moses Brown
Papers, II, 93.

16. Neither Drake, *Quakers and Slavery*, 89, nor Staples, *Annals of Providence*, 236, point out that the act had no effect on the slave trade; slaves
could be brought into the colony and kept there for a year, a far longer
period than any slave trader needed to dispose of his cargo. There was
already a sufficient number of slaves in the colony to supply the need for
domestic servants and farm hands. W. E. B. Du Bois in *The Suppression of
the African Slave-Trade to the United States of America, 1638-1870* (N. Y.,
1896), 35-36, comments on the act and recognizes its ineffectiveness.

fused, Moses decided to publish it in the newspapers: "I think it will be useful," he wrote, "to prepare the way to have an Amendment of the Act past last Session of the General Assembly."[17]   Arnold's address was the first of a series of anti-slavery articles which Moses sent to New England newspapers from 1774 to 1776.[18]   John Carter, publisher of the *Providence Gazette,* was sympathetic with Brown's campaign against slavery; until 1776, when the important developments of the Revolution pushed slavery into the background, Carter made the columns of his newspaper available to him.[19]

Moses also tried to mold opinion through private correspondence, writing to anyone who was the least bit interested in doing away with the slave trade or slavery.   "Understanding thou art an advocate for the freedom of the poor Africans," he wrote to Levi Hart of Connecticut, a complete stranger, on October 18, 1774, "and concerned in thy labours to discourage that iniquitious traffick of buying and selling of men I herewith send thee a small book containing a piece wrote by John Westly [Wesley] on the subject."   He told Hart that a reformation in slavery was "highly necessary at this juncture when such a[n] evident token of the Divine displeasure seems to be hanging over this American continent."[20]

Out of the correspondence which Brown had with Friends during his "tryals and exercises" in 1773 came a heightened concern for slavery reforms.   The most impor-

17. Aug. 23, 1774, Moses Brown Papers, II, 72.
18. For some of Moses' drafts of articles he prepared for the press, see Moses Brown Papers, Misc. MSS., III, 167 ff.
19. Moses' draft of the article is in *ibid.,* 167; the printed article appeared in the *Providence Gazette; and Country Journal,* Oct. 22, 1774.
20. Moses Brown Papers, Misc. MSS., K-AB.   Hart, a Congregational minister in Preston, Conn., was a man of influence in New England; he was an original member of the Missionary Society of Connecticut and a trustee of Dartmouth and Yale Colleges.   Moses and Hart later co-operated to abolish the slave trade in Connecticut.   Edward A. Park, *Memoir of the Life and Character of Samuel Hopkins, D.D.,* 2d ed. (Boston, 1854), 121.

tant of his new acquaintances was Anthony Benezet of Philadelphia, who had a significant influence on Moses' religious
and humanitarian thinking. Benezet was a man "whose first
appearance by no means does him justice," Thomas Arnold
wrote to Moses after a visit to his home. He was "but an indifferent person, and one who perfectly despises or neglects
the goods of this world, any further than they contribute to
a comfortable subsistance." But he was "a man of sense and
reading."[21] Brown obviously agreed. After reading Benezet's pamphlet on temperance, he became a foe of the demon
rum, attributing many of the social ills of the time to it. He
even went as far as to discontinue giving it to his field hands,
with the result that "I have my business done better and the
labourers come in and go out more quiet and sattisfactory
to them and their familys than they used to do when spirits
were freely given and used by them."[22] Moses also read
Benezet's *Thoughts on War, Some Historical Account of
Guinea,* and other anti-slavery writings. Although they had
never met, each had heard of the other, and their similar
beliefs and attitudes as well as their many mutual acquaintances made it quite natural that they should exchange
letters.[23]

Moses' position on slavery represents, in addition to an
enlivened religious spirit, "an awakened social conscience"
that Michael Kraus has said "is one of the outstanding characteristics of the eighteenth century."[24] In this he differed
somewhat from most of his Quaker friends. In 1754 Benezet
had attacked slavery as being "neither consistent with chris-
tianity nor common justice," and, although he later added
that it was "destructive of the welfare of human society,"

21. Sept. 8, 1774, Moses Brown Papers, II, 72.
22. *Ibid.,* Misc. MSS., B-814, Box 2.
23. Benezet to Moses Brown, Dec. 27, 1775, Gratz Collection, Case 8, Box 6,
Historical Society of Pennsylvania, Philadelphia.
24. Michael Kraus, "Slavery Reform in the Eighteenth Century: An Aspect
of Transatlantic Intellectual Cooperation," *Pa. Mag. of Hist. and Biog.,* 60
(1936), 53.

his most often repeated criticism was that it was unchristian. John Woolman's argument in his famous essay, "Some Considerations on the Keeping of Negroes," was also essentially a religious argument.[25] The early Quaker anti-slavery literature had been written primarily to appeal to Quakers, and it derived its force from its moral and ethical message. Moses was also convinced of the unchristian character of slave-keeping, and he often spoke of it in those terms. But he was more impressed with the non-Quaker writings of John Wesley and Granville Sharp than with the writings of Benezet and Woolman, for he thought the arguments of the former better suited to impress non-Quakers in Rhode Island. Wesley and Sharp stressed the idea that slavery violated the natural rights of man. During the Revolution, Moses couched his attack primarily in terms of the natural rights theory, pointing out that slavery was inconsistent with the political ideals which the Americans used to justify their resistance to British tyranny. It is significant that the sentence that caught his eye in Sharp's *A Declaration of the People's natural right to a share in the Legislature* was "the tolleration of domestick slavery in the colonies greatly weakens the claim of natural rights of our American brethren to liberty etc." Moses' argument against slavery was a strong one, for it combined the puritanical slant of the revolutionary movement with the very principles by which the Americans asserted their own freedom.[26]

During the fall and winter of 1774 Moses formulated his ideas about slavery, and in the spring of the next year he made a vigorous attempt to amend the act of 1774. He drew up a proposed act for prohibiting the importation of Negroes

25. Mary S. Locke, *Anti-Slavery in America, from the Introduction of African Slaves to the Prohibition of the Slave Trade, 1619-1808* (Boston, 1901), 29, 31.
26. Moses Brown to Levi Hart, Oct. 18, 1774, Moses Brown Papers, Misc. MSS., K-AB. Moses found this sentence in Sharp's essay, p. 28 *n;* see the 1775 edition in the John Hay Lib.

and sent it to the General Assembly and to each of the
deputies. He told them that he would press his attack "un-
till this proviso the enacting clauses corrisponds with the
justice of the preamble which manifests a benevolent design
to discourage slavery." Taking up the clauses of the act
one by one, he destroyed them bit by bit. Were there freemen in the colony, he asked, who were so lacking in humanity
and justice as to condone the cruelties to which slave owners
in the West Indies subjected their slaves? Masters frequently
gelded slaves, he informed the deputies, chopped off half a
foot to prevent them from running away, whipped them
until they were raw, then put salt and pepper in their
wounds, and inflicted numerous other cruelties on them.
Moses' purpose in narrating the long list of inhuman practices was to show that they had been produced by slavery
itself. Not only did they have a debasing effect on the slaves;
after a time these were felt by the whites as well. If Rhode
Island continued to allow slavery and the slave trade, he
warned, her people, like those of Jamaica and other places
where the institution had existed for a long time, would also
become accustomed to cruel and immoral practices. He
therefore proposed a speedy repeal of the provision in the
law allowing owners to import slaves into the colony for a
year.

He also urged repeal of the provision that allowed owners
to export native-born slaves without their consent or without themselves being liable to criminal prosecution. Such
treatment of Negroes, he argued, was a violation of their
natural rights as human beings. He said that the colony's
constitution ought to support the proposition that anyone,
black or white, born within the colony "was free as though
born in England." He reminded the deputies that the charter and the Declaration of Rights issued at the time of the
Stamp Act claimed for the colonists the same rights as Englishmen, and since Negroes were declared free in England

they ought to be free in America. Can a man be considered humane, he asked, "who deprives a child under his own roof of liberty?"

One of the most frequent objections Moses had to refute was that freed Negroes would become a charge to the community. This argument appealed to people who disliked to pay taxes, particularly taxes for poor relief. To avoid such a development several laws in Rhode Island prohibited masters from freeing their slaves. Moses' reply was a ringing defense of freedom and a reminder that it was expensive. Suppose, said Moses, that the town council does give freedom to an old Negro who has spent his best years in the service of some master, and suppose, by an accident, that he does become a charge to the community, "can liberty and the rights of man be restored without expence? Will not the publick interfere in its behalf? What are we spending not only our treasure and blood for but liberty. Shall we fear a little expence than to bring about a restoration of those rights, the infringement of which is one cause and perhaps the greatest that this land now groans under. . . . Liberty is the greatest blessing that men enjoy, and slavery the heaviest curse that human nature is capable of."[27] Moses saw nothing wrong with seeking government aid to secure the rights of the individual and to guarantee that even the weak and the poor were protected. He saw clearly that society was as healthy as its members, and to make sure that all the inhabitants were healthy was only common sense.

Moses was unable to persuade the deputies to amend the act of 1774; his failure shows how fortuitous its passage was in the first place. Moses and his friends in Providence had seized on a favorable opportunity to strike at slavery when the desire to retaliate against Britain was greater than the

27. Moses Brown's notes appear from the context to have been written after the First Continental Congress met in Sept. 1774, and before the Declaration of Independence. Moses Brown Papers, Misc. Letters, III, 175.

desire to continue the slave trade. But the forces that profited from the trade recovered quickly and were able to prevent the adoption of a really effective law.

Although Moses' efforts to amend the act of 1774 were not immediately successful, he was not discouraged; he obstinately returned to the Assembly session after session to repeat his objections and point an accusing finger at his friends who put profits before justice to the Negro, and their own ease and comfort before the welfare of the colony. The eventual success (in 1784 and 1787) of the anti-slavery movement was due in no small measure to Moses' leadership and perseverance. Unlike many other foes to slavery Moses always asked for complete abolition of the institution as well as abolition of the trade, although as a practical man he emphasized the latter.

In addition to his public propaganda effort and his activities in the Assembly, Moses carried on a private campaign to induce slave owners to free their slaves or to treat them better.[28] There were few slave owners in Rhode Island who were not visited by Moses and urged to free their slaves, and he met with remarkable success.

One of the most frequent and difficult problems Moses encountered was that of securing freedom for Negroes who had once been free but who had been seized by their former owners or by someone else and returned to slavery. They had no one to appeal to for help and, though legally free, they frequently spent the rest of their lives in slavery. Moses eagerly came to their assistance, but there were many obstacles to securing freedom for such Negroes. Often a court case dragged out for several years. He never tired in the

28. "A Deed of Manumission," signed by Caleb Greene, is in *ibid.*, Austin MSS., V, "Abolition," Moses Brown School Lib. It is dated Providence, Dec. 15, 1774; for another case see unsigned statement [Moses Brown], Aug. 1774, Moses Brown Papers, Misc. MSS., III, 168. See also Joseph Alpin to Moses Brown, July 19, 1775; Thomas Robinson to Moses Brown, May 23, June 19, 1776, Moses Brown Papers, II, 41, 58, 60.

fight for freedom, however, and his labors were appreciated, as a letter from John Quamine, a well-educated Newport Negro, illustrates:

Having some late understandings of your noble and distinguished character, and boundless benevolent engagements, with regard to the unforfeited rights, of the poor unhappy Africans in this province; and of your sundry petitions to the General Assemblies in their favours, [there] has existed [in] one of that nation, though an utter stranger, [a desire] to present thee with gratitude and thanks . . . , the only returns he is capable of, for all your ardent endeavours for the speedy salvation of his poor enslaved country men, and for what you were kindly disposed to do already of this kind, in freeing all your servants.[29]

When the war with Britain came to New England in 1775, people were too busy fighting Redcoats to pay much attention to Moses Brown or even the Continental Congress on the subject of slavery. Members of the Congress had resolved in October 1774 that "we will neither import, nor purchase any slaves imported after the first day of December next; after which time, we will wholly discontinue the slave trade, and will neither be concerned in it our selves nor will we hire our vessels nor sell our commodities or manufactures to those who are concerned in it."[30] This resolution had no direct effect on the Rhode Island slave trade. The General Assembly approved of what the Congress did and adopted a plan to enforce the retaliatory measures taken against Britain, but Moses was unable to get a majority of the deputies to bring the laws of the colony into line with the resolutions of the Congress.

The formative period of the anti-slavery movement in New England ended in the year of the Declaration of Independence. After 1776, as a result of the war, importation

29. June 5, 1776, Moses Brown Papers, II, 59. Quamine was associated with Samuel Hopkins in the early African colonization schemes.

30. Worthington C. Ford et al., eds., Journals of the Continental Congress, 1774-1789, 34 vols. (Washington, 1904-37), I, 77.

of slaves virtually ceased in Rhode Island. But the slavers in Newport and Providence had no thought of stopping their business permanently; after the war they would return to the trade with chances for higher profits than ever because of the greater demand resulting from the temporary curtailment of the supply. Apparently there were others in America similarly inclined, for in April 1776, Congress modified the boycott against English imports and served notice that the permanent abolition of the slave trade was no longer intended. The principles of the Declaration of Independence were not to apply to Negroes; the economic interests of the slave trade won out over the political principles of the Revolution.[31]

After 1776 the Society of Friends ceased to agitate against slavery or the slave trade in the Rhode Island legislature or elsewhere outside the Society. Quakers had little time for the subject because the war raised serious problems for them, and for the next eight years they were hard pressed to protect themselves. Although Moses doggedly persisted in his efforts to get the General Assembly to amend the act of 1774, he was a solitary figure harping on a subject in which few people had any real interest. By 1779 his efforts also flagged, as he was drawn into the fight the Society waged to keep pure its testimony against war, and to preserve its unity against attack from without and dissension from within.

31. Du Bois, *Suppression of the Slave Trade*, 47.

6

Quaker Neutrality and the American Revolution

THE AMERICAN REVOLUTION presented members of the Society of Friends with a terrible dilemma: whether to remain faithful to their religious principles as Quakers or to their political principles as Englishmen or Americans. As Quakers they condemned war as morally and spiritually evil; it resulted in hatred and bestiality and could not possibly solve anything—good could not come from evil. In Pennsylvania as early as 1756 many Quakers had withdrawn from participation in political affairs because of the government's policy of violence toward the Indians and its involvement in the French and Indian War.[1] Although Quakers had become unpopular because of their pacifism they had not been molested. In Rhode Island they had fared pretty much the same.

The approaching conflict with England, however, placed Quakers throughout America in a much more difficult position. Both royal and revolutionary governments began to question the sincerity of Friends' neutrality, and the Quaker elders and ministers began to enforce more strictly the So-

1. Theodore Thayer, *Israel Pemberton: King of the Quakers* (Phila., 1943), 81-96, 113-22.

ciety's testimony against war. Unlike Friends in the middle
colonies, New England Quakers had no great leaders such
as the Pembertons to hold the members steady. When the
war broke out in New England, Friends there began to grope
for leadership and guidance.

For Moses Brown the decision as to what course to follow
was not an easy one. Privately he sympathized with the
American cause. This was to be expected. He had been
deeply involved in agitation against British policy during the
preceding decade, and it would have been odd indeed if he
had become a Tory. Had he not become a Quaker, he would
probably have joined his brothers in their support of the
Revolution. His position was therefore a difficult one, and
he stated his views on public events carefully. In a long
letter to his good friend James Warren, member of the
Massachusetts revolutionary Provincial Congress, he tried
to define his position: "My religious principles thou art I
presume sinsible does not admit of my interfering in war,
but my love for my country, and sence of our just rights is
not thereby abated, and if my poor abilitys could be aney
way subservient to a happy change of affairs nothing on my
part shall be wanting."[2]

Publicly, Moses was until early 1776 an advocate of compromise and reconciliation. He sounded more like a British
sympathizer than a neutral Quaker. In April 1775 he pleaded
for "a restoration of all those benevolent and kind offices that
hath for more than a century subsisted between this and our
mother country."[3] In an appearance before the Providence
town meeting he endorsed the sentiments of the Secretary
of State for the Colonies, the Earl of Dartmouth, who urged
an "accomodation of the unhappy differences subsisting between the two countries." At the same meeting he persuaded

2. May 11, 1775, Moses Brown Papers, II, 32.
3. William Greene Roelker, "The Patrol of Narragansett Bay (1774-76),"
Rhode Island History, 8 (1949), 45-63.

the council to postpone the erection of an artillery battery until the General Assembly could meet to discuss proposals for reconciliation. At one point in his campaign he traveled to Boston to lay before the Massachusetts military governor, General Gage, more than half a dozen letters from men in Providence and Newport urging peaceful reconciliation.

Moses' motives in publicly advocating a policy that he privately rejected are not entirely clear. No doubt they were mixed. He was probably influenced by the advice of Friends in Pennsylvania who counseled reconciliation. But he seems to have been influenced to a greater extent by a dramatic event involving his brother John. One morning in April 1775, a rider galloped into Providence bearing news that John Brown had been seized in Newport harbor by Captain Wallace of His Majesty's customs patrol ship, the *Rose*, for carrying supplies to the Continental Army forming in Massachusetts to protect Americans against such attacks by the King's troops as those against colonial militia at Lexington and Concord less than a week before. Governor Wanton had tried unsuccessfully to obtain John's release. Captain Wallace was now sending him to Boston to stand trial.[4]

Mulling the affair over, few people in Providence could have been too surprised about what they heard. John Brown had been a thorn in the side of British officers and customs officials for years. Like most merchants he had openly engaged in illicit trading, and it was no secret that he had been the organizer and leader of the attack three years before on the schooner *Gaspee,* which had been patrolling Rhode Island waters in search of violators of the Acts of Trade. John Brown was also in the thick of the resistance to parliamentary reprisals evoked by the Boston Tea Party. He was active in the creation of committees of correspondence in the colony, and recently, following the skirmishes at Lexington

4. *Ibid.* The story of John Brown's seizure is based upon the manuscripts published in Roelker's account.

and Concord, in the raising of an army and supplying it with food and equipment. If the King's officers wanted to destroy the leadership of American resistance in Rhode Island, they had picked the right man.

Response in Providence to the seizure of its wealthiest merchant was immediate. The first thought was to free John from his captors, and the first method hit upon was force. Within hours of the arrival of the messenger from Newport, the fastest horse in town was saddled, and eighteen-year-old Elkanah Watson, an apprentice in John Brown's business and an ardent admirer of his master, was pounding over the Middle Passage Ferry road on his way to Plymouth. Watson was to inform the Committee of Safety there of the crisis, organize a party to intercept the vessel carrying the prisoner as it rounded Cape Cod for Boston, and rescue him. Hastily planned and poorly executed, the scheme failed; John Brown was taken into Boston harbor and imprisoned in the gunroom of a ship to await trial.

Meanwhile, in Providence, a legal and much more carefully devised approach was begun. The Rhode Island government had recently received a letter from the royal government suggesting that the differences between England and her colonies be negotiated. Heretofore, no one, at least no one except Moses Brown, had paid the slightest attention to the government's overtures. Moses now had a brilliant idea: was it possible that in return for consideration of the proposal for negotiation, officials in Boston might release John? He did not know, of course, but it was worth a try. Extreme measures, such as the ill-advised Watson expedition, might result in John's being shipped to England for trial—a terrible prospect!

In a sense, what Moses now proposed was a rather subtle form of blackmail: preparations to resist royal authority by force would be placed in abeyance, providing John was released. To make the appeal as strong as possible, a request

was sent to Newport town leaders for their co-operation in the affair. Moses and Joseph Brown were selected to deliver it. When the brothers reached Newport they called on Governor Wanton and several others to enlist their aid in securing John's release, and then rode directly to Boston.

When the brothers arrived on the outskirts of Boston, they noted the degree to which relations between England and her colonies had deteriorated. General Gage was defending the town with a double patrol and had all entrances heavily guarded. Moses and Joseph waited well into the night for permission to enter, and Moses almost landed in jail when he unwittingly surprised an officer of the guard who was giving the password to the sentinels. When they were finally admitted, they were the first to enter the city since the battle at Lexington. At General Gage's headquarters, they talked with a number of officers from the expedition, among them the commander, Major Pitcairn, who tried to convince them that Americans had started the fighting by firing on his troops, a claim Moses later found to be untrue.

When they met General Gage, he seemed to be more interested in pumping Moses about the proceedings of the Continental Congress at Philadelphia than in the fate of John Brown; when he found that Moses knew little about Congress, he sent him to see Admiral Graves, the officer who held John's fate in his hand. From the Admiral, Moses learned the charge against John: participation in the burning of the *Gaspee* in 1772. Moses denied any knowledge of John's complicity in the affair and asked to see his brother. Moses remembered that "when he came on deck he was as glad to see me as ever he was and manifested his feeling by his tears of joy." Big John was frightened—a few days in the brig had taken all the fight out of him—and he had drawn up a defense that Moses now presented to Admiral Graves.

In an effort to find out the nature of the case against John, Moses sought advice from his friend, Judge Andrew

Oliver, a member of the royal commission that had investigated the *Gaspee* incident. Judge Oliver flatly denied that there was a valid case against John: "the Admiral can do nothing with thy brother." When he repeated his opinion before Graves, the Admiral's attitude changed completely. He released John, reimbursed him for the confiscated supplies, and ordered his vessels returned to him. Moses wrote to his brother Nicholas that John's freedom had been obtained "through Divine as well as human favor."

John's release may have been the result of intervention by God and by Judge Oliver, but a more likely explanation, one that Moses either forgot or discreetly omitted in his recollection, is that in exchange for his freedom John promised to use his influence to get the Rhode Island Assembly to adopt a more moderate and conciliatory attitude toward the Acts of Trade and to send a delegation to negotiate with General Gage about a settlement of differences. Moses was a party to the agreement, and may even have suggested it.

Had General Gage and Admiral Graves been better acquainted with John Brown they would have thought twice before concluding the bargain. As the distance between John and the ship's brig widened and the effects of "sufferings by detintion" faded, his determination to keep his word weakened. Nevertheless, he did address the Assembly, counseling moderation and urging that a delegation be sent to negotiate with General Gage. The deputies promptly rejected his suggestions, however, for they realized that once the individual colonies began to deal independently with the British government, American resistance would be broken. With this speech, John evidently felt that his part of the bargain had been kept. When Captain Wallace refused to return John's vessels, the latter not only repudiated his agreement with Admiral Graves but brought suit against Captain Wallace for £10,000, and again assumed a position of leadership in the American resistance.

Before long Moses too must have begun to regret his part in the episode. He received news of John's about-face with a mixture of fear, shame, and indignation. He was fearful that John's business affairs would now be subject to constant scrutiny by Captain Wallace and the customs officials and that the slightest slip would land him in their net, from which he might not escape so easily the second time. John's business associates in Newport and Providence would likewise, Moses predicted, feel the wrath of the royal officials. He was ashamed to hear that John had repudiated his agreement with the officers in Boston, an agreement that had been solemnly sworn to and signed before witnesses. He was indignant because his own "character as a person professing religion" would be damaged, his reputation for "sincerity and honnesty thou knows I was thought to have in Boston" would be questioned, and he would now be "thought to be a deciver and a hyppocrite if thy conduct turns out so contrary to what thou engaged and I was a voucher and surety for." Moses was not, he said, so concerned about himself as he was about his "religious profession and faithful brethern," whose claim of neutrality would be suspected by the British if the word of a member was worthless. In an unusual display of temper Moses threatened to divulge the entire proceedings at Boston to the Committee of Correspondence and "to lay before the Admiral my intire disapprobation of such conduct for the clearing myself."

As it turned out, Moses' concern about damage to his reputation and to that of the Society of Friends was unwarranted. If John had not kept his part of the bargain, neither had Captain Wallace. Nevertheless, this incident placed a strain on relations between Moses and his older brother. In the first flush of his conversion to Quakerism, bent upon doing "nothing against the Truth but for the Truth," Moses found it difficult to forgive his brother. John, who could

generally adjust his moral code to fit the necessity of the
moment, must have resented his brother's insinuations that
he was insincere and dishonest. He probably thought Moses
was a sanctimonious bore.

Moses' strident advocacy of reconciliation ended shortly
after John's release. Thereafter he followed a policy of strict
neutrality in the rapidly developing conflict between America
and Britain. Neutrality did not mean noninvolvement. A
few months after his trip to Boston, he was again drawn into
the struggle, this time to organize a relief expedition to
alleviate the suffering of innocent victims of the Revolution.
When Moses intervened to save John in April 1775, he had
seen firsthand the results of British attempts to coerce
Americans into obedience. At that time the city was beginning to feel the effects of the acts passed by Parliament
the year before to punish Bostonians for their Tea Party
and to show other colonies that resistance to the royal authority could only result in disaster.[5] Labeled by Americans as
the Intolerable Acts, the retaliatory measures closed and
blockaded the port of Boston, rescinded the colony's charter,
provided that officers indicted for a capital offense committed in connection with revenue laws might be tried in
some other colony or in Great Britain, and allowed army
commanders to quarter troops in the town. King George
III also appointed General Gage, no friend to Boston or
America, as governor to replace Thomas Hutchinson who
had gone to England.

Americans retaliated by calling the First Continental
Congress to meet in Philadelphia in September 1774 to devise means to protect themselves. After drawing up several
petitions for a redress of grievances, Congress adopted a
nonimportation and nonconsumption agreement and recom-

5. For this survey, see Allen French, *The First Year of the American
Revolution* (Cambridge, Mass., 1934), 11 ff.

mended that each colony enforce it. All through the winter and spring, Americans were busy arming themselves, and in the summer of 1775 Congress reassembled.

In Rhode Island preparations for war were carried on with vigor. An army was raised and equipped, and committees of correspondence and safety were formed to whip up enthusiasm for resistance. Joseph Wanton, who had served as governor since 1769, Darius Sessions, the deputy-governor, and two assistants, members of the council, refused to sanction these treasonous acts and were removed from office.[6] Governor Wanton had resisted the British up to the final moment, then found that it was not within him to make a complete break. He was an old and a sick man, and when the British evacuated Newport in 1776 he accompanied them to New York. Joseph Wanton, Jr., the governor's son, for years a close political and personal friend of Moses, went along with his father more out of filial loyalty than sympathy for the British.

When hostilities between Americans and British soldiers in Massachusetts finally began, Friends all over America had shown an interest in the welfare of members in New England. John Pemberton of Philadelphia had investigated conditions in Boston in the fall of 1774, and decided that although Friends were not yet suffering, meetings in New England might have to assist them in the future. If any funds were raised, he opposed turning them over to the Boston Overseers of the Poor, who, he reported, were most likely to favor the party of violence. According to Pemberton, nine-tenths of the people in Boston were "in favor of the violent party," and if Friends gave help to Bostonians they would be con-

6. Bartlett, ed., *R. I. Col. Recs.*, VII, 247, 257-58, 260, 262, 269, 311. Darius Sessions, Moses' colleague in the struggle for the college in 1769-70, one of those who refused to go along with the rebels, recovered from his lapse of loyalty to the colony and declared himself "a friend to the Liberties of America"; *ibid.*, 398-99.

tributing to the attack on the legitimate government, something a Quaker could not do with a clear conscience.[7]

Pemberton's prediction about the welfare of the Friends
in Boston soon came true. After Gage closed the port, conditions grew worse: the food and fuel supply dwindled, prices
soared, and the unemployed soon ran out of money with
which to buy even the bare necessities. At first, the monthly
meetings in and about Boston gave help to suffering Friends,
and the Smithfield Monthly Meeting sent a committee into
the town with donations. But relief was sporadic and insufficient.[8] In Philadelphia and New York, "Meetings for
Sufferings"—Quaker relief agencies modeled after those that
had originated in England a hundred years before—had been
set up to take care of such emergencies, but no such organizations existed in New England. Halting steps in that direction had been made in the New England Yearly Meeting
in 1773, when a temporary committee had been appointed
to write to the governor of Massachusetts about suffering
Friends in that colony. But no cases were reported, and the
committee was dismissed after a few meetings.[9] Similar
abortive attempts had been made by the monthly meetings
in Salem and elsewhere. During 1774 and the early part of
1775, a little money was collected for needy Friends but its
distribution was haphazard.

    To systematize Quaker benevolence, Moses and others

    7. Quoted in Henry J. Cadbury, "Quaker Relief During the Siege of
Boston," Colonial Society of Massachusetts, *Publications,* 34 (1943), 43-44.
I have discussed in detail the subject of Quaker relief during the Revolution
in "Moses Brown's 'Account of Journey to Distribute Donations 12th Month
1775' with an Introduction," *R. I. Hist.,* 15 (1956), 97-121.
    8. James Purinteen to Moses Brown, Feb. 19, 1775, and Ebenezer Pope
to Moses Brown, Feb. 19, 1775, Moses Brown Papers, II, 27, 28; Israel Pemberton to Moses Brown, Aug. 21, 1774, *ibid.,* Misc. MSS., B-814, Box 6; John
Hadwen and Caleb Carpenter, Yearly Meeting Committee Letter to Israel
Pemberton, Dec. 1, 1774, *ibid.,* Misc. MSS., K-AB; Smithfield Monthly Meeting Records, V, Moses Brown School Lib.
    9. New England Yearly Meeting Records, June 10, 1773, 300, Moses Brown
School Lib.

in Rhode Island tried to organize a permanent relief agency, but the conservative leadership in Philadelphia rebuffed their efforts. "It does not appear to us," Israel Pemberton wrote Moses in January 1775, "to be time yet to send anything that will give cause to any to think we approve of their conduct."[10] Despite the antipathy of Philadelphia Quakers for the Bostonians, Rhode Island Friends decided to go ahead with the relief. In March, Moses noted that he would raise the subject of relief for sufferers in Boston at the Preparative Meeting the next week, "Friends thinking it best to do what is done for them as a meeting and not as private members."[11]

The New England Meeting for Sufferings was founded at Newport on June 9, 1775, eight days before the Battle of Bunker Hill.[12] As the committee's most energetic and influential member, Moses rapidly became the center of a wide correspondence and placed his services and his modest fortune at the disposal of the committee to help the poor, the sick, and the persecuted Friends. But the relief program was not restricted to Friends. Since it was designed to relieve general suffering, he thought that it would enhance the reputation of Quakers in the eyes of all Americans; at the same time it would allow Friends to remain independent of both the British and the American revolutionaries.[13]

When Israel Pemberton heard of the program, he informed Moses that many Friends had wanted to start a subscription but had held back because there was no Meeting for Sufferings in New England to handle the funds. Now that such a committee had been formed, he added, they were

10. Moses Brown Papers, Misc. MSS., B-814, Box 6. See also John Townshend to John Pemberton, Sept. 11, 1775, Pemberton Papers, XXVIII, 59, Hist. Soc. of Pa.

11. Feb. 19, 1775, Moses Brown Papers, II, 27.

12. Cadbury, "Quaker Relief," Col. Soc. of Mass., *Publications*, 34 (1943), 8.

13. See Arthur J. Mekeel, "New England Quakers and Military Service in the American Revolution," in Howard H. Brinton, ed., *Children of Light: In Honor of Rufus M. Jones* (N. Y., 1938), 244-46, for a somewhat different reason for the establishment of the New England Meeting for Sufferings.

confident that "before the winter a large fund will be raised."[14] When the Pembertons and others in Philadelphia seemed to think that Nantucket should be relieved before Boston, Moses needled them to send aid to Boston, which now was not only occupied by the British but also under siege by the Americans. In his correspondence, he developed the idea that relief should be for "benevolence only"; if it was publicized as such, it would help convince people that Friends were not Tory in their attitude toward the "commotions," but were really neutral. At Moses' suggestion, Thomas Lapham, Jr., the clerk of the New England Meeting for Sufferings, wrote to the Philadelphia Meeting that the distribution should be made on a charitable basis only "to remove and prevent the jealousies which have arose, or may arise in the minds of any, that is disigned or aplied to any other." Unless they adopted a policy avoiding "distinction of religious sect, or political party," the Society would be severely criticized by both sides.[15]

In the fall of 1775, the Pembertons initiated subscriptions in the middle colonies and collected a sufficient sum to send to the New England committee for the relief of sufferers. By November, over £4,000 in Pennsylvania currency had been raised.[16] There was some disagreement over how much of this sum should be forwarded to New England, and some members in Pennsylvania and New Jersey meetings were dead set against sending any money at all. Not only did they doubt the wisdom of distributing relief to non-Quakers, especially to Boston radicals; they had been frightened by a re-

14. July 9, 1775, Moses Brown Papers, Misc. MSS., B-814, Box 6; Minutes, Pennsylvania Meeting for Sufferings, June 29, 1775, 9, Friends Bookstore, Philadelphia, Pa.
15. Committee of New England Meeting for Sufferings to the Pennsylvania Meeting for Sufferings, Aug. 14, 1775, New England Yearly Meeting Records, 24, 27-29, Moses Brown School Lib.
16. Pennsylvania Meeting for Sufferings to New England Meeting for Sufferings, Nov. 2, 1775, Minutes, Pa. Meeting for Sufferings, 37-42, Friends Bookstore, Philadelphia, Pa.

cent experience of the Mennonites in Pennsylvania who had raised a large sum of money for relief only to have a treacherous treasurer apply it to military purposes.[17]   Fortunately, the majority of the members were convinced of the necessity of supporting the project.   Moreover, they adopted the principle of nonsectarian, nonpolitical relief which Moses and others in New England had called for from the beginning, emphasizing that "it is not our intention to limit the distribution to the members of our own or any other Religious Society nor to the places of their present or former residence."[18]   The Philadelphia Meeting for Sufferings sent half the amount that had been raised—£2,000—to New England; David Evans and John Parrish delivered it to the committee on November 20.[19]   Moses added £500 of his own money to this sum.

All that remained was to distribute the money, but that task was complicated by new developments in Boston.   Moses heard that there were only four families of Friends left in the town and that they were not in distress; the "most worthy objects" of relief had been evacuated from Boston and were scattered throughout the towns to the eastward.   If that was the case, it would require considerable time to locate them.[20]   Finally, the committee also received word that "free ingress and egress" to Boston was possible only under flags of truce issued by the commanding officer of the British Army, a procedure that could be complicated and unpredictable.

Despite these complications, the Providence Meeting for Sufferings appointed a committee to distribute Quaker relief in Boston.   All but one of the committee, David Buffum, withdrew because of illness or other business.   A new com-

17. Israel Pemberton to Moses Brown, Jan. 7, 1776, Moses Brown Papers, Misc. MSS., B-814, Box 6.

18. Nov. 4, 1775, *ibid.*

19. Minute to the Pennsylvania Meeting for Sufferings, Nov. 21, 1775, Quaker Commonplace Book, William L. Clements Lib., Ann Arbor, Michigan.

20. William Richman to John Pemberton, Aug. 9, 29, 1775, Pemberton Papers, XXVIII, 25, 41, Hist. Soc. of Pa.

mittee—Thomas Steere, David Buffum, Thomas Lapham, Benjamin Arnold, and Moses Brown—then decided to start their errand of mercy on December 12.[21] Buffum and Brown agreed to meet the other members at Mann's Tavern on the outskirts of Cambridge. The two were old friends, and they made a good team for the task ahead.[22]

The trip to Boston was a long one, particularly during the winter months—almost ten hours by fast coach during good weather. The weather was cold and the highway muddy when the two men mounted their horses at the farm. Both men traveled light, with no blankets or extra clothes, something they were to regret, for the two- or three-day visit they anticipated stretched to almost three weeks. As they rode along, the two men discussed their mission. They were more or less in the dark about what they would do when they reached the outskirts of Boston, because the news of the situation there was sketchy, and probably not reliable. But they were armed with a letter to General Washington, Commander of the American forces besieging Boston, and hoped that he would allow them to talk with Friends James Raymor and Ebenezer Pope, who were in Boston and could bring them up to date about conditions.[23] Perhaps, when they met the others at Mann's Tavern, they would have some fresh news.

Unfortunately, their three friends could tell them little

21. Thomas Steere, Jr., Thomas Lapham, and David Buffum were residents of Smithfield. For the former, see James Pierce Root, *Steere Genealogy* (Cambridge, Mass., 1890), 81-82. For Buffum, see *Representative Men and Old Families of Rhode Island* (Chicago, 1908), I, 571, and *Memorials of Deceased Friends of New England Yearly Meeting* (Providence, 1841), 58-61.

22. The story of Moses' trip to Boston is based on his very detailed diary account, which I have edited as "Moses Brown's 'Account of Journey to Distribute Donations 12th Month 1775,' With an Introduction," *R. I. Hist.*, 15 (1956), 97-121. Clarkson Collins, librarian of the Rhode Island Historical Society, kindly called my attention to this valuable document, which is in R. I. MSS., 1750-75, XII, 110. All quotations which follow are from the diary unless otherwise noted.

23. Cadbury has printed the Address in "Quaker Relief," Col. Soc. of Mass., *Publications*, 34 (1943), 51-52.

they did not already know. On their way to Washington's headquarters at Cambridge the next morning, they saw evidence of the ravages of war.[24] All around the encampments, the countryside was a scene of desolation: "Fruit, range, and other trees, fences, etc., some buildings, taken smooth away" by soldiers to make fires to keep themselves warm. At his headquarters in Craigie House, General Washington received them kindly. After the committee had presented the address from the Meeting for Sufferings and asked permission to enter Boston, he told them that no one was allowed through the lines "except a man or his wife that had been separated." Although he was in sympathy with their mission, he could make no exceptions. Even if he could, an outbreak of small-pox made it unsafe to enter Boston. He therefore suggested that Friends in Boston meet the committee on the lines and offered to do anything he could to help them.

With Washington's permission, Moses decided to write to General Howe and Friends James Raymor and Ebenezer Pope. Washington referred the committee to General Nathanael Greene, commander of the Rhode Island troops, adding that if Greene approved the letters, he was likely to agree: "He is a Quaker, and knows more about it than I do."[25] Nathanael Greene and Moses were old friends and the General promptly approved the committee's plan, then asked them to have dinner and spend the night in his headquarters.

In the letter to Howe, Moses asked permission to hold a conference on the lines with some of the Friends in Boston so that they could decide upon a sum to be delivered to the distressed inside the town. Washington approved the letter and ordered an aide-de-camp to send the papers the next

24. For a description of Boston under siege, see French, *The First Year of the American Revolution,* 545-56; Richard Frothingham, *The History of the Siege of Boston . . .* (Boston, 1849), 276.

25. George W. Greene, *The Life of Nathanael Greene, Major-General in the Army of the Revolution* (N. Y., 1867), I, 142-43.

morning, December 15, to General Ward at Roxbury with an order for a flag of truce.

When these arrangements had been completed, the five travelers returned to Greene's headquarters for dinner and rest. During the course of the meal the conversation turned to the Quakers and their role in the struggle between America and Great Britain. According to General Greene, Moses recorded in his diary, Friends "should keep to their Religious Principles . . . if they did and medled not in the dispute by promoting of parties etc. they would meet with protection from both but if they did not they must expect to suffer." Moses and his friends remained silent, and the conversation turned to the question of the future of the American colonies, a subject that was on every man's mind.

James M. Varnum, a Newport man with a volatile disposition, thought that the colonies should announce their independence,[26] but Moses, unable to hold his tongue any longer, replied "that we ought (and I hoped every one did that were principles in this unhappy controversy) to keep an eye to a peaceable Union and not think of independency, which from some circumstances the people of England had too much reason to suspect particularly from Adamses letter etc." Greene agreed and said that "he believed in the beginning of this unhappy warr no one entertained such an idea"; but "if the warr continued," he added, "he could not promice for the consequence etc." (Within a month he was to change his mind and call for an outright "declaration of independence," the first American, it was said, to have used those exact words.)[27]

The next day, while three of the committee were making

26. Varnum was in the first class to graduate from Rhode Island College in 1769. Ironically enough, at the commencement exercises he defended the thesis that America should not become independent. He was commissioned a colonel in the 1st Regiment of the Rhode Island Infantry in May 1775. See Frederick W. Coburn in *DAB* s.v. "Varnum, James Mitchell."

27. Greene, *Life of Nathanael Greene,* I, 122.

arrangements with General Ward for the flag of truce, Moses and Benjamin Arnold attended the Provincial Assembly session in Watertown to pick up further intelligence respecting the poor inhabitants of Boston and Charlestown. The Speaker of the Assembly was James Warren, Moses' good friend from Plymouth, but he had little information on conditions in Boston. He did, however, introduce Moses and Arnold to William Cooper, the town clerk of Boston now serving as a member of the Assembly. Cooper gladly gave them a list of the poor, sick, and otherwise distressed people who had left the town. Joseph Palmer, another of Moses' friends, was a member of the Council, and he also supported the committee's efforts.

After a restless night in a crowded Cambridge dwelling, Moses and Benjamin saddled up and rode to Roxbury, where they found their three companions waiting for an answer from General Howe. Moses and Thomas Lapham went out to meet the flag of truce and learned that Howe had refused them a conference with Raymor and Pope, but had agreed to send Sheriff Joshua Loring to talk with them.[28] Moses suspected that Howe's subordinates were responsible for the decision, and he asked the officer in charge of the flag of truce, Sir Henry Calder[29]—who admitted that he knew nothing of their business—to write to General Howe, requesting the desired conference.

Negotiations continued for two days, but Howe still refused to allow the Boston Friends to talk with the committee on the lines. Determined to do something, the committee decided to risk sending in a draft on Henry Lloyd for £100 lawful money which they advised their friends to "dispose of to such poor necessitous persons in Boston, as are not con-

28. Loring had been appointed by General Gage. His relations with the committee seem to have been amiable. For a different estimate of Loring, see French, *The First Year of the American Revolution*, 341-42.

29. See Worthington C. Ford, comp., *British Officers serving in the American Revolution, 1774-1783* (Brooklyn, 1897), 160.

cerned in promoting or carrying on military measures, without regard to religious sect or political party, taking care to preserve our religious testimony against wars and fighting pure." They urged that a strict account be kept of the names of the persons, the numbers of children or other relations, occupation, and religious profession, and they enclosed a sample form to be followed in recording the information. They also advised all Friends in Boston to leave the town and find some quiet place in the country where they could "live peaceable with all men."[30]

The next morning Moses and Benjamin made a final attempt to arrange a conference, but to no avail. They learned, however, that the suffering in Boston had been grossly exaggerated and confirmed earlier reports that the needy people were no longer in the town but scattered among towns to the eastward. Heading for Marblehead, the town where the greatest suffering was reported, they encountered a number of poor children begging "Master give me a copper to buy a biskett." The situation in Marblehead convinced them that the task before them was too great for their small company. They therefore requested the selectmen of the town to assist them; dividing into three groups, with a selectman in each, they spent the day in a house-to-house canvass distributing money to the poor according to their needs, "relieving between 60 and 70 familys who appeared really Necissitous, and such scens of poverty I had before been a strainger too."

Unable to attend to all the needy people in the town that day, the committee designated two members to complete the

30. The draft was never honored. See Thompson, "Moses Brown's Account," *R. I. Hist.*, 15 (1956), 116, the correspondence in Moses Brown Papers, II, and Thomas Steere (for the committee) to James Raymor and Ebenezer Pope, Dec. 15, 1775, Quaker Commonplace Book, William L. Clements Lib. The letters comprising the committee's negotiations with the British and Quakers in Boston are in this commonplace book. See also Cadbury, "Quaker Relief," Col. Soc. of Mass., *Publications*, 34 (1943), 59.

job. Moses and his friends pushed on to Salem with "sattisfaction of mind," and the next day they repeated in Salem the procedure that had worked so well in Marblehead. Although conditions were not as bad as at Marblehead, they found many "real objects of charity." Four of the committee (Thomas Steere was left behind to finish the work at Salem) set out for Cape Ann and points east the next morning, stopping to relieve those in need as they heard about them. On the twentieth they arrived in Gloucester and repeated the previous procedure. Here the weather turned extremely cold and after long hours in the saddle, the committeemen began to experience suffering themselves.[31] "Yet the necessitys of the poor were such as prompted us to go through much sufferings on that account without complaint and I may say scarce a relenting thought."

At Gloucester the depth of poverty exceeded anything they had yet witnessed. Many of the more well-to-do inhabitants had left town, fearing an attack by Captain Mowatt and his raiders, who had recently burned Falmouth (now Portland, Maine). The poor, now without employment, became even poorer. Most of these people had depended on the fishery for a livelihood, but since that was no longer open to them, they were swiftly becoming destitute. "Some families," Moses recorded, had had "no other bread but potatoes for some time, which with checkerberry tea was seen the only food for a woman with a sucking child at her breast." There were many children, widows, and old people among the hundred-odd families they visited that day. Later, when he had returned to Providence, he wrote to William Wilson that "we here nor with you have very little idea of their poverty, yet their children seemed healthy, crawling even into the ashes to keep them warm."

31. For the weather in and about Boston during Dec. 1775, see "Diary of Samuel Cooper, 1775-76," *American Historical Review*, 6 (1901), 328-29, and "Diary of Ezekial Price, 1775-76," Massachusetts Historical Society, *Proceedings*, 7 (1864), 219-25.

During their stay in the Cape Ann region, the four companions lodged at John Low's inn. Low was a very respectable and tender man, Moses noted, and he gave them every assistance during their stay. Moses, who had developed into an accomplished proselytizer during his short time as a Quaker, became very friendly with Low, who had led a rather dissolute life, and tried to convert him to Quakerism. Like Moses, Low had recently lost his wife, and her death had caused him to reflect about his past and to decide on a personal reformation. As the first step, he had freed one of his slaves and was considering freeing the others. When the committee left Cape Ann, Moses and Low "tenderly and affectionately bade each other farewell," and Moses, moralizing on his own experiences, let Low "know of my loss of a companion the usefulness of affliction and expressed a desire he might with me rightly improve it." Later Moses wrote to Low and sent him a set of Barclay's *Apologys,* in hope that it would hasten his reformation.

By the time the five men had returned to Salem, they had been on the road eleven days, spent mostly on horseback braving the winter weather, which had become progressively worse. Moses caught cold during the trip; on the twenty-third he did not leave his quarters in Salem, although he received a number of poor women who came to get aid. The twenty-fourth was a stormy day with a fierce wind and driving snow, and the committee concluded its work with a series of meetings at Jeremiah Hacker's house. On Christmas Day, they left Salem and spent three days working their way slowly toward Chelsea and Point Shirley. Along the way they saw numerous signs of the exodus from Boston and heard many tales of hardship and privation. They encountered a number of people from Boston who had been quartered at Point Shirley for twenty-one days because they had been exposed to smallpox. The unceremonious evacuation had been handled by one of General Howe's men,

who had confiscated their money, clothes, and furniture. Moses piously hoped that the British would "be duly informed of this and provide against it by giveing the direction to a man of virtue."[32]

He was equally pious about American soldiers. At one of the inns where the committee met with the selectmen of a town, there was "a noisy company of soldiers fidling and dancing after super." Moses spoke to the selectmen about the noise and boisterous behavior of the soldiers, condemning it as disturbing and wrong in itself and "contrary to every prospect of the present time and even the Congress discouraged it by resolves." The selectmen admitted it was not very agreeable, but said that since the culprits were soldiers, and riflemen at that, and since it was a "Christmas frolick and they had been up all the night before," it must be allowed.

The party lasted well into the early hours, and Moses and his friends got little sleep that night. They were so eager to leave that evil place that they rode directly to Cambridge before having breakfast. There, waiting for them, was a letter from Thomas Lapham telling them that he had not yet heard from Raymor and Pope, but that he hoped to receive word the following day. Moses and his colleagues decided not to wait. The next day they headed home and after stopping in Smithfield to attend the monthly meeting, they arrived at Moses' farm about nine o'clock on the twenty-ninth of December. "May I be duly thankful," Moses wrote, "upon every rememberance of the favourable assistance of Divine goodness and presarvation through this journey which I have been presarved to return to my family and friends in health and a good degree of sattisfaction." He had reached home just in time, for the next day a fierce storm broke.

During the eighteen-day trip Moses and his friends managed to give away three-fourths of the £2,500 they had

32. Thompson, "Moses Brown's Account," *R. I. Hist.*, 15 (1956), 121.

started with. The donations had been "18 [shillings] on an
average to a family" and would have been larger had they
known in advance the number of people in need. Three
days after the committee returned to Providence, Moses
wrote letters to the Pembertons and to William Wilson,
giving them an unofficial synopsis of the trip and remarking
to Wilson that "the name of Quaker though little known
in these parts will be remembered and perhaps some may
no more think it reproach."[33]   Israel Pemberton replied,
sending his congratulations on a job well done, but he made
one mild criticism—the committee had "been much too spar-
ing" in the size of its donations, and he expressed the "hope
you have ere this made such a farther distribution and the
poor people most certainly want much in this very cold
season."

The Pembertons at first had been hesitant about raising
money to give to the Bostonians; once committed to the
project, however, they became tireless workers for the cause.
And when it was over, they knew how to use the results to
good advantage. The news of the mission's success, Israel
informed Moses, had quieted the criticism that had been
leveled at the project in the beginning, and meetings that
had not made contributions were willing to open wide their
purses if more money was needed in New England. Noting
that some newspapers had printed accounts of the distribution, Pemberton suggested to Moses that "some farther hints
of that kind in other papers might not be unseasonable, if
rightly given for there are many here who deny anything."
Pemberton fully recognized the importance of the relief
expedition as a means of softening criticism aimed at the
Quakers.[34]

Throughout most of 1776 the Meeting for Sufferings,
under Moses' direction, continued to distribute relief in New

33. Dec. 27, 1775, Moses Brown Papers, Misc. MSS., B-814, Box 6.
34. Feb. 2, 1776, *ibid.*, K-AB.

England. He headed a second expedition which aided about one hundred and sixty more families in fourteen towns within a distance of forty miles of Boston, averaging about thirty-two shillings for each family. At the end of the trip, Moses had between £60 and £70 left, and he wrote Friends on Nantucket telling them to draw on him for that amount if there were any families in need. Additional money received from Philadelphia was sent to committees in Salem and Lynn to be distributed at Marblehead, Cape Ann, Falmouth, and other towns in that area. Sufferers in Newport and Plymouth were also given assistance.[35] By September the New England Meeting for Sufferings had received £3,195 from Philadelphia and distributed it among seven hundred persons.

The clear, detailed reports that Moses sent to the Philadelphia Meeting for Sufferings were important: they dispelled apprehensions many Friends had had about supplying funds; they served as models for reports of similar future projects; and they etched in sharp detail the nature of Quaker humanitarianism. The praise Moses received from his friends in Philadelphia was well deserved. The Pembertons henceforth considered him to be the most reliable, trustworthy, and principled Friend in New England, and they directed most of their correspondence concerning affairs of the Society to him.

Ultimately the problem of providing relief in New England on an extensive scale was solved by circumstances beyond the control of Quakers. In March 1776, General Howe decided that Boston was not worth the sacrifice it would cost to hold; he loaded his army and eleven hundred Tories on Admiral Shuldham's ships and sailed out of the harbor, leaving the town to Washington's triumphant American army and a jubilant populace. As the war moved south, conditions in New England improved, even for Quakers. There were times when the Meetings for Sufferings had to come to

35. Israel Pemberton to Moses Brown, Feb. 20, 1776, *ibid.*

the aid of poor or distressed Friends, particularly during the severe winter of 1777-78, but for the remainder of the war they fared about the same as the other people; in fact they might have been better off because of the well-organized system of poor relief that operated in each monthly meeting.

One of the important results of Moses' relief expedition was that it convinced him of the virtue of neutrality. He was no longer merely content to follow the advice of Friends in Philadelphia. Shortly after his return from the first relief trip, he had an opportunity to state his attitude toward the Revolution when the Philadelphia Friends called on all Americans to reject the revolutionary governments and to give their loyalty to England. In a letter to John Pemberton, he voiced his disapproval: "Some of us would have liked friends address better if it had not been directed to the people in general but as usual [to Friends] thereby taking away the handle the people make against friends by a publick answer which hath much confirmed the common people this way that friends as a Society are meddling beyond and contrary to their profession." He discountenanced public announcements on the war by Friends or by meetings as detrimental to their testimony for peace, but more especially because they brought Friends under attack from the people.[36] Several times he cautioned the Pembertons and others in Pennsylvania and New Jersey against taking sides in the Revolution. And he exercised proper restraint himself. When Thomas Paine's *Common Sense* was published in January 1776, he thought of answering it because Paine's attack against neutrals was an indirect slap at Quakers; but he realized that any attack on *Common Sense* would cause the critic to be labeled as pro-British and bring discredit to the Society.[37]

36. Mar. 20, 1776, *ibid.*
37. See the "caution" sent to Philadelphia Friends by the committee of the New England Meeting for Sufferings on Mar. 12, 1776, *ibid.*

Rather than try to stem the irresistible tide of sentiment for independence, he turned his attention to what he considered a far more important task: preserving the Society of Friends from disintegrating under the mounting internal and external pressures. The position he adopted and quietly but stubbornly defended was similar to that advanced by Isaac Penington in the seventeenth century. Like Penington, he called on each member to discipline himself, to tend to his own business, to perform his own services in the Society, to follow his own practices, and to allow others to do the same. He saw that for the Society to adopt an extreme position on any controversial part of Friends' doctrine would place a great strain on many of the members and force some of them out of the Society. Above all, differences of opinion should not be aired in public. The church government, such as it was, should not become authoritarian, forcing members into a conformity of opinion about matters on which Friends differed.[38]

During the Revolution, Friends in New England, and in Rhode Island in particular, managed to remain more unified than in the middle and southern colonies—a smaller percentage was put out of the Society. Moses Brown deserves most of the credit. His natural self-effacement, which prevented him from publicly stating his views, partially accounts for the failure of the historians of Quakerism to recognize his importance in preserving the unity of the Society during the Revolution.

After 1776, during the long years of the Revolution, Moses, like many other Quakers, remained neutral in deed if not in thought. He looked on in silence when the Declaration of Independence was issued; he did not participate in the creation of the independent state of Rhode Island nor contribute to the birth of the new nation under the Articles

38. For an excellent discussion of Penington's views, see Arnold Lloyd, *Quaker Social History, 1669-1738* (London, 1950), chap. 2.

of Confederation; and he confined his public remarks about the military defeats and victories of the American army to lamentations about the needless loss of life and urgent pleas for an end to hostilities.

Although Moses maintained an attitude of strict neutrality after 1776, he became convinced by 1779 that Great Britain could never conquer America. Once he realized this, America's future relations with England attracted his attention. Although he had no desire or expectation that the former political ties between America and England would be restored, he did want America to remain a part of the English-speaking world. He reflected the anti-French prejudice common in America, a prejudice caused partly by religious differences and by the wars that England, and perforce the colonies, had fought with France for over half a century. He disliked the French, their language, their customs, their manners, and most of all their Catholic religion. "What are Great Brittain and America about," he asked one of his former business agents in London; "are they not exhausting each other to become prey to the Romish Yoke? . . . [Is it] the Divine purpose to chastise the Protestants herewith for their unfaithfulness not only in neglecting to carry the Reformation further, but for falling from the simplicity and sincerity of the first reformers?"[39]

During the war Moses associated with French army officers when they were Providence; and entertained some of them in his own home, probably out of curiosity and in hope of converting them to Quakerism, but he was never impressed by their intellect, their conduct, or their piety. In eighteenth-century America, the French had a reputation for extravagant living and loose morals, and to an orthodox Quaker who was perhaps more puritanical than the Puritans,

39. Moses Brown to John Roberts & Sons, Aug. 30, 1779, Moses Brown Papers, III, 22. See also Moses Brown to George Hayley, May 2, 1779, Oct. 20, 1780, and Mar. 5, 1781, *ibid.*, 7, 40, 50.

and a vegetarian and avid temperance advocate to boot, their company could scarcely have been congenial.

Moses watched with no little anxiety and alarm the close economic and political ties that developed between the United States and France during the war. Fearful that these would be followed by close cultural connections, he objected to French influence in any form: "I greatly desire to see peace once more established, and the reciprocal advantages of trade and intercourse between Great Brittain and America again restored which at present is running into other channels, to stop which and prevent the change of manners which with the manufactures and connections here to fore not approved are gaining ground."[40] Confident that trade would return to its prewar channels, he relied upon "time with language, blood, . . . the mutual interest of the two countries," to mend the wounds of war. One way to hasten re-establishment of Anglo-American trade after the war was for American businessmen to discharge their old prewar debts to English creditors. In 1781, while Britain and America were still at war, Moses noted "with much sattisfaction" that most of the local merchants were making remittances through France and Holland to discharge their indebtedness.[41] He might have added that they did so partly because of his efforts. By that year Moses had become a free, unsolicited agent for British mercantile firms, using great freedom in urging his friends to make their remittances and to discharge their obligations. He did this, he said, not only because of a wish to see justice done to English creditors but also because of a desire to lay the groundwork for a re-establishment of commercial relations after the war with England. His reward was "sattisfaction in bearing testimony against retaliation." A far-sighted as well as a practical man, he saw that there would be many people in England who

40. Moses Brown to John Roberts & Sons, Aug. 30, 1779, *ibid.*, 22.
41. Moses Brown to Shubal Coffin, Mar. 5, 1781, *ibid.*, 40, 50.

would call on their government to use its economic strength
to seek revenge for the loss of territory and prestige. This
he hoped to avert.

Moses' interest in a restoration of commercial and cultural ties between Great Britain and America continued
during the first two years of peace. By the end of 1784,
however, he was disillusioned somewhat by the uncompro-
mising commercial policy of England and felt that the solution to America's problems lay elsewhere than in commercial
expansion along prewar lines, perhaps in the development of
domestic manufacturing.

7

Emergence of a Quaker Leader

IN THE COURSE of the long years of the Revolution, Moses Brown emerged as the leading Quaker in New England. The basis of his leadership was an ability to hold the diverse groups within the various meetings together in the face of economic disaster, public ridicule, and divided loyalties. The solidarity of the Society of Friends was threatened not only by external enemies but by internal disputes. The war raised many problems that Friends had never had to deal with before, and the individualistic tendencies of their beliefs encouraged many to challenge the authority of tradition and the collective will of the meetings. To Moses the internal conflicts brought on by the war were as serious as dangers from battle or from governmental authorities, and he made strenuous efforts to minimize their effects.

The most divisive threats to the Society were posed by paper money and taxes. These two issues were intimately connected with the much broader question of acceptance or rejection of the new governments which used the taxes and money to support their civil and military establishments. In the early years of the Revolution, some Friends felt that

currency issued by the rebellious governments should not be accepted, and this attitude became the official position of the Society, although it was more strictly adhered to in the middle states than in New England.[1] Moses thought that the distinction made by Quakers between specie and paper money was ridiculous; one promoted the war as much as the other. His position was determined by sympathy for the American cause and by common sense: it was fortified by his experience when distributing the donations to the poor sufferers around Boston from 1775 to 1777. There he found that while some Friends accepted specie, others refused to take the new paper currency "from a principle of its promoting the war as well as on account of the authority making it."[2]

The Quaker refusal to accept the new paper currency contributed to its depreciation in New England and helped drive hard money out of circulation. In Rhode Island, those who contributed to this evil were looked upon by many people as scarcely better than common criminals.[3] Friends who refused to accept paper money were accused of doing so because of selfish motives or because they were pro-British, and not because of religious scruples. There was just enough truth to the charge, and a willingness on the part of many

1. Pemberton to Moses Brown, Aug. 28, Nov. 9, 1775, Moses Brown Papers, Misc. MSS., B-814, Box 6. The Pembertons' refusal to accept paper money issued by the revolutionary governments may well have been an expression of their pro-British feeling rather than an effort to maintain the Quaker discipline, although admittedly the two motives are hard to differentiate. For an argument that Israel Pemberton "did not defend the acts of the British government," see Thayer, *Israel Pemberton*, 207.

2. April 30, 1776, Moses Brown Papers, Misc. MSS., K-AB.

3. In the August session of the General Assembly the two houses "voted and resolved, that if any person or persons shall refuse to take the paper money emitted by this colony, the paper money emitted by the Continental Congress, or by any of the American colonies, . . . he shall incur the displeasure of this General Assembly; and ought to be held and esteemed as an enemy to its credit, reputation and happiness"; Bartlett, ed., *R. I. Col. Recs.*, VII, 374. The resolution was printed in the *Providence Gazette; and Country Journal*, Sept. 16, 1775.

to believe it, to make it stick. Among Friends themselves there was great diversity of opinion. Moses discouraged the Yearly Meeting and the monthly meetings from adopting any fixed rule on the subject and suggested that each member be guided by his own conscience. He exerted his moderating influence through letters and conversation. In his characteristically pragmatic way, he based his decision on what he thought was best for the Society and for Rhode Island and not on adherence to abstract principles. His practical approach paid dividends, for toward the end of the war he could write to Friends in Pennsylvania that "it may be said in justice to the people in the government that there is now so little appearance of a spirit of persecution of Friends as in any of the Colonies."[4]

Closely connected with the currency question was that of taxes. All Quakers agreed that members should pay taxes for the support of civil government, but they were not agreed as to whether they should pay taxes to support a government engaged in war. This difference of opinion was serious enough, but there was an added complication: the government they were asked to support was a revolutionary government. Prior to the American Revolution, Friends in England and in America had not scrupled to pay their taxes during wartime. But as early as 1775 there were indications that American Friends were at odds over whether they should continue to pay taxes to governments that were organizing resistance to royal authority.

There were two main reasons for this change in attitude. Many members had been strongly affected by the reforming spirit developing within the Society, and they wanted greatly to bring their actions into line with their professed testimony of noninterference in civil affairs. Many Friends sincerely believed that their testimony for peace prevented them from

4. Moses Brown to John Pemberton, Apr. 30, 1776, Moses Brown Papers, Misc. MSS., K-AB.

paying taxes to support a revolutionary government in any way whatsoever.

The second reason for the change in attitude was that there were many Friends whose sympathies lay with the home government and who refused to be a party to overthrowing it. While they could not participate actively on the British side, they could express their opposition to the changes taking place by refusing to pay taxes to the revolutionary governments. The hard core of this pro-British sentiment was in Pennsylvania, particularly in Philadelphia, and in some areas in New Jersey. On many questions the sense of the Philadelphia meetings was accepted as the sense of the entire Society. In a letter to Moses as early as July 9, 1775, Israel Pemberton expressed his desire for conformity on the question of taxes.[5] In his opinion the circumstances under which taxes were levied were irrelevant; Quakers should not pay taxes to the revolutionary governments. He agreed with an ancient Friend, John Richardson, who said that Friends should mind their "own way in the truth and look not out," which meant that they should continue to support England. But Moses dissented from Pemberton's tendency to consider the tax question in abstract terms, nor did he think that Friends should lean too heavily on the writings of early Quakers to support arguments for the payment or nonpayment of taxes. In his opinion, payment of taxes would be right under some circumstances, wrong under others. The Society should not force members to conform to any one position. Each man should be governed by his own conscience. This, he thought, would have the least divisive effects.

Throughout the war, many Friends claimed a policy of neutrality in the war, but, like the Pembertons, they defined neutrality as continued support for the old governments and refusal to support the new. Others thought that Friends

5. Moses Brown Papers, Misc. MSS., B-814, Box 6.

should pay all taxes and not be concerned about how the money was spent; generally, these people sympathized with the Revolution. It was from this quarter that the trouble came. In July 1775, Moses received a long unsigned address on the subject of taxes. Although he noted that "the author appears to be willing to serve mankind without the vanity of seeking to be known," he probably knew that his friend Timothy Davis of the Sandwich Monthly Meeting on Cape Cod had written it.[6] Moses had become acquainted with Davis at the New England Yearly Meeting at Newport in 1773. The two men had exchanged letters, and Moses had visited Davis only a short time before he received the address.

The greatest threat to the unity of the New England Yearly Meeting during the Revolution came from Davis and his followers. Davis' argument was clearly and persuasively stated. Admitting that Friends both in America and in England differed about paying taxes in wartime, he pointed out that Friends in Massachusetts had paid taxes even though the greater part had been spent for war. But because it was very difficult to separate war taxes from taxes for civil government, he asked "what did our predecessors do?" Aside from "Priests Rates," he showed that Friends in England had always paid taxes. He asserted that Friends in Massachusetts Bay should support the new government because it was better than no government at all; "in a word let a man be under any form of government that he can imagine to himself, where he received any advantage of it, and while he remains under it, he ought to bear his proportion of the charge of it." To support his case Davis quoted from Scripture and from respectable Quaker authorities. In the final analysis, however, he fell back on the authority of the individual's

6. Anonymous [Timothy Davis] to Moses Brown, July 16, 1775, *ibid.*, II, 40. Arthur Mekeel has discussed the Timothy Davis affair and Friends' policy on taxation in his article, "Free Quaker Movement in New England During the American Revolution," Friends' Historical Association, *Bulletin*, 27 (1938), 72-82.

conscience. "It is a time that calls aloud for everyone," he wrote in protest against the spirit of conformity in the Society, "closely to examine their standings; tradition or education although of the best, will be but a poor support in the time that is swiftly approaching; nor will others being firmly established on the immovable rock of ages, as an everlasting foundation, be any alleviation to us in the days of our distress; we must experience this for ourselves, or, sink into perditions."

Davis had been prompted to state his views on taxation because he disagreed with the advice of the Meeting for Sufferings in Philadelphia in January 1775 that Friends should "discountenance and avoid every measure tending to excite disaffection to the King as supreme magistrate" and oppose "every usurpation of power and authority . . . combination, insurrections, conspiracies and illegal assemblies." He also resented the insistence of the Philadelphia Friends that members should subordinate their views to those of the ministers and elders. Davis' first address was not printed and not widely circulated, but in the fall, a second address, written along the same lines, was published by Benjamin Edes at Watertown, the temporary seat of the Massachusetts Provincial Government, and circulated throughout New England. This too was unsigned but everyone knew who the author was.[7]

Philadelphia Quakers objected both to Davis' ideas and to the fact that he had published them without the permission of the Society's official censorshop body, the Meeting for Sufferings. Had he submitted it to the Meeting, of course, it would have been suppressed. Moses objected to the pub-

7. [Timothy Davis], *Letter from one Friend to Some of his Intimate Friends on the subject of Paying Taxes,* published by Benjamin Edes (Watertown, Mass., 1755). The only extant copy is in the Ridgeway Branch of the Library Company of Philadelphia. See Mekeel, "Free Quaker Movement," Friends' Hist. Assn., *Bulletin,* 27 (1938), 72-82, for a discussion of Davis' letter.

lication of Davis' article not so much on these grounds but because his harping on the tax issue in public emphasized a divisive issue. "It is a time of tryal, but there is need of unitying in endeavours to preserve one another from falling in the many snares now spread to entangle and wound the body."[8]

Moses and a number of Friends visited Davis at Dartmouth early in 1776 to talk him into recanting or remaining silent.[9] Failing in this, they asked him to attend the Yearly Meeting soon to be held in Newport in hopes that there, under the guiding light of the members, he would see his way clear to change his mind. Davis seriously considered accepting this last proposal because he did not want "to do anything rashly," but finally he informed Moses that no good would come from his presence, since some of the members intended "to pursue the matter with uncommon severity."[10] During the following months Davis was visited by other committees from the Meetings for Sufferings in New England and Pennsylvania; well-wishing and sympathic Friends, among them Moses Brown, urged him to give up his stand on taxation and return to the communion of Friends. Even when faced with disownment, however, Davis refused to give ground.

The Society did not move swiftly in ejecting Davis from membership. His was not a voice crying in the wilderness; he had the support of most of the members of his monthly meeting at Sandwich. They might not agree with his remarks on taxation, but they could see no reason why he should be disowned for nonconformity. His case was thus referred from the monthly meeting at Sandwich to the quar-

8. Moses Brown to Jonathan Macey, Joseph Mitchell, and William Rotch, Mar. 13, 1776, Moses Brown Papers, Austin MSS., III, "History of Friends," Moses Brown School Lib.

9. Epistle of New England Meeting for Sufferings to Pennsylvania Meeting for Sufferings, Mar. 12, 1776, Minutes, New England Meeting for Sufferings, I, *ibid.*

10. Apr. 22, 1776, Moses Brown Papers, Austin MSS., XII, "Personal," *ibid.*

terly meeting, and then to the New England Yearly Meeting which met in June 1778. After still further delay, the Sandwich Monthly Meeting, prodded by the Philadelphia Meeting for Sufferings, finally disowned him on December 4, 1778.[11]

The Timothy Davis defection illustrates very well a development within the Society of Friends that is all too often overlooked or ignored. The distinguishing characteristic of Quakers had been their belief that the light of Christ was in each man guiding him to the "Truth"; responsiveness to this inner prompting was the only sure guide to freedom and authority. As a social control and steadying influence over the anarchistic tendencies of this doctrine, the monthly, quarterly, and yearly meetings had been developed to the point at which the fallible opinion of the individual was subordinated to the authoritative determination of the members. By the end of the eighteenth century, the weight of the elders and ministers in the meetings was becoming decisive. If, as a famous Quaker historian has pointed out, "the right coordination of the spiritual guidance of the individual with the spiritual discernment of the community occasioned the chief internal difficulties of early Quakerism," then the problem was still unsolved in New England at the time of the American Revolution.[12]

To be sure, the conflict between the "individual spiritual guidance" and the "spiritual discernment of the community" was never so acute in New England as it had been in Old England or as it became in Pennsylvania. Nor had the proponents of the corporate authority of the meetings won as decisive a victory in New England as they had elsewhere. The fact that New England Quakers had found no need to create a Meeting for Sufferings until the American Revolu-

11. Mekeel, "Free Quaker Movement," Friends' Hist. Assn., *Bulletin,* 27 (1938), 79.

12. Quoted from W. C. Braithwaite, *Spiritual Guidance in the Experience of the Society of Friends* (London, 1909), 61, in Lloyd, *Quaker Social History, 1669-1738,* 17.

tion points up this fact. But under the pressure of trying circumstances in New England during the seventies, and assisted by the spreading influence of the Philadelphia Friends, the meetings came to exercise more and more control over the members. Rules that had been loosely applied were now strictly enforced. The newly created Meeting for Sufferings was charged not only with the responsibility of protecting the material welfare of the members but also of exercising powers of censorship over what Friends could write and publish. Diversity of opinion was still tolerated, but if a member insisted on publicly voicing unorthodox views, he could expect to feel the weight of the monthly meeting or receive a visit from a committee of the Meeting for Sufferings. That is precisely what happened to Timothy Davis. There was no fundamental difference between his views on taxes and those held by Moses Brown, but Moses did not insist on making his public. Perhaps his sympathy with Davis accounts for the fact that Moses did not approve of his expulsion, although he acquiesced in it.

Disownment of Davis did not end the matter; it merely dramatized the divergence of opinion within the Society over the question of paying taxes to the revolutionary government. Davis was orthodox on all other matters, and he would not forgo his religion. With upwards of half a hundred members of his meeting, he began to hold public meetings for worship after his disownment. The monthly meeting dealt with these members in summary fashion, ousting thirty out of thirty-five Friends who were involved.[13] Later, in the Dartmouth Monthly Meeting, eleven others who held similar views and who refused to accept the decision of the meeting were disowned. How many left the Society voluntarily or were deterred from becoming Friends because of the dispute is, of course, unknown.

13. Mekeel, "Free Quaker Movement," Friends' Hist. Assn., *Bulletin,* 27 (1938), 78.

Although Moses attempted to reclaim Davis for the Society, the nonconformist refused to abandon his position.
The Davis affair tended to make orthodox Quakers less tol-
erant of differences of opinion on the question of paying
taxes during the Revolution. The longer the war lasted the
more difficult it became for men like Moses to keep the
various meetings from taking an extreme position one way
or the other. Under Moses' moderating influence, the Smithfield Monthly Meeting had evolved early in the war a formula which accommodated those few members who refused
to pay taxes. By 1780, however, the sentiment for nonpayment of taxes had grown stronger, and there was great pressure in the meeting to convert the "apology," which had been
originally drawn to satisfy a minority, into the official position. Moses was suspicious of the motives of some of those
who led this movement. He wrote to Anthony Benezet that
"the principle difficulty, with some of them [who endorse the
"apology"] and those of us who decline is we fear some take
up the Testimony more on account of the authority that
demand the taxes than because they are used for war."[14] The
publication of any definite testimony on the subject of taxes,
Moses argued, would have damaging effects on the Society.
No matter what might be decided it would place many
Quakers in an impossible position. If a member did not
agree with the testimony he would either have to give up
his convictions or run the risk of disownment. Moses was
greatly "depressed and discouraged" at the diversity of
opinion, but he told Benezet it would be a mistake "to make
our union to consist in a conformity of sentiments and practices in matters in which faithful men are not agreed from
their different apprehentions of what the Gospel requires."
Although Moses strongly opposed publication of the

14. Moses Brown to Benezet, Oct. 2, 1780, Moses Brown Papers, Austin
MSS., XII, "Personal," Moses Brown School Lib. See also Samuel Allison to
Moses Brown, Nov. 23, 1780, Moses Brown Papers, Misc. MSS., K-AB.

"apology" by the New England Meeting for Sufferings, he did not follow Timothy Davis' lead and present his views to the public. When the Smithfield Monthly Meeting and the New England Meeting for Sufferings overrode his objections and forwarded its action to the Philadelphia Meeting for Sufferings for approval, he wrote letters to the Pennsylvania committee cautioning against precipitous action. Since the "apology" was never published, Moses' advice must have been heeded. Nevertheless, the question of the payment of taxes remained a troublesome issue for the Quakers until the United States and Britain agreed to peace in 1782. Quakers, even those who looked with disfavor on the government of the new nation, then submitted to the inevitable and quietly paid their taxes.

In 1776 Moses became involved in another episode that threatened the unity of the Society of Friends—the Jemima Wilkinson heresy. Although not as important as the Timothy Davis affair, it was far more dramatic and potentially more dangerous. In the Narragansett country, two or three small groups of Friends, affected by the enthusiasm of the Great Awakening, had split off from the regularly established Friends' meetings. These people were variously referred to as "Newlites" or "Separators."[15] They denied the necessity of any external authority and exalted the authority of the individual conscience as a guide for conduct, regardless of the consequences. This variant Quaker sect derived strength from the reaction of many Quakers against the intensification of reforming zeal that animated the more orthodox members of the Society, who desired more careful regulation of the daily life of members and were intolerant of any deviation from the strict discipline of the meeting. Only the more pious members, or those willing to accept the leadership of the elders and ministers, were able to comply with the

15. Caroline Hazard, *Narragansett Friends' Meeting in the XVIII Century, with a Chapter on Quaker Beginnings in Rhode Island* (Boston, 1899), 97.

rigorous standards that had now become necessary for membership.

One of the "Newlites" was Jemima Wilkinson, a young Quaker girl from Cumberland, the daughter of Jeremiah Wilkinson, a well-to-do farmer and ironmonger who had served on the town council in the 1750's and was a friend and business associate of the Browns for many years.[16] Jemima's mother had died when she was a young girl, and she had received little training at home and even less in school. In 1770 she had heard George Whitefield preach one of his "hellfire" sermons, and became absorbed with religion. A great deal has been written about Jemima and her colorful career, most of it nonsense, based on second-hand or hearsay evidence. Moses Brown and his uncle Elisha were eyewitnesses to most of the early events of her notorious life, and the letters they exchanged tell an interesting, and probably accurate, story.

After Jemima heard Whitefield preach she no longer showed much interest in attending meetings or in keeping the Quaker discipline, and in February 1776 she was disowned by the Smithfield Monthly Meeting. A few months later, she came down with a fever, and her family feared for her life. Overnight, she miraculously recovered. Her explanation for her recovery was truly remarkable. She insisted that she had died and gone to heaven, where her body had been renewed by a spirit who would reveal God's will to man. Insisting that she was no longer Jemima Wilkinson, she asked to be called simply "The Friend"; later she elaborated on this and called herself "The Publick Universal Friend." Like the "Separators" she rejected all church organization as superfluous and claimed direct and continual

16. The best account of Jemima's career is that by Robert P. St. John, "Jemima Wilkinson," New York State Historical Association, *Qtly. Journal,* 11 (1930), 158-75. See also John Quincy Adams, "Jemima Wilkinson, The Universal Friend," *Journal of American History,* 9 (1915), 249-63.

guidance of the spirit. She told people she could predict the future, read people's minds and hearts, and cure the sick.

Jemima was a tall, handsome woman, with a well-proportioned figure, black hair, a glowing complexion, and dark, expressive, penetrating eyes.[17] She possessed an earnestness and personal charm that melted the souls of many who had remained untouched by Whitefield. Among her converts were scores of "Separators" and orthodox Quakers who inclined toward enthusiastic religion, among them some of the most respectable citizens of the state. Stephen Hopkins was her friend and adviser; Joshua Babcock of Westerly—a graduate of Yale College and friend of Benjamin Franklin and Washington—and Judge William Potter of South Kingston, were among her followers. At first she spoke in the Friends' meetinghouses but they were soon denied to her because of her popularity and her refusal to accept the guidance of the elders and ministers.[18] She then established meetings in Warwick, South Kingston, and East Greenwich, Rhode Island, in New Milford, Connecticut, and in a few other places in southern New England.

The Quakers struck back at Jemima. Attendance at her meetings was considered a serious breach of the discipline, and if a member continued to follow her after he had been warned, he was disowned.[19] Meetings refused to take any public notice of her; what was said about her in private was not a matter of record. There is no question but that she was very badly treated by Friends. Uncle Elisha Brown, who

17. See the detailed description of her in the *Providence Gazette; and Country Journal*, Mar. 17, 1787. The piece was an extract from the *Freeman's Journal* (Phila.), Feb. 14, 1787.

18. In 1778 Jemima, her sister Mary, and Rhoda Scott of Bellingham, Mass., received permission from General Sullivan to make a religious visit to England. William Aldrich and some others petitioned the General Assembly for permission to accompany them, and the petition was granted, provided Aldrich and his company did not return to the state. Later the General Assembly withdrew its consent. Petitions to the Rhode Island General Assembly, 1778-80, XVII, 35, R. I. Archives.

19. Hazard, *Narragansett Friends'*, 171.

had been captivated by Jemima's preaching and repelled by
the strict discipline of Friends, wrote Moses he thought that
"God in his enfinst wisdom had rased hur as it ware from
the ded to declare his everlasting truth at a time when the
friends have no person scarcely boold enuf but feare [and]
chus to hid thare talents under a bushel."[20] Moses had visited
Jemima on several occasions and heard her say "she had
been dead and that she was not the same person of Jemima
Wilkinson but was the Comfortor. I charitably hoped she
ment no more than she was a Comfortor to the people. . . .
But how to reconcile her being actualy dead and not the
same body I must confess I know not."[21] Moses told his
Uncle Elisha, rather patronizingly, "as a person conscientiously believes and acts so is he and I doubt not she with
thy self, in the general means well." To his knowledge,
Jemima had not committed any dishonest acts, and had led
a moral and respectable life. He later remembered that she
had an extraordinary memory and could recite long passages
from Friends' writings and the Bible without notes. She
frequently attended funerals and executions of condemned
spies and army deserters, and prayed for their souls, as well
as for the souls of the executioners.

Jemima's new religion, or revival of an old one—she
resembled in her actions some of the enthusiastic sects of the
seventeenth century—presented a real threat to the Quakers
in New England during the Revolution. In 1783, Abner
Brownell attacked Jemima and her heresy in a scurrilous
pamphlet entitled "Enthusiastical Errors, Transpired and
Detected."[22] By this time, however, Jemima had decided
that the New England climate was too cold to nourish her
new religion, and she departed for points south, accompanied

20. Jan. 4, 1779, Moses Brown Papers, III, 2. In this letter Elisha reviews
the history of the Quakers' treatment of Jemima as he had witnessed it.
21. Feb. 12, 1779, and Elisha's reply, Mar. 18, *ibid.*, 4, 5.
22. See Charles Evans, *American Bibliography* . . . , 14 vols. (Chicago,
1903-59), VI, 160.

by a few of her faithful followers. But the threat she had posed was not forgotten, and the movement to define doctrine and control religious practice continued.

With the Jemima Wilkinson affair fresh in his mind, Moses in 1780 began to formulate the idea of a uniform discipline for the entire Society in America, based on the New England discipline and those followed in New York, Maryland, and England. He thought that if all the meetings could agree to a set of queries consistent with the principles of the "Truth," yet general enough to allow regional and cultural differences, criticism of the Society for inconsistency and insincerity would subside. In 1783 he wrote to Friends in New Jersey and Pennsylvania that he favored "one general code of laws among the American meetings."[23] James Pemberton sympathized with Moses' suggestion and thought that properly handled it was possible. Any formula would have to be drafted by a general session representing the various regional Quaker meetings, he cautioned, and some of his friends thought it impracticable to adopt the same rules for all.[24] But they also thought it would be difficult to frame a code which would fit the diverse circumstances of the different Quaker communities. The real objection to Moses' plan, Pemberton wrote, was that some Friends feared that a reliance on written rules might lead to a decline in the exercise of their spiritual gifts. Pemberton himself said that this fear was not justified, for if the decisions of the meetings collectively flowed from the promptings of the "Inner Light," they would find solid support among Friends who were concerned about the maintenance of the discipline "and strengthen their hands against such who are weak, or superficial," and the sense of the meeting would be infused with truth.

Actually, Pemberton must have known that in many

23. Nov. 11, Allison Collection, Haverford College Lib., Haverford, Pa.
24. May 21, 1784, Moses Brown Papers, Misc. MSS., B-814, Box 6.

instances decisions arrived at in the meetings did not represent such nice co-ordination between individual spiritual
guidance and collective spiritual discernment, but were
rather the judgments of elders and ministers, the real leaders
in the Society. On the other hand, Moses, who expressed
great surprise when his suggestions were rejected, did not
realize how strong and obdurate were those Friends who
placed greater trust in the still small voice of the Divine
Teacher in their souls than in the word of the elders and
ministers, and objected to attempts by the leaders to force all
members into a strict conformity to the discipline. He apparently had forgotten his earlier reluctance, in connection
with the controversy about tax payments and most other
issues, to coerce members in matters of opinion. Although
he did not fully understand why his desire to make the discipline uniform met with such resistance, Moses did not push
his plan to excess; instead, he worked quietly and successfully in the meetings in New England to persuade the members to adopt his scheme. In 1785 New England Friends
were the first to adopt and publish a uniform discipline.

Moses' bold step in formation of a uniform discipline was
indicative of his religious development and of his rise to a
commanding position in the Society of Friends. For the first
few years of his membership he had been like a novice among
experts, willing to accept leadership of Pennsylvania and
English Friends while he waited for the illumination of the
divine light. But his expectations were not fulfilled. He
experienced few "openings" after his conversion. In this
important respect he had found his conversion to Quakerism
a disappointment. He was not a mystic. Slowly he came to
emphasize the form rather than the spiritual element of his
faith, regulating his life according to a strict code of ethics
based on the discipline and his own sense of right and wrong.
Preference for a well-ordered life caused him to set aside a

certain part of each day for meditation or "silent waiting," during which he reviewed his past life and planned his future. Some Friends questioned the propriety of such a practice; it was contrary to the spirit of Quakerism, they said. Moses justified himself with the reply that a well-regulated life, rather than waiting to be moved by the spirit, gave him more time for specific, practical work for the welfare of the religious community. No one could deny that his plan worked.

Moses' contacts with Friends in other states in America increased substantially during the war. In the last years of the Revolution, when the armies had moved to the southern states, Friends from New England and the middle states exchanged visits to strengthen each other in their testimony for peace, and to further the reformation within the Society. Moses entertained numerous traveling Friends at his spacious Elmgrove mansion. James Lloyd of Philadelphia visited him in June 1780; the two rode over to Dartmouth, Massachusetts, to try once more to draw Timothy Davis back into the fold, but to no avail.[25] Lloyd was much impressed by Moses and valued him as a worthy Friend. George Churchman, a well-educated and pious Friend from the Nottingham Monthly Meeting in Maryland, visited the farm in the summer of 1781 with a number of other Friends, and Moses accompanied them to meetings along the coast of Massachusetts. Churchman later wrote to John Pemberton about his trip, and observed that "as to brightness and purity . . . Moses for what I know, is one of the brightest, if not the most so in those parts."[26] On his return home, Churchman wrote to Moses thanking him for his hospitality, and remarking that "my affection seems to flow towards you in an uncommon manner; perhaps full as much, if not more so,

25. Sept. 8, 1780, *ibid.*, III, 36.
26. June 30, 1781, Pemberton Papers, XXVIII, 35, Hist. Soc. of Pa.

than towards any other person with whom I have had so short an acquaintance; I feel you near in the nearest Relation."[27] Moses had always been able to command the respect of his associates, but his ability to cultivate friendships was a development in his personality that ripened only after he became a Friend.

Warner Mifflin, a Delaware pacifist, inveterate traveler in the cause of "Truth," and indefatigable foe of slavery and the slave trade, also visited Moses in 1781. Like Moses, Mifflin had become convinced of the sinfulness and injustice of slavery, and in 1774, in a ceremony similar to that performed by Moses the year before, he freed all his slaves. The two men talked about slavery, Timothy Davis' defection, Friends' schools, and the war. Mifflin, like Churchman, thought Moses a hospitable and worthy Friend. Some months after his visit he wrote Moses that he had "often thought [of] the nearness I feel toward you when under your roof, which I thought felt like my own, as I many times thought I could [have] gone into your closet and helped myself to some refreshments as free as I could to my own, which I thought was a liberty that Truth gave me."[28]

Frequent contact with Friends from different parts of the country was very important in Moses' life. Most of these visitors were well educated, some of them well fixed financially; all were leaders in the Society. Through prolific personal correspondence with these people Moses was able to keep in touch with national developments, to hear new ideas, and to compare his own thoughts with minds superior to those in Quaker circles in the New England Yearly Meeting. Moreover, as a result of his association with traveling Friends, he gained a reputation throughout America that subsequently became useful to him in his humanitarian and re-

27. July 27, 1781, Moses Brown Papers, Misc. MSS., K-AB.
28. July 27, Oct. 3, 1781, *ibid.*

ligious activities. He rapidly became known as a man who could be counted on to perform needful services for Friends in other areas, no matter how remote.[29]

In January 1783, Moses' work was formally recognized. He was made an elder in the Smithfield Monthly Meeting, a position he held for the rest of his life.

29. June 7, 1780, *ibid.*, III, 29. Wilson sent this letter to Moses with a covering letter dated June 28, 1780. See also a follow-up letter from Wilson, June 29, *ibid.*, 34.

8

A Guarded Education for Friends' Children

MOSES' EMERGENCE as the leader of New England Quakers toward the end of the war was partly the result of his educational work among Friends. In the early years of the Revolution, Friends had turned their attention from their worldly problems of persecutions and sufferings inward to problems of the Society. An increased interest in education characterized the general reforming spirit that pervaded the entire Society and touched all phases of Quaker life.[1] Moses was exceedingly responsive to the reforming spirit in education, an interest which antedated his conversion. In the 1760's he had helped found the New Brick School House in Providence, and he was still one of its proprietors. His successful campaign to get Rhode Island College located in Providence had focused attention on higher education and contributed to its growth. Although wounded soldiers now crowded the college, he maintained a lively concern for its future and looked forward to the day its doors would open to resume the peaceful cultivation of the mind.

1. See Rufus M. Jones, *The Quakers in the American Colonies* (London, 1911), 571, for a discussion of the reform movement within the Society.

After his conversion, Moses' main educational concern centered on the advancement of the educational opportunities of Friends. In a letter to Anthony Benezet in 1780 on the education of Friends' children in Philadelphia, Moses reported on the efforts of a few of the faithful in New England to open Friends' schools, a movement he had helped to get underway two years earlier.[2]

Moses was the originator of the idea for a monthly meeting school and its strongest supporter. In March 1777, Moses suggested and the Smithfield Monthly Meeting adopted a minute declaring that the care of the young was "much relaxed within our yearly meeting, from what our Discipline requires" and recommending "to the solid attention of the Quarterly Meeting this important subject." They were convinced that if the minds of Friends were "united in a living concern therein," it would "be an acceptable step in the Reformation."[3]

After great effort, Moses and a few other Friends managed to set up a school in the lower meeting in Providence.[4] It failed within two years. The explanation is simple: there was an almost total lack of qualified teachers, a scarcity of funds, and an attitude among local Friends that varied from indifference to outright hostility. Moses noted that the poorer members did not send their children to the school and that only a few of the more well-to-do Friends supported it. Occasionally, members sent their children to private schools in and about Providence, but most put them out as apprentices to learn a trade. Other meetings in New England made feeble efforts to set up schools, but they too failed

2. Mar. 9, Moses Brown Papers, Austin MSS., XII, "Personal," Moses Brown School Lib. For details of Benezet's educational activities, see George S. Brookes, *Friend Anthony Benezet* (Phila., 1937), 29-59.

3. Smithfield Monthly Meeting Records, I, 208-9, Mar. 25, 1777, Moses Brown School Lib.

4. The progress of the Smithfield Monthly Meeting may be followed in its Records for April, May, and June 1777, 157 ff., *ibid.*

for similar reasons. The progress of education among Friends in New England was disappointing.

Far-sighted members of the Society—Moses Brown, William Buffum, Thomas Hazard, Moses Farnum, Elisha Thornton, and a few others—did not give up. If the financial resources of the monthly meeting were too meager to finance a school of any size, they would turn to the greater resources and stronger leadership of the quarterly meeting. But the quarterly meeting failed to induce the monthly meetings to establish schools for much the same reasons that led to the failure of the school sponsored by the Smithfield Monthly Meeting: "Want of suitable persons qualified for the service," inadequate funds, and lack of genuine interest on the part of Friends.[5]

Since the establishment of Friends' schools was considered a "Step in the Reformation," Quakers may justifiably be charged with inconsistency when they refused to support them. There were, however, two sides to the "Reformation." In addition to the movement in the direction of a closer conformity to the practices of the "Truth" through education, the re-emphasis on the spiritual element of religion led many Friends to rely on the "Inner Light" as the sole guide for conduct and to look suspiciously at any movement that emphasized conformity to rules. Indeed, some Friends felt that education led to a decline in religious feeling. Moses was of two minds on the subject. Like Anthony Benezet he recognized the necessity for children to learn a trade so that they could earn a living, but he often expressed a distrust of higher education and said that where there was much education there was apt to be a decline in attention to religion. Later, when the yearly meeting school was first established, he was to emphasize the need for a "guarded education," the instruction of the children in the principles of the Society and the inculcation in them of a respect for

5. Mar. 9, 1780, Moses Brown Papers, Austin MSS., XII, "Personal," *ibid.*

its traditions and practices. He hoped, as a result, that they would remain true to their birthright membership and become faithful followers of the truth.

In the summer of 1779 efforts of the small group of Friends supporting the educational movement began to bear fruit. In June, Moses laid before the Yearly Meeting a recommendation of the Rhode Island Meeting School Committee that the school question be considered. In response to his appeal, the Yearly Meeting appointed a committee of sixteen to study the quarterly meeting's proposals. Moses was a member and helped draft the report endorsing the "speedy establishment" of a yearly meeting school that would qualify "a sufficient number of Instructors and School Masters" to educate children so that they could take their places in the business world.[6] The quarterly and monthly meetings were asked to promote "Free, Liberal and voluntary subscriptions, donations, bequests, and divices, adequate to the design and importance of the subject; as a fund, to remain foreever, the interest or income of which to be applyd to the support of education." These subscriptions were to be promoted annually until the income from the fund was adequate to sustain the school. To increase the size of the operating fund, the committee recommended that non-Quakers be allowed to attend the school as long as they complied with the rules. Moses and the members of the committee were not easy about taking in outsiders, but, because of the lack of funds and the unwillingness of members to support the school, they felt that it was necessary. Time and the visible benefits accruing to those children who did attend might cause a change in the Quakers' parsimonious attitude.

Once the Yearly Meeting had approved of the plan, its implementation was turned over to the Meeting for Sufferings. Moses was treasurer of this meeting and almost all the documents dealing with the school bear his signature.

6. Smithfield Monthly Meeting Records, Oct. 26, 1780, *ibid.*

Predictably, the treasurer's chief problems were financial; too many Friends did not have an "openness" to contribute. There was also the vexing question of currency. Would subscriptions in paper money be acceptable, or would only hard money be received? Since specie was very scarce in New England during the Revolution, the Meeting for Sufferings, interpreting the school as "a matter of Freedom and benevolence," decided that paper money would be acceptable.[7] Moses undoubtedly had a hand in formulating this practical solution to a difficult problem.

Plans to open the school were twice discarded because of lack of funds, and on the eleventh of November, 1782, the Meeting for Sufferings, in desperation, sent a lengthy appeal to all the quarterly and monthly meetings. Although submitted by a committee of four—Thomas Hazard, Samuel Smith, Moses Brown, and David Buffum—this document has the stamp of Moses' thought and expression on it. The central thought was that the salvation of the Society depended upon a proper attention to the education of members' children. "Our principles," the appeal read,

lead to a separation from the world, its customs, habits, language, and manners; how then can we hope for faithful successors in our posterity, or that they will come up in principles and practices agreeable there to, if we continue so far to neglect the early care of our offspring, as to send them to schools where principles and practices so repugnant are inculcated and taught: It is essential to the continuance of every society, upon the foundation of its rise and establishment, that its first principles be often recurred to.[8]

Funds for the school increased with agonizing slowness despite continual efforts by a few people to "excite [in] our

7. Moses' extracts of the Minutes of the Yearly Meeting School Committee, Moses Brown Papers, Austin MSS., IV, "Education," *ibid*. These "extracts," give a connected account of the progress of the yearly meeting school. They also contain information not found in the Minutes.

8. *Ibid*. Moses signed the document as clerk; it was printed by John Carter as a broadside.

Brethern propper sentiments of the propriety and usefulness of such an institution." But the plea that friends "promote so benevolent a design toward the poor and those of small circumstances as to the things of this life" produced scarcely a stir among the members of the Society.[9] Nevertheless, the Meeting for Sufferings decided in November 1782, notwithstanding the fact that the subscriptions for opening and maintaining the school were disappointingly inadequate, to appoint a committee to select the location and the master of the school.

Eventually the choice of a location narrowed down to Providence, Portsmouth, Smithfield, and Lynn, and a committee was appointed to investigate the suitability of these towns and inquire about a master.[10] By October 1783 reports on all the towns except Portsmouth had come in; the committee decided on Smithfield as the place and Elisha Thornton as the master.[11] Final action on the matter was postponed until the report on Portsmouth was received. When Portsmouth finally submitted its proposal, the committee reversed its tentative decision and awarded the school to Portsmouth. The desperate need for funds probably dictated the decision. Isaac Mott and Isaac Lawton, members of the Rhode Island Monthly Meeting and firm supporters of the school, used their influence to get the Portsmouth meeting to contribute £60 a year out of the income from its rents on a number of lots in Newport. Furthermore, the meeting at Portsmouth provided a place for the school in its meetinghouse, and Isaac Lawton agreed to assume the arduous duties of schoolmaster if the school was located in his town.

Lawton was an excellent man to take charge of the school. Short and lithe in stature, he was quick and lively in his

9. *Ibid.*
10. D. Howland to Moses Brown, Jan. 25, 1783, *ibid.*
11. Moses' extracts of Minutes of the Yearly Meeting School Committee, *ibid.*

movements, intelligent and agreeable in conversation, affable
and polite in his manners.[12] Already known as an "eminent
and eloquent minister," he was a favorite with the children,
believing that kind and sympathetic treatment would produce better scholars than the conventional strict and authoritarian procedures. He was undoubtedly Moses' choice, for
the two men had been intimate friends since Lawton visited
Moses during his "tryals" in 1773. For a decade they had
fought side by side against the slave trade and slavery, and
for toleration for Quakers during the Revolution.

The final decision to open the Portsmouth school was
taken with the clear understanding that unless members
contributed generously to its support it would surely fail.
But Moses was so convinced of the vital need for a school
where Friends' children could get a "guarded education"
that he refused to believe that Friends would not rise to the
need. Like his friend Benezet, he attributed Friends' apathy
to "a self seeking worldly spirit the emasing of wealth for
posterity and liveing in ease and luxury etc."[13] Since becoming a Friend he had often thought "that there was too
much striving to ware eat and get possessions equal to the
greatest stewards." Moses himself bore a cross because of
his easy circumstances and large property holdings, and the
thought frequently occurred to him that he set a bad example
for poorer Friends who envied the "*supposed* easy scituation
of their brethern in affluence."

During the formative stages of the school movement
Moses began to develop his ideas about the curriculum. Dis-
cussing with Benezet the value of foreign languages, he remarked that it might be all right for some "geniouses who
may be concerned in physick etc. to know the Lattin as it
is a language most of the European Nations write in. If so

12. Rayner Wickersham Kelsey, *Centennial History of Moses Brown School,
1819-1919* (Providence, 1919), 12.
13. Moses Brown to Anthony Benezet, Oct. 2, 1780, Moses Brown Papers,
Austin MSS., XII, "Personal," Moses Brown School Lib.

it will be necessary that there be a school capable of teaching it although it may not be useful but to a few."[14]   When he made these remarks in 1780, Moses had not yet decided whether the yearly meeting school should offer instruction in foreign languages.   He observed that Friends in New England had never had a desire for "high learning" and, from his observations, were "an illiterate and I may justly say an ignorant set of people compared with others."   In the entire New England Yearly Meeting, only five or six members knew any foreign language and many could not even write their names.   He realized that in Benezet's home town of Philadelphia education had been stressed, but he was not certain of the benefits.   "I am sensible," he noted, "where there is a dependency on learning as an essential qualification for a Gospel Minister or office in the Church there will be darkness [on the part of the ministers] and disappointment [within the meeting]."   He agreed with Benezet that excessive learning tended to divert the mind from religious truth.

Moses was not consistent in matters of education.   Distrusting "high learning" and preferring subjects to be taught that would have some immediate practical value, he nevertheless made sure that his son was taught French, mathematics, and other subjects not strictly utilitarian.   He himself spent long hours reading and studying history, literature, and science, and he contributed numerous books and a philosophical apparatus to the college and encouraged some of his young friends to increase their learning.   But Moses' penchant for the practical and the useful blinded him to the intangible values of higher education, at least for Quakers. His objective in educating Friends' children was limited. He thought that the young should be taught to make a living and to become Quakers.   To do this, they needed only to learn to read, write, and do simple figuring; this would

14. Oct. 2, 1780, *ibid.*

enable them to learn a trade and become independent. The
acquisition of useful knowledge, however, was merely a
means to an end: it should be supplemented by the proper
religious training in the school, the home, and the Meeting
for Worship, which would make the member an "ornament
to the society." Later, when Moses had acquired more
knowledge and experience about education, he was to change
his mind on some of these subjects.

Moses' pessimistic attitude about the future of the yearly
meeting school was changed somewhat when he learned of
the success of the Ackworth School established by the late
Dr. John Fothergill in England. He was filled with "sollid
delight at the beneficience of Friends" who contributed to
the school and hoped the example would be useful in New
England to induce Friends to support the yearly meeting
school. "If such laudable example will not envite the generous feelings of humanity to action," he wrote William
Rotch in 1782, "and constrain us to a greater discharge of
our duty in the virtuous education of our children and
youth, I dont know what will."[15] He said that he had almost
despaired of Friends recognizing the importance of education and had often questioned his own feelings on the subject
because of the indifferent attitude of so many others. Moses
made extensive use of the success of the Ackworth School in
his fund-raising campaign, and the school itself served as a
model for the yearly meeting school.

Considering Moses' pessimism and his ambivalent attitude towards education, his perseverance and dogged determination to establish a yearly meeting school are remarkable.
Although he does not deserve the entire credit, it is incon-
ceivable that the school would have opened when it did
without him. He consulted with Benezet on the preparation
and publication of a suitable grammar for the students,

15. Mar. 17, 1782, *ibid.*, IV, "Education." All the quotations that follow
are from this source unless otherwise noted.

worked with the committee to draw up rules and regulations for the scholars, and talked with Isaac Lawton about the many problems incident to its eventual opening. And he was a member of the committee placed in charge of the school when it opened. The day came at last on November 8, 1784.

Before the school had been in operation six months, difficulties arose. Friends who could afford it did not send their children to Portsmouth, and the parents of needy scholars did not accept the invitations that went to the seventy-five monthly meetings urging members "to exert themselves so that all friends may be educated for business." In May 1785, the school committee appointed three of its members to find out how many poor children the fund could support the next year and to draft an appeal for greater attendance. Acting on the sub-committee's recommendation, the school committee sent an appeal to all the monthly meetings, noting that "besides the necessary litterary instructions the children are to be taught habits of regularity, of decency, of respectfull subordination to their superiors, of forebearance, affection and kindness towards each other, and religious reverance toward their maker, and those habits of silence and recolection *Taught and practiced in the Antient Schools,* and inculcated in the Holy Scriptures." Again the response was disappointing: at the end of the first year, the school committee noted that the school was still small, "consisting of about 20 schollars, two of which [are] of the first class of Poor."

By the middle of 1786, the school was also in serious financial difficulty. Members had not only refused to send their children to the school; they had also refused to send financial assistance. William Rotch and Moses Brown were the principal supporters, and a small donation was made by Newport Friends, but most of the meetings, particularly those in the northern rural areas of New England, contributed nothing. Far removed from the school, they failed

to see how it could help them; they preferred to spend their money on local schools over which they might have some control, or to put their children to work. The school committee was, therefore, forced to take action. Isaac Lawton's salary as master was reduced, and the committee went to court in an attempt to collect the back rents on the lots in Newport. The initiation of a suit indicates the precarious financial state of the school, for Friends seldom sued to recover a debt unless they were desperate.[16] Failure to collect the rents forced the committee seriously to consider closing the school.

Before coming to a final decision, a committee was appointed to frame an appeal to Friends in England. Several years before Shubal Coffin of Nantucket had gone to England seeking school funds; perhaps the salvation of the school yet lay in England. In the past, English Friends had always come forward with help for their American brethren when they had received the call—Rhode Island Friends could still remember the generous gifts of money that came from England and Ireland during the war. As clerk of the school committee, Moses sent an appeal to the Meeting for Sufferings in London calling attention to the imminent failure of the school unless help was received soon. He attributed failure to the depressed economic conditions in America, particularly the "depreseated state of paper currency in this state, and the laws making it a tender for silver and gold," which made the collection of rents in Newport difficult and prevented Friends from making contributions.

With the latter Moses also sent personal appeals to Samuel Neal and David Barclay, influential Friends in London, describing in greater detail the "state of this part of the society in New England respecting education."[17] He listed three

16. See Joseph Mitchell to Moses Brown, Oct. 25, 1785, Moses Brown Papers, V, 46.

17. Mar. 15, Mar. 23, 1787, *ibid.*, VI, 3.

reasons for the "great neglect" of education among Friends: first, many members still had a mistaken notion that since education was not a necessary qualification for the gospel ministry it served no useful purpose. One of the results of this hostility towards education was that in many meetings there were not even enough members qualified properly to conduct the business of the meetings. Second, because Friends were scattered over a wide area, mainly in the country, only small groups of students could be collected at any one place for schooling; this required a large number of teachers, of which there was a great shortage among Friends, and usually they were not qualified to teach even simple reading, writing, and arithmetic. Third, the generally depressed state of Friends, caused by distraint of taxes and property during the war, the depreciation of currency following the Peace of 1783, and the legal tender laws recently enacted made it difficult for them to contribute to the school fund. These, then, were the fundamental reasons for the almost certain failure of the yearly meeting school. Moses' analysis was as accurate as it was candid; he neither exaggerated Friends' apathy and suspicion of education nor was he insincere about their inability to support the school; his advice was based on firsthand knowledge of the history of the school and of conditions within the Society.

Passing from the causes for the "great neglect" of education to ways in which English Friends might help, Moses suggested that if they did not find an "openness" to contribute to a school dedicated principally to teaching the poor, perhaps they might contribute to a special fund to employ a schoolmaster capable of teaching a few students of "genious and capacity" "Lattin, French, or some other language with usefull parts of mathematics which at present cannot be learned in any school we have in Society here." He would, he wrote, "willingly add £100 to my subscription as a fund for that purpose in my life time instead of its standing in

my will, which has for some time been the case, to lay a foundation for such an establishment in a future day." He had no expectation that the demand for higher learning would come soon but he mentioned the matter in case English Friends wanted to contribute to that cause, "as but a few, a very few friends here, thinks any more than common reading writing and arithmatick necessary."

In 1787, Friends in England were having their own difficulties and they could not send aid to New England. Since the school committee's resources were exhausted it decided on June 18, 1788, less than four years after the doors were opened, to close the school. Although Moses knew that it had been started with insufficient funds and had been operated on a shoestring, its failure was a staggering blow. His reaction was similar to what it had been when his wife died, and when he thought he was going to die: for a time he withdrew within himself and made few references to the event in his correspondence. But his reaction was in some respects different this time. In the past, he had become engrossed in his religious activity. Now he resigned himself to the realization that the education of Quaker children would have to await a more favorable time.

Although he realized that there were extenuating circumstances in the failure of the school, Moses interpreted the refusal of Friends to support it as a great internal weakness of the Society, almost as serious as the basic problem confronting the Society: a rapidly declining membership. Indeed, a successful school might have helped ease the drop in membership. During the early years of Quakerism, there had been a small but significant stream of converts into the Society about equal to the number who departed from the path of "Truth"; in addition, the percentage of Friends' children who became members had been large. During the last quarter of the eighteenth century, however, the number of converts to Quakerism dropped sharply, and the children

of members did not live up to their birthright membership. The only way Moses could see for the Society to survive was for the leaders to stimulate the children to become sincere members. To expect children to be good without teaching them that which was good and guarding them from that which was evil was, in his estimation, to expect too much.

If Moses was disappointed at the failure of the school, he did not become cynical or pessimistic. As treasurer of the school committee, he continued to attend the numerous meetings where the financial problems of the school were discussed. In 1795 subscriptions were sent out again, and the next year Moses reported that some progress had been made but that the funds were still insufficient to reopen the school. He also noted additional reasons for delaying action: "The dispersed scituation of friends in most meetings, which would prevent most of their children takeing benefit of such school . . . without the further expense of boarding out their children"; the difficulty in getting schoolmasters "under the present state of learning suitably qualified among friends to take the charge of such schools"; and "a proper concern and liberality, proportioned to the importance of a pious education."

Throughout the 1790's Moses carefully invested the committee's collections, waiting for the day when the fund would be large enough to make another try. Determined to avoid another failure, he urged the members to delay reopening the school until its success could be assured. In this he was wise, for another failure might have resulted in outright abandonment of the plan. Not until thirty years after the children had been sent home on a vacation in 1788 did the yearly meeting school reopen its doors. When it did, the building occupied by the new scholars was not in Portsmouth but in Providence, on a plot of ground, located on Prospect Hill, given to the Society by Moses Brown.

Moses' efforts during the war to provide a "guarded edu-

cation" for Friends' children coincided with changes in his
personal life. In January 1779, Moses and Mary Olney appeared in the Smithfield Monthly Meetinghouse and declared
their intentions of marriage. Mary was one of Moses' fellow
enthusiasts about providing education for Friends' children.
She had been his friend for years and a companion on many
a religious journey since his conversion to Quakerism. The
formal, conventional entries made by the clerk in the meeting's minutes tell us all we know about the event. The
meeting appointed Benjamin Arnold, his companion on the
trip to Boston in 1775, and Joseph Mitchell, a friend he had
brought to Providence from Nantucket, to "inquire into his
clearness." They reported favorably the next month, and on
March 25, 1779, at the Lower Meetinghouse in Providence,
the marriage was "conducted in a degree orderly." Sixty-
nine witnesses signed the declaration of marriage, including
members of the family and many of Moses' old friends.[18]
The gathering was one of the largest that had attended a
Friend's wedding, and Moses must have been gratified to
see so many of his old friends present.

Moses' second wife, Mary Olney, was the daughter of
Richard and Hannah Olney of Providence. She was thirty-
five when she married Moses, who was five years her senior.
What she looked like, whether pretty or plain, tall or short,
blond or brunette, is unknown. Although she rode all over
New England attending Friends' meetings, she was not a
well woman when she married Moses, and was frequently ill
during the remaining eighteen years of her life. She was a
pious Quaker, clerk of the women's monthly and quarterly
meetings, and a tireless worker for the Society. The marriage caused no immediate changes in Moses' life, and his
correspondence reveals nothing of his feelings.

Only a year after his marriage in 1779 Moses suffered a

18. Smithfield Monthly Meeting Records, Jan. 28, Feb. 25, 1779, 201, 205,
207, Moses Brown School Lib.

serious illness. In November, he was struck down by a "nervous complaint" which became painfully severe when he wrote or read even a few lines. His head and neck ached, his eyes swelled and became red and watery, and he suffered from chills, particularly in the hands and feet. Some days the pain was so great he could do nothing but remain in his bed or sit propped up in a chair before the fire. His pulse was "small and not frequent," he noted, but increased when he moved about, "an effort I expect of nature to supply the upper extremitys and a mark of a debility of the circular powers."[19] He had first noticed this "Virtigo," as he called it, the previous winter when he was "greatly exposed in attending every meeting from our own to the quarter." He had made use of some purgative medicines, kept his head covered with a wool cap, and had had no "further attack of what our family has been subject to; viz the palsey and appoplexy."

In the spring, however, his "tryals" had been increased by the illness of his wife and his daughter Sarah and the difficulties of his friends on Nantucket Island who, accused of being spies and traitors, had been taken to Boston for safekeeping. Then his old friend and co-worker in the Society, Moses Farnum, suffered a series of "paraletick fits" that disturbed Moses greatly. Added to these cares was the slow progress of the "Reformation," particularly in education. "These things," he wrote John Pemberton, "brot on rather more debility than usual and I felt the symptoms approaching towards a fit. But by means imidiately used to restore an even circulation as the feet in warm water and the Divine Blessing there on I recovered from this languid state though for some time, weeks, I was nearly at a stand."

Moses recovered during the summer, but the next attack, which came on in the winter, was more severe. It was

19. Moses Brown to John Pemberton, Dec. 22, 1780, Moses Brown Papers, Austin MSS., II, "Republic of Letters," *ibid.*

brought on, so he said, by his concern in the difficult matter
of writing a refutation of Isaac Backus's *History of the
Baptists,* which contained some unflattering and "erronious"
materials concerning the Quakers.[20] To John Pemberton,
Moses wrote that he knew he should give up some of his
activities, but as they were mostly concerned with affairs of
the Society he didn't see how he could.[21]

Moses probably exaggerated the severity of his illness.
Abraham Chovets, the doctor whom John Pemberton consulted for Moses in Philadelphia, diagnosed his disorder as
"an atonia, or relaxation of the nerves that enter the composition of the coats of the blood vessels of the head to direct
the vital actions, probably from too great attention of the
mind and an hereditary weakeness in his native constitution."
Chovets said that unless Moses curtailed his activities, he
might develop palsy, or epilepsy, although he held out "great
hopes of preventing these accidents" if Moses made use of
the "antispasmodic and tonick medicines" he recommended.[22]
How accurately Moses described his illness, or how accurately Dr. Chovets diagnosed it without seeing the patient,
is impossible to determine. Considering the state of the
medical profession in the eighteenth century, Moses was
probably fortunate that he was in Providence and Dr.
Chovets in Philadelphia. At least his weak constitution was
not further weakened by bloodletting, purging, and the
dozen and one remedies that might well have proved fatal.
Moses later said that the medicines Dr. Chovets prescribed
were of great help. At any rate, he had soon recovered sufficiently to resume his activities.

For the next three years Moses suffered from frequent
attacks of "apoplexy," but although he was forced to stop

20. Moses Brown to William Rotch, Mar. 7, 1781, Moses Brown Papers, III,
51.
21. Jan. 14, 1781, *ibid.,* Misc. MSS., K-AB.
22. Diagnosis by Abraham Chovets, Philadelphia, Jan. 14, 1781, *ibid.*

his business activities altogether, he did not allow his illness to interfere with his religious work.[23] His attitude was that if it was the Divine Will to take him from this world, there was little he could do about it, and he proceeded to make the most of his remaining time. When he was unable to write, he dictated his letters to his daughter Sarah or his son Obadiah.[24] Outdoor exercise seemed to give him some relief from the pains in his eyes and neck, and he spent a great deal of his time riding to the numerous meetings in New England. Although he preferred to ride horseback, he bought a chaise, and traveled in it when the weather was bad. His illness had caused him to have head chills; as protection against the cold he began to wear a wool stocking cap under his large, wide-brimmed hat.

One of the central themes of Moses' early life as a Quaker was his attempt to reconcile his desire "to retire from all outward objects" with his deep sense of public responsibility. During the first years of the Revolution the balance was in favor of retirement from the world, but towards the end of the war, despite his work for the Society and his frequent attacks of vertigo, Moses became more involved in the affairs of Providence and the state of Rhode Island.

During the war the people of the town had suspended maintenance of their public services—streets, drainage ditches, pest house, public dock—and after years of neglect, they had fallen into disrepair. As peace approached, town leaders turned their attention to these matters. One of the most important projects was the repairing and paving of streets. Moses had played a leading role in the original effort to pave Providence streets some twenty years before, and now that his services were once again in demand, he could not resist

23. Jonathan Easton, Jr., to Moses Brown, Mar. 1, 1783; Moses Brown to Thomas Wagstaffe, Nov. 5, 1784, Moses Brown Papers, IV, 34.
24. Moses Brown to Samuel Allinson, Sept. 19, 1783, *ibid.*, Misc. MSS., K-AB.

the call; he assumed almost sole direction of the movement.[25]
He surveyed and selected the streets to be repaired, and
organized, financed, and supervised the projects. The town
council had such confidence in his ability and his integrity
that they gave him virtually a free hand.

As a result of his activities as Surveyor of Streets—his official title—Moses was drawn into the financial affairs of the
town. He and the town treasurer were appointed by the
council to work out "the best manner and form of issuing
the town treasurers notes" to pay for paving the streets.
Earlier Moses had expressed concern about the effect his
passiveness during the war might have on his public reputation, but by the end of the conflict it became evident that he
was as influential and as popular as ever. Indeed, there were
few public projects in which he was not active or about
which town officials did not seek his advice.

He was active in quasi-public affairs too. In 1784, in
order to hasten the economic growth of the town, Moses,
John Brown, Jabez Bowen, and a few other far-sighted citizens had several meetings to discuss the establishment of a
bank.[26] (Banks in Boston and Philadelphia had been a boon
to the prosperity of those towns.) They got as far as fixing
a time to start the subscription, and actually raised some
money; but before they could proceed very far, the state was
plunged into a depression, and the project fell through. It
was six years before they revived the scheme and pushed it
to a successful conclusion.

The end of the war also found the townspeople interested
in reviving the college. In January 1783 it reopened with

25. Moses' activities in paving and repairing Providence streets may be
followed in the Providence Town Records, Aug. 1782–Aug. 1784, VII, No.
2988, Oct. 25, 1783 and No. 3012, Nov. 17, 1783, R. I. Hist. Soc.; for records
of his activities from 1780 to 1783 see Nos. 3081-82, 3084, 3086, 3089; and for
the period Aug. 1784–Aug. 1785, see VIII, No. 3211, Aug. 1784. See also
Town Council Records, 1774-87, July 19, 1785, V, 823, *ibid.*

26. Thomas Truman to Moses Brown, Mar. 2, 1784, Moses Brown Papers,
IV, 74.

much fanfare and great prospects for the future. Doctor Benjamin Waterhouse, professor of the theory and practice of physic in the newly established Harvard Medical School, was elected a fellow, and John Innis Clarke, John Smith, Esek Hopkins, Rufus Hopkins, Thomas Jenkins, Ebenezer Thompson, and the Reverend Enos Hitchcock were chosen to fill the vacancies on the Board of Trustees.[27] A few months later Moses was also elected a trustee to replace Jenkins, who had moved to New York.[28] Moses declined to serve, however, and in a letter to the corporation stated his reason: " 'tho I profess myself to be a friend to literature and every institution which tends to promote virtue and good morals in the riseing generation, which I trust is the aim of the governors of this institution, yet from several circumstances I feel most desirous to mannifest my attention to those objects in private life and therefore hope to be excused from the appointment."[29]

Moses did not particularize about the "several circumstances" which determined his decision, but a summary of his numerous activities and of other events at this time provide a plausible explanation. He was wholly engaged in promoting the Quaker school and probably did not want to be diverted from that important task. He was also very worried about his physical condition; he felt that he had to budget his time and energy carefully, and he preferred to devote it to the yearly meeting school and to the work of the Society rather than to the college, which already had many supporters. About the same time, Moses was shaken by the tragic death of his brother Joseph. In November

27. Minutes of Meeting of the Corporation, Jan. 27, 1783, Rhode Island College Misc. Papers, 1783-1804, II, 3, John Hay Lib.

28. Annual Meeting of the Corporation, Minutes, Sept. 1, 1784, *ibid.*, 41. The announcement of his election appeared in the *Providence Gazette; and Country Journal*, Sept. 4, 1784.

29. Sept. 7, 1784, Rhode Island College Misc. Papers, 1783-1804, II, 83, John Hay Lib.

1784, Joseph suffered the first of a series of severe attacks of what Moses called apoplexy or palsy, which impaired his mental as well as his physical faculties; death followed in a little over a year.[30]   Despite the fact, as Moses once wrote William Rotch, that he found in Joseph "something wanting respecting the necessary business of his life that sometimes is trying to my patience,"[31] Moses was deeply affected by his brother's sudden illness and death.   The two had been very close.   Of the brothers, Joseph had been the least disturbed by Moses' conversion to Quakerism, and he had early come to share his views on slavery.   But perhaps the most important reason for Moses' rejection of the college trusteeship was that he was also once again turning his attention to the struggle against slavery.   He later hinted that one of his reasons for declining the appointment was that some of the members of the college corporation were slaveholders or engaged in the slave trade.   Undoubtedly he wanted to be free to lead the crusade against slavery and the slave trade as he had a decade earlier.

30. On June 25, 1785, Moses wrote to Champion & Dickason in London that "Brother Joseph has had several attacks of the paralatick kind since my last, 'tho he is abroad as comfortable as can be expected.   His activity in Business is no more to be expected; his recollection is impaired and 'tho his inspections turn accordings to his genius remains visible his usefulness in that way as well as business is greatly spoiled."   Moses Brown Papers, V, 38.

31. Mar. 17, 1782, Moses Brown Papers, Austin MSS., IV, "Education," Moses Brown School Lib.

9

Anti-Slavery Crusade: Culmination, 1784-1794

IN THE SUMMER of 1783, even before peace was officially declared, Moses heard rumors in town that the trading company of Clark and Nightingale was outfitting a slaving ship for the Guinea Coast. When he made inquiries, he learned that the owners were indeed sending a ship to the African coast, but to trade in "ivory, wax, and gold dust," not slaves. Skeptical about this explanation, he visited John Clark, a friend of many years, gave him a pamphlet condemning slavery, and talked to him about the evils of slave trading. Apparently Clark gave Moses no assurances that he and Nightingale would not engage in the slave trade, for in August Moses wrote a long letter to his friends begging them not to participate in "so great an evil as I have found that Trade to be." Moses recalled to them his own feelings on the subject almost twenty years before when, as a young man, he had engaged in the "traffick." At that time, he remembered sadly, "the convictions of my own conscience were such as to be averse to the voyage, yet in reasoning upon that subject with those who were for pursuing it, my holding slaves at that time so weakened my arguments, that I suffered myself, rather than break my

connections, to be concerned." If he had known how other people felt about the slave trade, he observed, or if he had had someone to dissuade him, he would "have been preserved from an evil, which had given me the most uneasiness, and has left the greatest impression and stain upon my mind of any, if not all my other conduct in life." He hoped by writing to his friends to perform the service for them that others had neglected in his case.[1]

Moses' letter to Clark and Nightingale may have shamed them, but it did not cause them to abandon their plans to send a ship to the Guinea Coast. The importance of the incident was that it prompted Moses to reopen the attack on the slave trade, an attack that culminated in abolition of slavery in Rhode Island.[2]

Revival of the slave trade was not confined to Providence; there was a general movement at the end of the war involving not only American merchants but English as well.[3] The reaction of the anti-slavery leaders on both sides of the Atlantic was prompt and vigorous. Anthony Benezet and James Pemberton in Philadelphia, Warner Mifflin in Delaware, David Cooper in New Jersey, James Ramsay, Granville Sharp, Thomas Clarkson, and William Dillwyn in England were the leaders of a renewed effort to prevent revival of the traffic in Negroes and to abolish slavery. Moses Brown in Providence was in correspondence with most of these men and received the literature that poured from their pens. In Newport, the Reverend Samuel Hopkins again became active when merchants there began to outfit ships for the

1. Aug. 26, 1783, Moses Brown Papers, IV, 56.
2. Elizabeth Donnan, *Documents Illustrative of the History of the Slave Trade to America*, 4 vols. (Washington, 1932), III, 335 n; Moses Brown's notes, Oct. 20, 1784, Moses Brown Papers, Austin MSS., V, "Abolition," Moses Brown School Lib.
3. Drake, *Quakers and Slavery*, 91-95. For the revival of the slave trade in Rhode Island after the Revolution, see Donnan, *Documents*, III, 333 ff.; Donnan, "The New England Slave Trade after the Revolution," *New England Quarterly*, 3 (1930), 251-78; Park, *Samuel Hopkins*, 115-54; Locke, *Anti-Slavery, passim*; Du Bois, *Suppression of the Slave-Trade*, 39-52.

African coast. The fact is, however, that in America agitation was not well co-ordinated; its success depended upon the tireless efforts of a few individuals in particular areas.

In his new crusade in Rhode Island, Moses followed closely the plan he had used ten years before; he sent articles to John Carter, printer of the *Providence Gazette*, who inserted them in his paper; he purchased large numbers of anti-slavery pamphlets and sold them through Carter's printing shop at Shakespeare's Head; and as treasurer of the Meeting for Sufferings and member of the Yearly Meeting Anti-Slavery Committee, which had been appointed to seek legislative prohibition of the slave trade, he was able to bring the Society into the fight. Sometime in October, Moses and several other Friends—Thomas Hazard, Thomas Aldrich, Isaac Lawton, David Buffum, and Thomas Arnold— drew up a remonstrance to present to the next session of the General Assembly.[4] Moses made a list of the deputies and calculated that of the sixty-six members, sixteen would approve the petition, twenty-five were certain to vote against it, and twenty-five were doubtful.[5] Of the Providence deputies, Moses could count on the support of Ebenezer Thompson and Captain Paul Allen, but he was not sure how brother John or John Smith would vote.

Moses and his friends delayed presenting "The Petition and Remonstrance of a Committee of the People called Quakers in New England" until December 1783, after the mid-year elections, in the hope that the Assembly would then be more favorably disposed towards their request. At that time, the lower house appointed a five-man committee to consider the petition and report at the next session. The

4. *Providence Gazette; and Country Journal,* Aug. 30, Sept. 20, 1783. The second article included "A Proposed Act for the Abolition of Slavery" similar to the bill eventually passed in 1787. Moses probably submitted these articles to the *Gazette* for there are numerous drafts of them in Moses Brown Papers, especially Misc. MSS., III, 168 ff. For the Friends' petition, see *ibid.,* 171.

5. "List of Deputies in October Session 1783," *ibid.*

upper house concurred the next day and added two of its
members, Thomas Wells and John Smith, to the committee.
Of the seven men, four were in favor of the petition. On
December 25, the committee drew up and presented a bill
to the lower house. It is evident that some of the members
of the Friends' committee had a share in drafting it.[6]

The proposed bill contained almost all that the Friends
had asked for.[7] Beginning with the familiar words, "whereas
all men are entitled to life, liberty, and the pursuit of happiness," it went on to declare that slavery was a violation of
the rights and privileges of Negroes and that government was
"instituted to promote the welfare of mankind and the
security of their rights, and ought to be administered for
the attainment of that end." The main principle underlying
the bill was reconciliation of freedom of the slaves with the
welfare of their owner and of the public. It would have
freed all Negroes or mulattoes born after March 1, 1784,
and urged that they be "educated in the principles of the
christian religion, and instructed in reading, writing, and
arithimatick." Owners would be permitted to retain slaves
for a maximum of four years after they came of age. If an
owner freed males under twenty-one or females under eighteen he was required to see to it that they did not become
public charges. The bill also permitted anyone to free his
slaves with the condition that those freed should be of sound
mind and body and not over forty-five years of age. On the
subject of the slave trade the committee endorsed the anti-
slave trade resolutions of the Continental Congress of 1774,
and realistically put teeth into its recommendations: the
master of a vessel clearing the state for the coast of Africa

6. *Ibid.*, 172. There is an official copy of the Friends' "Petition and
Remonstrance" in Petitions to the Rhode Island General Assembly, 1783,
XX, 102, R. I. Archives.

7. "Report of the Committee," Acts and Resolves of the Rhode Island
General Assembly, 1783-84, XXIII, 106, R. I. Archives.

would henceforth be required to post a bond of £1,000 that he would not engage in the slave trade.

Moses must have been extremely pleased with the bill, particularly the bonding provision. Although the act did not provide for the immediate extinction of slavery, the ultimate achievement of that goal was assured by acceptance of the principle of gradual abolition.

The Friends' committee appeared at the December session to speak for the bill. There must also have been some debate in the lower house when the bill was brought in on the twenty-fifth, and some changes made, because the version printed in the newspapers differed slightly from the draft submitted by the committee.[8] At any rate, the lower house referred the bill to the February session in order to give the deputies a chance to consult their constituents for instructions in town meeting.

Moses now turned to the freemen of the northern towns. In an effort to secure their votes for the bill, he provided John Carter with articles for almost every issue of his paper.[9] He also supplied anti-slavery material to Bennett Wheeler's new journal, the *United States Chronicle: Political, Commercial, and Historical,* which began publication on January 1.[10] Moses' most important action, however, was to enlist the clergy on his side. Since he was convinced that people who believed slavery to be morally reprehensible and unchristian would refuse to condone it, he sought out the religious leaders in the town to carry his message to the members of their congregations. "Men of virtue," he reminded them in a circular letter, "should unite to put a stop to the continuance of the slave trade."[11] The town meeting had

8. *Providence Gazette; and Country Journal,* Jan. 10, 1784.
9. For example see *ibid.,* Jan. 31, Feb. 21, 1784.
10. See also issues of Jan. 29, Feb. 12, 19, 1784.
11. Jan. 26, 1784, Moses Brown Papers, IV, 72. The town meeting was called for Jan. 31, 1784; Providence Town Papers, VII, No. 3070, 106, R. I. Hist. Soc. Either this meeting did not take place or nothing was decided,

scheduled the bill for discussion on Saturday, January 31, he
noted, and it was rumored that objections would be raised.
Since this was a matter "which may effect the best interest
and reputation of the town, the lives of many innocent
Affricans even those in infancy and unborn[,] as well as continue the stain which that trade has made upon the Christian
profession and the benign doctrines of the Gospel." Moses
urged Providence religious leaders "to lay before such of
your respective members and friends your sense and feelings
on the subject for their attention at the town meeting to
prevent so injurious and disreputable a measure." Sorrow-
fully he recalled that he had once been a "transgressor in
that iniquitious practice," and had long felt "reproof and
remorse on the account." But he had often thought "that
had a few pious men mannifested their disapprobation . . .
I might have been preserved from the evil, which I mention
for your incouragement to labor as well as to mannifest the
hope I have of success from the joint endeavors of those
whose light hath shined to show them the evils attendant
on the slave trade."

The Reverend Messrs. Snow and Manning willingly
co-operated with Moses. Joseph Snow was ill, but he called
a number of friends to his house, showed them Moses'
letter, and advised them to vote at the town meeting according to their consciences. President Manning personally led
a delegation of friends to the meeting to support the bill.
Other religious leaders undoubtedly used their influence
among the members of their congregations.[12] As a result of
Moses' efforts, the Providence town meeting instructed the
local deputies to support the bill in the General Assembly.

The lower house debated the bill on February 25 and 26.

---

for on Feb. 3, nine freeman signed a request for another meeting to discuss
the anti-slavery bill, *ibid.*, No. 3074, 107.

12. Moses Brown to Elder Hopkins, Mar. 3, 1784, Moses Brown Papers, IV,
74.

Much to Moses' embarrassment and chagrin, but not to his surprise, brother John violated his instructions from the town meeting—instructions he had urged and voted for— and "was deep in the opposition"; in fact he was the leader.[13] John excelled at the art of self-deception. He could always find sufficient reasons for doing what suited his convenience or self-interest, and he usually adopted the views of the last man to whom he talked on a subject, provided those views coincided with what he wanted to do rather than with what he knew he ought to do. In this instance, he was probably approached by Newport slave traders and convinced that he should change his mind about supporting the bill. When it was introduced, John spoke against the measure at great length, using every argument he could think of: he introduced a slave captain named Benson to support his claim that since "the slaves in their own country were to be destroyed if not sold, it was therefore a piece of humanity to bring them away and make slaves of them";[14] he urged that action be postponed because the subject was before Congress; he insisted that the Resolve of 1774 was of no consequence now that America was independent; he attacked the Quakers for inconsistency because they still used products produced by slave labor; and he painted a dark picture of the financial consequences for the Newport merchants and distillers in Newport if the trade was stopped. John was supported by Esek Hopkins, commander of the American Navy during the Revolution and a former employee of the Brown brothers (he had captained the ship *Sally* on its ill-fated voyage), and by Nathan Miller, the only dissenting member of the Assembly committee that drafted the bill. Miller argued that

13. Moses Brown to Elders [in Newport], Feb. 5, 1784, *ibid.*, 72; Town Meeting Records, 1783-1804, VII, 9, City Clerk's Office, Providence; *United States Chronicle*, Feb. 12, 1784.

14. Moses Brown Papers, Misc. MSS., III, 173. On Feb. 29 Moses added a note to the above account that "I make little or no mention of our arguments on the Subject they did not prevail against Interest and Influence."

slavery was justified by scripture, an argument not heard very often at this time, but one that was to become much more popular in a few years.

When the vote was finally taken in the Assembly on the original version of the bill, it was defeated by a two-to-one majority, but an amended bill was passed subsequently, though it was not as important as it appeared. Although the new law prohibited the future importation of slaves into the state, provided for gradual abolition of all newborn Negroes, and abolished the restrictions against manumissions, the fines for violation of the act were omitted, and there was no prohibition against Rhode Island slave traders carrying on their business outside the state. On the complicated subject of the maintenance of freed Negroes, public opinion was about equally divided between those who thought that the charge should be paid by the public and those who felt that it should be paid by the former owners. Moses favored the second plan for Quakers who had freed their slaves; for others he thought that a satisfactory solution would be to split the charge of schooling and religious training between the public, that is, the town meeting where the slave resided, and the former owner.[15] The deputies, however, decided that the responsibility should devolve upon the towns where the slaves resided.[16] Neither Moses nor the Quakers appear to have had anything to do with this amendment, but they must have agreed with it.

The decisive influence against the original bill came from an unexpected quarter. Moses noted that Speaker William Bradford from Bristol, one of his political allies during the days of the Ward-Hopkins controversy, "turned the scale principally" against the bill. From the chair he showed partiality to the pro-slavery speakers and closed the debate by reading a letter from a correspondent, to the effect

15. *Ibid.*
16. Bartlett, ed., *R. I. Col. Recs.*, X, 132.

that this "little state had gone far enough in stopping the importation into this state, and it would be like the smallest spot on the face of the sun and would no more stop the trade if we past the act than the spot would the light."

In addition to the "speakers weight," Moses noted that another important reason for the defeat of the original measure was "an unwillingness that the Quakers should be instruments of doing so much. We were much flung at by several." It was this feeling against the Quakers that stopped Moses from organizing a society for the abolition of slavery in 1784, for he thought that the public would not support an organization started by a Quaker. Only much later, after other methods had failed to stop the trade, did he change his mind and organize an abolition society.

Moses summed up his feelings about the law in a letter to Samuel Hopkins: "I am not without hopes the consequences of our endeavours 'tho not so effectual as we desired may prove to [be] the spreading of the concern and raising more advocates for those injured people."[17] The influence of the commercial interest in the House was "greatly exerted," he told Samuel Hopkins, and "the justices of the subject thereby overbourn." He mentioned Bradford's decisive role in the debate and suggested that pressure be brought to bear on the Speaker to induce him to change his mind before the subject was again introduced in the Assembly. As for brother John, Moses said that he did not think he would give them any more trouble in the General Assembly. Since he had violated his instructions the town was not likely to return him at the general election in April.

John had already received notice that his defense of the slave trade had not met with the approbation of all his constituents. Zephaniah Andrews, a master mason and builder who had worked for all of the Brown brothers at one time or another and was important in local politics, wrote to him

17. Mar. 3, 1784, Moses Brown Papers, IV, 72.

the day after the debate on the bill, demanding to know why he had voted contrary to his instructions. John replied that if he followed the instructions of each and every constituent, he would "not only be as polittically dead to this town as Benedict Arnold is to the United States, but I should allso be useless to my family and friends in a civil and commercial line as you seem to wish me to be in a political line."[18] Justifying his defense of the slave trade on the basis of the self-interest of the merchants, the welfare of Newport, and the prosperity of the state, he excused his violation of the town meeting's instructions by saying that after he had promised to vote for the bill, he had "received more lite and a much graiter conviction that the majority of the town was misled." The town meeting, he told Andrews, could decide whether he had acted dishonorably. Whatever the freemen of Providence may have thought of John's honor, they demonstrated their faith in the principle of instructed representation by refusing to return him to the General Assembly in April.

Moses' optimistic letter to Hopkins could not conceal the disappointment he felt about rejection of the provision prohibiting Rhode Islanders from participating in the slave trade, for which he held his brother responsible. He did not, however, allow his disappointment to blind him to the fact that the episode had shown that the people, at least in Providence, were in advance of their representatives on the subject of the slave trade. Complete triumph of the anti-slavery forces was only a matter of time, provided he and his friends pressed the attack with zeal and perseverance.[19] His plan was to wait until a favorable opportunity presented itself, then make a last assault.

Samuel Hopkins was not so sanguine. His pessimism was based in part upon what he saw and heard in Newport.

18. Feb. 27, Mar. 1, 1784, *ibid.*, Misc. MSS., III, 177.
19. Moses Brown to James Pemberton, Mar. 20, 1784, *ibid.*, K-AB.

Numerous shippers and distillers resided there, and many townspeople derived profit from their activities. Public opinion would have to change radically, he thought, before Newport would support measures to suppress the trade. Nevertheless, the Congregational minister sent his congratulations to Moses and the Quakers for their "laudable example in bearing testimony against the slave trade, and exerting themselves to suppress the slavery of the Africans; and I must say, [you] have acted more like Christians, in this important article, than any other denomination of Christians among us. To our shame be it spoken!"[20] Hopkins had had little to do with the fight over the bill except to send to the Newport press a few articles clipped from other newspapers. So unhealthy was the local climate of opinion that the printers declined publishing his material for fear of economic ruin and physical harm.

While Hopkins remained relatively inactive in Newport, Moses mapped his strategy to secure further legislation. The existing law should not be repealed, as some advocated, until another act had been passed, for, he warned, pro-slavery interests might succeed in blocking the adoption of a new law. If a new act were adopted, the present law could be repealed in the concluding paragraph. He also emphasized the necessity of a program to educate the people to recognize the immorality of the slave trade. Continued publication of anti-slavery articles in the newspapers, he wrote Hopkins, and distribution of pamphlets and newspaper clippings in other states were essential. To clinch his point, he sent Hopkins a number of recent pamphlets. One of Hopkins' schemes—the colonization of expatriated slaves—failed to win Moses' support, even though Hopkins proposed to educate some of the freed men as preachers. Surely, he wrote Hopkins, you are not "insensible of our [Quaker] particular prin-

20. Apr. 29, 1784. For what follows, see Park, *Samuel Hopkins*, 119-20, 129-36, 139.

ciple in respect to spreading the Gospel that it requires a
special call and qualification?   Should these appear in any
blacks I hope we should not be wanting to incourage and
assist them in that great work."   But Moses doubted that
any Negroes were under the Divine favor; "till some special
gifts and call to individuals takes place," he wrote, "or some
christian state be drawn to pattronice such an attempt it may
not produce the desired effect."   In any event he was intent
on abolishing the slave trade and refused to be diverted from
that task.   "At present," he told Hopkins, it "seems my
business to suppress the pernisious trade from this state
particularly."[21]

Moses' concentration on the slave trade was based on the
theory that once the trade was stopped slavery would soon
die out.   The most effective way to achieve this goal was
through state legislation; clearly Congress neither would nor
could do anything about slavery, and it was up to the states
to act independently.   That they had the authority he had
not the slightest doubt despite some statements he had heard
to the contrary.   After the slave trade was abolished there
would be plenty of time to consider colonization schemes, if
these seemed desirable.   Moses' insistence on state action
stemmed partly from his feeling that the abolition of slavery
and the slave trade was the people's responsibility, and that
they were morally bound to act.   His efforts, he thought,
should be directed toward awakening the people to their
moral responsibilities.

For three years Moses waited for a favorable opportunity
to present a new anti-slave trade law.   Following the suggestions he had made to Hopkins in 1784, he conducted a ceaseless educational campaign that approached in intensity the
one launched by Thomas Clarkson in England a few years
later.   As a result of his efforts, poems, essays, addresses, and
articles from other newspapers, English as well as American,

21. Drake, *Quakers and Slavery*, 121-22.

were printed in the *Providence Gazette* and the *United States Chronicle.*[22] Hopkins sent Moses his *Dialogue Concerning the Slavery of the Africans,* first published in 1776, and asked him whether he thought it worth reprinting. Moses apparently thought it was, for it came out again in 1785.[23] Hopkins also sent a new essay he had written and asked Moses to get John Carter or Bennett Wheeler to publish it, "because I thought if it *first* appeared in our paper, the author would be more likely to be suspected, which would answer no good end, but the contrary."[24] Hopkins' essay, signed "Crito," was considered an effective performance and Moses and Hopkins sent it to their friends in many states, where it appeared in the newspapers and was distributed in pamphlet form.[25] Thomas Clarkson's *An Essay on the Slavery and Commerce of the Human Species* and extracts on "Negro Trade and Slavery" from Dr. Price's *Observations on the Importance of the American Revolution, and the means of making it a Benefit to the World* were also widely circulated. Articles like these, strategically spaced in the local press, gave readers a steady diet of anti-slavery reading matter.[26]

The campaign registered some degree of success. Moses wrote to Hopkins in March 1785 that "the Testimony gains ground for freedom, divers [slaves] having been set at liberty in this Town." Indeed, the Providence town council frequently freed slaves under the terms of the 1784 law.[27]

22. *Providence Gazette; and Country Journal,* Jan. 22, 1785, Mar. 3, June 21, Sept. 8, Oct. 6, 13, 1787; *United States Chronicle,* Mar. 7, 1785, Jan. 12, 19, 1786, Aug. 2, 1787.

23. Samuel Hopkins to Moses Brown, Apr. 30, 1784, Moses Brown Papers, IV, 80. This essay was first printed in Norwich, Conn., by J. P. Spooner in 1776. It was reprinted by R. Hodge in New York in 1785.

24. Nov. 17, 1784, *ibid.,* V, 14.

25. For the history of the Hopkins essay, see Donnan, "New England Slave Trade," *New Eng. Qtly.,* 3 (1930), 253, and her "Agitation Against the Slave Trade in Rhode Island, 1784-1790," in *Persecution and Liberty: Essays in Honor of Lincoln Burr* (N. Y., 1931), 473-82.

26. Moses Brown to Samuel Hopkins, Mar. 4, 1785, Moses Brown Papers, V, 21.

27. *Ibid.,* 44.

Moses was personally instrumental in obtaining freedom for many others. He refused to serve as executor to the estate of his old friend, James Angell, until the heirs agreed to free the half dozen slaves of the estate, and he talked John Carter and several Friends into manumitting their slaves.

Moses put great store in the influence that the progress of one state might have on another, and he did everything he could to further the cause outside Rhode Island, particularly in Massachusetts and Connecticut.[28]   He sent pamphlets to Governor James Bowdoin, Peter Thacher, and many others in Massachusetts, and corresponded with Jonathan Edwards and Levi Hart of Connecticut. And he maintained his heavy correspondence with Quakers in the middle states.

In the summer of 1784, James Pemberton sent him the rules of the recently revived Philadelphia Society for the Abolition of Slavery and hinted that perhaps Moses could form a similar society in Rhode Island.[29]   When Samuel Hopkins heard of the formation of an abolition society in New York, he asked Moses if it was "worth while to try to form one in this State?"[30]   Moses had considered such a move in 1783, but had decided against it. Not until 1786 did he draft a plan for an abolition society in Rhode Island. When he sent it to Hopkins, however, the Newport minister was ill and Moses was too busy to follow it up singlehandedly. But he did try to dissuade Quakers who were reluctant to enter into an anti-slavery association with non-members. When Joseph De Laplaine, New York printer and bookseller, objected that the Society's discipline might be corrupted if the members co-operated with non-members, Moses replied in his typically common sense way: "I have been sinsible of the danger thou mentions . . . yet to avoid doing what appears useful to our fellow men mearly from fears of some difficulty

28. James Bowdoin to Moses Brown, Feb. 2; Peter Thacher to Moses Brown, Sept. 21, 1787, *ibid.*, V, 56; VI, 13.
29. May 21, 1784, and Moses' reply, *ibid.*, Misc. MSS., K-AB.
30. Mar. 16, 1785, *ibid.*, V, 25.

seems to give way to our own weaknesses as it must *be* con-
fest were we established in principle and practice according
to our Testimony our being in promiscuous company could
not exert much less excite the reasons thou refers to."[31]
Actually, Moses still thought the most effective plan was to
urge the influential religious leaders in the state to approach
their congregations through the pulpit and to bring the subject up in their church conferences. The dissenting clergy
in England had done this, he reminded Hopkins, and he
was hopeful that the American clergy would imitate their
example.[32]

By 1786 Moses began to lay great stress on the intellectual
equality of Negroes and whites. Although he was influenced
by James Ramsay's remarks in his influential *Essay,* his personal experience was probably more important in shaping his
thought. The evidence was all about him that Negroes,
some of whom were not even free, possessed talents and capabilities equal to those of whites. He had to look no farther
than his former slaves to be convinced that their degraded
condition could be traced to environmental factors and was
not inherent in a dark skin. Many years before the Revolution, he had hired tutors to teach his slaves to read, write, and
figure; they had responded to instructions and made useful
employees in the countinghouse. Anthony Benezet, on the
basis of his long experience with Negro education in Philadelphia, had assured him that Negroes could be educated the
same as anyone else. For Moses this evidence confirmed the
scriptural injunction that all men are equal in the sight of
God, a precept that Quakers interpreted literally.

31. May 29, 1786, *ibid.,* 66.
32. Jan. 20, 1786, *ibid.,* 55. He mentioned the Cambridge University prize
medal "to be given to the best essay exposing the enormities of the slave
trade." Moses had proposed to President Manning of Rhode Island College
that the college establish a similar reward, but his suggestion was refused,
"as there are some of the Corporation in the trade." If Hopkins wished to
try Harvard, Yale, Princeton, Moses promised to give twenty dollars toward
such a prize.

By 1787 Moses thought the time was ripe to try again for a law prohibiting citizens of the state from participating in the slave trade. In the Yearly Meeting at Newport in June, he sponsored a memorial which a Friends' committee presented to the state Assembly on the thirteenth. It laid great stress upon the deplorable economic conditions in the state, which it interpreted as divine punishment for failure to abolish the slave trade. No specific recommendations were made; the memorialists merely asked that a law be passed "as you in your wisdom judge the most effectual to prevent that cruel and unjust trade, and finally to abolish that barbarous custom of holding mankind as slaves." William Almy, soon to become Moses' son-in-law, signed the memorial as clerk of the Yearly Meeting.[33]

As was usually the case when controversial legislation was proposed in the Assembly, the deputies referred it to the next session so that they could test public opinion. Moses stepped up his propaganda campaign, particularly among the ministers in the northern part of the state who had been so helpful in 1784; and he urged Samuel Hopkins to use his influence among his colleagues in the south.[34] As usual, Hopkins was pessimistic. He doubted that the Assembly would do anything at the next session; "I have pretty good evidence," he wrote Moses, "that some of them speak fair words to you and your friends, who yet are determined against doing anything against the slave trade." Benjamin Edes, the printer of the *Newport Herald*, had been so intimidated that he had refused to print an article in favor of the bill. "Thus that wicked

33. The memorial is in Petitions to the Rhode Island General Assembly, 1786-87, XXIII, 127, R. I. Archives. Only the *United States Chronicle*, Aug. 2, 1787, carried the memorial before it was debated in October.

34. *Providence Gazette; and Country Journal,* July 21, Sept. 8, 1787; *United States Chronicle,* Aug. 2, 1787. Hopkins's "Crito" essay was printed by Carter in two installments, one on Oct. 6, and the other on Oct. 13. From Joseph Crukshank, the printer in Philadelphia, Moses received a large supply of anti-slavery articles; James Pemberton to Moses Brown, Jan. 12, 1787, Moses Brown Papers, V, 85.

set of men in this town have got the printer in their hands,"
Hopkins said, "and have silenced the press, as other tyrants
have done before them."   Nevertheless, Hopkins did circulate a memorial among the ministers, but he could not convince them that it would serve any useful purpose, and it was
allowed to die.[35]

In August, Moses received encouraging news when
brother John, who had sent two vessels on slaving expeditions
to Africa in 1786, wrote that he was going into the East India
trade, "in which case [I] shall not be any more concerned
in the guiney trade."   John added that he was stepping down
as a deputy (after his rejection by the voters in 1784, John
had been returned to the Assembly in 1786), and suggested
that Moses take his place, for "if you are in the House you
can do what you think right respecting the proposed pro-
abbition to the Guiney trade, or raither the slave trade."[36]
John's departure was not the only change that had occurred
in the Assembly since the passage of the law dealing with
slavery in 1784.   William Bradford, who had played such a
decisive role earlier, was still Speaker, but Esek Hopkins was
no longer present, and John Smith and John Brown had been
replaced by Welcome Arnold and Benjamin Bourne, both
opposed to the slave trade.   In fact, only seven deputies who
had been in the lower house in 1784 were present when the
anti-slave trade bill was brought in for consideration in
1787.[37]

The heart of the new bill was a section which prohibited
citizens or residents of the state, "or any other person whatsoever," from participating in the slave trade.   The fine for
violation of the law was fixed at £100 for every person imported or transported, and £1,000 for every vessel that en-

35. Samuel Hopkins to Moses Brown, Aug. 13, 1787, Park, *Samuel Hopkins*,
I, 121.

36. Aug. 18, 1787, Moses Brown Papers, VI, 11.

37. But see Donnan, *Documents*, III, 344 *n*, for a different analysis of the
composition of the Assembly.

gaged in the trade.[38]   When debate on the bill opened on
October 31, the Friends' committee, headed by Moses Brown,
was allowed to speak in answer to the objections that had
been raised.   The discussions were almost as brief as the
victory was complete; the vote was forty-four in favor and
only four against, "all of which were concerned in the trade
or in distilling for it."   The Friends' committee then carried
the bill across the building to the chamber where the upper
house was meeting.   At first, Governor John Collins suggested postponing final action until one of the neighboring
states had prohibited the trade, but Moses and some of the
assistants dissuaded him and it was adopted unanimously.
Moses informed Samuel Emlen in Philadelphia that "the
Governor appeared to be as well sattisfied as any and ordered
a copy taken for himself to send to President [John] Jay of
New York Society for freeing Negroes etc. who had written
him sometime past expressing his disapprobation of the
trade."[39]   Although Moses was not surprised at the outcome,
he had not anticipated such an easy victory.   He was particularly pleased that the bill had been passed not "upon mere
commercial views but the more noble and enlarged principles
exprest in the memorial and act."

Moses' correspondence during this period suggests that
he thought the nation as well as the states should recognize
the immorality of the slave trade and of slavery.   Because of
these views, he privately opposed the adoption of the Federal
Constitution on the grounds that it condoned the slave trade
and perpetrated slavery; publicly he maintained a neutral

38. For what follows see Moses Brown to Committee of Mass. Assembly on
the Memorial of Friends, Nov. 1, 1787, and Moses Brown to Samuel Emlen,
Nov. 6, 1787, Moses Brown Papers, VI, 17.   The original bill, with the con-
curring endorsements on the reverse side is in Petitions to the Rhode Island
General Assembly, 1786-87, XXIII, 127, R. I. Archives.   The anti-slave trade
bill became law on Wed., Oct. 31, 1787; Journals of the House, Oct. 1787–
Mar. 1788, R. I. Archives.   It was announced in the *Providence Gazette; and
Country Journal* on Nov. 3 and in the *United States Chronicle* on Nov. 8
without editorial comment.

39. Letters, 1785-88, XX, 80, R. I. Archives.

stance. Only a month after the conclusion of the Philadelphia convention, he condemned two articles in the Constitution "which according to the construction of friends here millitate against our Testimony in support of liberty, or against slavery." Those articles were: Article I, Section 9, which denied to Congress the power to prohibit the slave trade until 1808; and Article IV, Section 2, paragraph 3, which denied freedom to slaves who entered the states whose laws freed them. He was reluctant, he admitted, to say anything against "that respectable body in this respect," but if Friends meant to keep their testimony clear, he thought they must oppose those sections of the Constitution that "give countenance to if not directly encourage slavery."[40]

Summarizing the reaction of Friends in Rhode Island to the articles on slavery in the Constitution, Moses noted that "there is no sensible friend I have conversed on this subject but has not been disagreeably affected." He was greatly "afflicted," he continued, "to have an article in the constitution of these states so repugnant to the principles of liberty, truth and rightousness." As he interpreted Section 9 of Article I, although it considered the poor Africans "the subject of unrightous revenue," it "left out of the power of Congress to consider them as men and so entitled to liberty, and their protection, nor yet are they yielded by the states to Congress as commerce, but left to the averice or oppression of the subjects of any state." The importation of slaves, he observed, had been concurred in by the convention as a right, not to be interfered with for twenty-one years; thus "incouragement of a reformation is abstracted and the states may fall back from their present light on the subject into darkness and the recovery from this gross evil for which this land mourns, be long obstructed." That a twenty-one-year continuation of slave importation would undo the work done by the states and fix the institution on the nation perma-

40. Moses Brown Papers, Misc. MSS., K-AB.

nently was a very real fear to Moses and others in Rhode Island.

Moses admitted that he had no knowledge of the debates in the constitutional convention; Rhode Island did not even have a delegate present, he said ruefully. But he suggested that if the southern representatives insisted on protecting slavery and the slave trade, then Congress and the other states could not trust them in any matter. The principle of liberty, he declared in a belligerent tone quite unusual for him, would be a "fit subject to have divided [the nation] upon"— it alone was sufficient reason to keep Rhode Island out of the Union. "Let those states that still insist on enslaving their fellow men together with their principles of slavery and the others unite in equal liberty," he remarked ironically. Although he did not see how Friends could approve the Constitution when it contained the article on slavery and the slave trade, he was sorry that they were put in a position of having to oppose a needed reformation of the Union and the establishment of a new frame of government, to which in other respects he had no objection.

Moses knew that the Confederation Congress would do nothing to stop the slave trade and he was convinced that the new Constitution, if adopted, would deny to Congress the power to deal with the trade for twenty years. After the abolition of the trade by Rhode Island, therefore, he turned his attention to the other New England states. In Massachusetts and Connecticut, he found that the movement against the trade was already strong, and he merely added his weight to increase the momentum by supplying pamphlets and articles to the press and sending encouragement to the leaders. As a member of the New England Yearly Meeting Anti-Slavery Committee, he visited both Boston and Hartford with memorials, similar to the one submitted in Rhode Island, and presented them to the state legislatures.[41] By

41. Samuel Hopkins to Moses Brown, Oct. 22, 1787, *ibid.*, VI, 15; William

late 1788, he was pleased to learn that the anti-slavery cause
had triumphed in those states.[42]

But the enactment of prohibitory laws did not eliminate
the slave trade. Moses was aware that the Rhode Island
law was not being observed and that the government was
doing very little to punish violators.[43] The only way to
enforce the act, he wrote Edmund Prior, one of the leaders
of New York's abolition society, was "by incouraging a society similar to yours in N Y and Philadelphia as the number
in favour of the trade are powerful in money and influence
tho' not large."[44] To the Reverend Jonathan Edwards in
New Haven he lamented that progress had been so slow in
Connecticut and that he could do so little to help, for
he was busy in New Hampshire where he had heard that
vessels from Rhode Island were being fitted out and cleared
for the African coast.[45]

In order to halt this practice, Moses decided to organize
a society for the abolition of the slave trade. He already
had a plan, drawn up in 1786, modeled after similar organizations in America and England. There were many people
in the state eager to emulate their friends in New York and
Philadelphia. Meetings were held in Providence during
January 1789, and on February 20, in the Friends' meetinghouse, the Providence Society for the Abolition of the Slave
Trade was officially organized with ex-Congressman David
Howell as president, Thomas Arnold, merchant and Friend,
as secretary, and Moses Brown as treasurer.[46] Samuel Hop-

Rotch to Moses Brown, Aug. 11, 1787, Moses Brown Papers, Austin MSS.,
III, "History of Friends," Moses Brown School Lib.; Moses Brown to [James
Pemberton], Nov. 13, 1787, Archives, No. 954, Friends Library, Philadelphia.

42. Jonathan Edwards to Moses Brown, Oct. 20, 1788, Moses Brown Papers,
VI, 45.

43. Moses Brown to Samuel Eliot of Boston, Jan. 5, 1788, Moses Brown
Papers, Austin MSS., V, "Abolition," Moses Brown School Lib.

44. Oct. 25, 1788, Moses Brown Papers, VI, 16.

45. Dec. 16, 1788, ibid., 49.

46. See the announcements in the *United States Chronicle,* Feb. 5, 12, 19,
26, 1789.

kins sent his congratulations but objected to the title given the society as being "too confined. It should, at least, be extended *to the whole state*. And I think it ought not to be confined to the *Abolition* of the Slave Trade. It ought to promote the freedom of those now in slavery, and to assist those who are free, as far as may be, to the enjoyment of the privileges of freemen, and the comforts of life." Hopkins was not as insistent about the second change as he was about the first. At the outset he refused to join the society unless its title was altered to make it a Rhode Island rather than a Providence organization. There were others in Newport and the southern part of the state, Thomas Robinson, and William Almy among them, who agreed with Hopkins. Their objections were overcome, however, and they signed the constitution.[47]

Heretofore, apologists for the slave trade had remained relatively silent, and very few articles had appeared in the press justifying it. But the legal prohibition of the trade, the creation of a private organization of influential citizens bent on enforcing the act, and the possibility that violators would be made to answer for their misdeeds in court goaded one of their number to break the silence. Even before the final steps were taken in the formation of the abolition society, "A Citizen," writing in the *Providence Gazette,* attacked the proposed society and defended the slave trader. Implying that the society would be controlled by the Quakers, the author charged that its purpose was to ruin any citizen engaged in the slave trade who had refused to give assurances to private do-gooders that he would discontinue his business in that line. In an age of unrestricted public debate, the ensuing battle in the columns of the Providence newspapers was the most bitter and unrestrained controversy that had ever taken place in Rhode Island history—not even

47. Samuel Hopkins to Moses Brown, Mar. 7, 1789, Moses Brown Papers, VI, 57.

the invective of the Ward-Hopkins controversy could equal
it. What started as a discussion about the pros and cons of
the slave trade, soon degenerated into an acrimonious debate
in which politics and personalities became the main subject.

As "A foe of oppression," Quaker Thomas Arnold, secretary of the abolition society, answered "A Citizen" with a
denial that the society intended to ruin anyone and challenged him to produce evidence to support his charges.
Arnold ended his defense by saying that "it is vain to expect
to lurk behand the Figlean scream of a fictitious signature,
there are to few in town who speak the language of slavery
to make the discrimination difficult." Indeed, there were
few who did not know that "A Citizen" was John Brown.

Arnold himself was not so readily identified. John
thought that David Howell, the president of the society,
had written the article. He and Howell had at one time
been on the same side of the political fence (they had both
opposed the national impost duty in the early 1780's), but
they had parted company during the debate over the Constitution. John had become an ardent Federalist while
Howell was still unalterably opposed to the establishment
of a strong central government. John's second article was
therefore an undisguised attack against Howell, but he
directed his fire in all directions, with little regard for
accuracy, hoping to hit Howell, the abolition society, the
Anti-Federalists, and the Quakers with one blast. Those
who had opposed the 5 per cent impost and the Constitution
and had approved legal tender laws and paper money, he
declared, were the same people who now opposed the slave
trade. He urged the people to adopt the new Constitution
because it would protect slave owners from attacks on their
property. The traffic in Negroes "is right, just and lawful,"
John insisted, "and consequently practiced every day." Two
years before, he charged, when the Quakers had petitioned
the Assembly to repeal the legal tender laws, they had made

a bargain with the deputies to drop that subject if the Assembly would pass a law prohibiting the slave trade. He attempted to denigrate Thomas Arnold by saying that he had been elected both secretary and councilor of the abolition society because there were so few respectable members that it was difficult to fill both positions, and because the Friends, who ran the society, needed his influence and money. In a final blast, he fulminated against Arnold and Moses, whom he accused of having already destroyed property worth £30,000 by encouraging slaves (he called it slave stealing) to leave their masters.

Making very little effort to conceal his identity, Moses entered the fracas on March 7 with a calm, impersonal letter in the *Providence Gazette* which answered each of his brother's arguments and asked that John and Arnold "Bury the hatchet." John sent him a curt note: "I wish to know weither you are the author of the pc [piece] signed 'a friend 'tho a monitor to a Citizen' as printed in the last Saturdays paper."[48] If Moses thought he could get either side to discontinue the argument merely by making the suggestion, he was mistaken. Even before he wrote in the *Gazette*, Thomas Arnold had sent another article to the newspapers, in which he matched John's invective, insinuation, unsubstantiated charges, and personal abuse.[49] John replied in kind, and so the exchange of unpleasantries raged. According to John, Arnold was a wolf in sheep's clothing, who had assisted in luring Negro slaves away from their masters; he had turned Quaker only to marry a pretty girl (Nancy Brown) and to gain a fortune; he had carried on a trade to Jamaica in time of war with false papers, contrary to the laws of the state. Arnold, on his part, charged that John was a tool of the

48. John Brown to Moses Brown, [Mar. 9, 1789], *ibid.* The date of the letter is established by Moses' note on the bottom: "Received and Answered 9th 3rd mo. 89."

49. *United States Chronicle*, Mar. 5, 1789. Arnold cloaked his identity with the pseudonym, "Monitor the Younger."

slave traders; that he did not have feelings like other men; that public records had been defaced for his private interests; that he had a very relaxed conscience (to defend the slave trade); that he would not free his Negro slaves when others had freed their part; and that he was dishonest in business.[50]

Towards the end of March, Moses and Howell tried to smooth over the fight between John and Arnold. Rather belatedly, Moses observed that "as public altercations, which become personal, are apt to wound the feelings of friends, and connexions who are innocent, I have concluded to suspend further observations on the matters agitated." He reserved the right to advance such arguments as might be singly and pertinently applied to the subject of the slave trade, and, when he had time, to correct errors in factual references made by the combatants.[51] In other words, he proposed to continue the attack, but on his own terms. But one newspaper commentator said that the argument between Brown and Arnold should not be stopped, "for if it goes on the *whole truth* may come out; and, who have been led to suppose that very rich men [John] and very plain dressing men [Arnold], were very good men, may be convinced that riches or plain coats do not always designate *honest men*."[52]

The struggle had continued too long and the charges and countercharges had become too serious for either side to withdraw with honor. The debate now became primarily a political and personal contest between Arnold, representing the Quakers, the abolition society, and the Anti-Federalists, and John Brown, representing the anti-Quakers, slave traders, and the Federalist forces. Moses found the public debate distasteful, but he continued to submit to the newspapers extracts of articles attacking the slave trade and to write to the editors correcting misstatements of fact about Negroes

50. *Ibid.*, Mar. 12, 1789.
51. *Providence Gazette; and Country Journal*, Mar. 21, 28, 1789. Moses signed his articles "M. B."
52. *United States Chronicle*, Mar. 26, 1789.

and slavery.[53]   By May, the bitter debate between John Brown and the members of the abolition society had petered out.   In retrospect, the whole argument must have appeared academic to many people.   After all, the bill against the slave trade had passed, and a majority of the public seemed to disapprove of the practice and expected slavery to disappear in a short time.

Despite the passage of the anti-slave trade act, however, state authorities were apathetic about enforcing it, and it seemed questionable whether the abolition society's charter gave it the right to initiate suits against violators of the state laws.[54]   By the spring of 1790, some of the traders were once again outfitting their slave ships in Rhode Island ports, and the controversy between John Brown and the society flared up again.[55]

When John forcibly sent "a Negro man on bord one of his vessels, after the Societys committee had agreed to support the man in his right to freedom,"[56] the society decided to prosecute him in an effort to free the man.   John denied that the charter of the abolition society gave it the right to sue, but the issue was compromised rather than settled.   When John agreed to restore the Negro to freedom, the society

53. *Ibid.*, Mar. 12, 26, 1789.   Samuel Hopkins to Moses Brown, Mar. 30, 1789, Moses Brown Papers, VI, 61.   Hopkins wrote: "I am pleased to find you are enabled to maintain such a degree of calmness and fortitude, under the abuse which you and your friends have received from one who, unprovoked, is casting firebrands, arrows, and death, and fighting with creatures of his own imagination."   The reference was, of course, to John Brown, whom Hopkins disliked intensely.

54. Unsuccessful efforts to prosecute slave traders are reflected in William Rotch, Jr., to Moses Brown, May 6, and May 16, 1789, Moses Brown Papers, VI, 67, 70; Moses Brown to James Pemberton, July 27, 1790, *ibid.*, Misc. MSS., K-AB; Samuel Hopkins to Moses Brown, Aug. 17, 1789, Park, *Samuel Hopkins,* 127.

55. Moses described the state of the slave trade and the nature of the opposition to it in a letter to James Pemberton, Apr. 13, 1789, Moses Brown Papers, VI, 63.

56. Moses gave the details of the case to James Pemberton, Apr. 26, 1790, Moses Brown Papers, Misc. MSS., K-AB.   See also Samuel Hopkins to Moses Brown, Mar. 11, 1790, Park, *Samuel Hopkins,* 128.

dropped the case against him. John's action forced Moses back into the thick of the fight. Although he had no doubt that the society's charter gave it the right to instigate actions against violators of state laws against the slave trade, he wanted to remove any doubts. Accordingly, he spearheaded a movement to get an explanatory act through the Assembly. It was passed in June 1791 by a vote of 37 to 22, "the opposing party exerting themselves to their utmost."[57] Nevertheless, the society still faced difficulties in its fight to enforce the anti-slave trade laws. Moses noted that the supporters of the slave trade hired the best attorneys in New England, who used all their skill to prolong cases indefinitely in the state courts. Attorneys scared or bought off witnesses, and slave traders hid behind legal technicalities in order to escape punishment.

Moses' correspondence in the early 1790's tells a monotonous story of unproductive efforts to enforce the anti-slave trade laws in New England.[58] Confronted with public apathy, inefficient state officials, and the power of the slave traders, Moses gradually abandoned his position that the issue was one for the local governments to solve and threw his support behind the movement, already underway in the middle Atlantic states, to transfer the problem to the federal government. After Congress enacted the Fugitive Slave Law in 1793, he joined other New England Quakers in petitioning Congress against the slave trade; in the following year he went to Philadelphia as a New England delegate to the American Convention for Promoting the Abolition of Slavery and Improving the Condition of the African Race.[59]

57. For this and what follows, see Moses Brown to James Pemberton, July 19, 1791, Moses Brown Papers, Misc. MSS., K-AB.
58. The corresondence in Moses' papers concerning this aspect of the anti-slave trade agitation is extensive. His activities may be followed in volumes VIII-IX. See also Abolition Society's Book, Minutes for meeting on Nov. 18, 1791, 26-29, Moses Brown School Lib.
59. For the trip and Moses' activities, see Samuel Collins to Moses Brown, Dec. 29, 1793; Theodore Foster to Moses Brown, Jan. 21, 1794; Warner

Moses was a member of the committee that appeared before Congress, and he also spoke privately to important administration leaders. Congress responded by passing an act, with much less opposition than had been expected, prohibiting foreign vessels engaging in the slave trade from being equipped in United States ports.

Back in Rhode Island, Moses devoted himself to the cause of the freed Negro. Appeals for financial assistance received prompt and generous attention, and he was always ready to go to the aid of a Negro who was in trouble with the authorities. Slaves who had escaped from their masters and Negroes who were in danger of being sold into slavery found sanctuary in his home, one of the main stations on the Underground Railroad that ran from Quaker homes in New Bedford to inland Massachusetts. Despite the secrecy which shrouded the business on the escape route—few records were kept—numerous references in Moses' correspondence suggest that the traffic to and from his house was heavy. Indeed, his activities as well as his correspondence make it clear that he was considered the leader of the anti-slavery movement in New England.

Mifflin to Moses Brown, Jan. 24, 1794; John Murray to Moses Brown, Mar. 3, 1794; Joseph De La Plaine to Moses Brown, Mar. 19, 1794; Moses Brown to James Phillips, May 7, 1794; Moses Brown Papers, VIII, 40-43, 46; Moses Brown to Almy & Brown, Feb. 17, 1794, *ibid.*, Misc. MSS., I, 61.

10

American Economic Independence and the Textile Industry, 1788-1790

A T THE END of the war Moses realized that the old political ties between America and England were forever broken. But he was convinced that a resumption of commercial activity would be advantageous to the new nation and he did everything he could to promote it. He saw increasing indications, however, that harmonious economic relations between America and England were by no means certain. In the summer of 1783 he learned that the British West Indian Islands would henceforth be closed to American ships; and at the end of the year Parliament placed a prohibitive duty on whale oil. To this discriminatory policy, Moses attributed the postwar depression in America, although he knew that American merchants had contributed to their own problems by purchasing more English goods on credit than the economy could absorb. For several years he watched with anxiety while his friends tried various schemes in an attempt to extricate themselves from the growing web of debt.[1]

1. See Robert A. East, *Business Enterprise in the Revolutionary Era* (N. Y., 1938), 213-38, but particularly p. 216. Moses' views on the causes of the depression may be gleaned from the numerous letters he wrote to his agent, Champion & Dickason, in London, which are in Moses Brown Papers, VI.

Typical of Rhode Island indebted merchants was Moses'
brother John. In an effort to find new sources of income
to pay his creditors, John built a large fishing fleet of fifteen
schooners, entered the tobacco trade, engaged in illicit trade
with the British and French West Indies, developed an extensive coastal trade, built and operated a gin distillery, and,
finally in 1786, sent two vessels to the African coast on slaving expeditions in search of large and quick profits.[2]   His
expectations from the slave trade were dealt a severe blow
in 1787, when the General Assembly passed its anti-slave
trade law.   Forced temporarily to abandon the slave trade,
and only moderately successful in his other commercial activities, he was driven by his ceaseless ambition and energy to
seek new avenues to wealth.   Like his father and uncle before him and his brother Nicholas in his own time, John
had the unique ability to adapt his business projects to
changing circumstances.   Hearing of the fabulous profits
that might be won in the East India and China trade, the
"Providence Colossus," as he was called by some of the
townspeople, sent the *General Washington* in 1787 on a
two-year voyage to the Orient.[3]   Successful from the beginning, John reaped large profits from the China trade for over
a decade.   Other Rhode Island merchants followed his lead.

Moses, on the other hand, had concluded that the remedies for American economic dislocation were not to be found
solely in re-establishment of commercial connections with
Great Britain, or in development of trade with the East
Indies and China.   He could see very little evidence that
either line of enterprise did much to alleviate the distress
of the unemployed, whose numbers were increasing daily.
Importation of English manufactured goods merely retarded

2. John Brown to Moses Brown, Nov. 27, 1786, Frederick S. Peck Collection,
1786-92, Box VIII, No. 10, R. I. Hist. Soc.

3. Gertrude Selwyn Kimball, "The East-India Trade of Providence from
1787 to 1807," *Papers from the Historical Seminary of Brown University*,
ed. J. Franklin Jameson (Providence, 1896), 3-6.

domestic industrial development, he concluded, and East India imports were luxuries the people could well do without.

Moses was particularly alarmed by the effect of deteriorating economic conditions on Friends. Many members of the Society had suffered great losses during the Revolution and postwar depression; and their strict code of ethics, which encompassed their business as well as their religious life, made their situation still more critical. They were prevented from engaging in such profitable enterprises as the slave trade or the illicit trade with the French and British West Indies, and some members would not deal in goods produced by slave labor. Quakers, moreover, were distinguished by their refusal to take advantage of the legal tender laws to hold off creditors or to discharge indebtedness. Those who did offer depreciated state paper for payment of a debt contracted in silver or gold were likely to be censured by the monthly meeting. The miserable state of affairs among Friends was brought home to Moses very forcefully when he saw the yearly meeting school, established in 1784 after so much effort and sacrifice, fail in 1788. Although he attributed its failure to the declining moral state of the members, he thought that poor business conditions were partly to blame.

For a number of years following the war, Moses tried to find ways to ease the plight of Friends in New England. Whaling and fishing—occupations that had attracted many Friends in the colonial period—had been destroyed during the war; Friends had to find other means of livelihood. To this end Moses, assisted by Thomas Arnold, experimented with new methods of producing pot and pearlash—duty-free products which brought good prices on the English market. His plan was to develop a new process by which a higher grade of potash could be produced from only half the amount of raw product, so that Friends might develop the industry

into a profitable business. These efforts were partially successful, but they did not produce the results he had hoped for.

Moses had numerous other schemes to help Friends, including plans for crop improvement, suggestions to sheep growers about how they could increase the productivity of their herds, and new methods of making cider.[4] But he realized that these were merely stopgaps. The economic condition of Friends could not improve materially until the economic conditions of the country improved as a whole. Despite his objections to the Constitution, he agreed with many of his friends that the solution to the depression depended in part upon a drastic change in the organization of the national government, a change that was already under way, but he felt that governmental reform should be accompanied by the development of American economic independence.[5] To achieve this independence he believed America must develop domestic industries and manufactures that would give employment to American workers, redress the imbalance of trade and debt with England, and stop the drain of specie from the country. After a careful study of the American economy, he concluded that the development of an American textile industry would best achieve these ends.

Moses realized that formidable obstacles hampered the development of a domestic cloth industry capable of offering serious competition to England: an inadequate supply of raw materials, a poorly trained, inexperienced, and insufficient labor force, lack of technological skill, poor distribution facilities, and primitive marketing techniques. In 1787

4. Moses Brown Papers, Misc. MSS., II, 68-69. For his plan to winter sheep, see Shubal Coffin to Moses Brown, Mar. 24, 1788, *ibid.*, VI, 31. Moses was also interested in raising bees. David Lawton to Moses Brown, Mar. 6, 1787, *ibid.*, 1.

5. Caroline F. Ware, *Early New England Cotton Manufacture* (Boston, 1931), 8-9.

virtually all domestic yarn in Rhode Island was manufactured in private homes on conventional spinning wheels and then made into cloth on weaving looms. Although Hargreave's spinning jenny was known in America, it was not yet in general use and the organization of the cloth manufacturing industry had not changed materially for decades. Shopkeepers bought the raw product, put it out successively to pickers, spinners, and weavers, and finally sold the yarn or the finished cloth from their stores. Moses had done this in 1767-69 during the period of nonimportation.

Cloth produced by household manufacture was not only inferior in quality to English imports; it was also more expensive. This was particularly true of cotton cloth, because cotton yarn could not be made strong enough for the warp in the spinning jenny, and expensive linen yarn had to be used. This technological barrier was a serious deterrent to the development of a domestic cotton cloth industry. In England the answer to the problem was Arkwright's new spinning frame, a water-driven machine that did something Hargreave's jenny could not do; it gave cotton thread a twist that made it strong enough for use as warp in the manufacture of cotton cloth. Until American workmen obtained the use of Arkwright's remarkable machine and mastered the technique of perpetual spinning, little progress could be made.

Moses' greatest industrial achievement was to sponsor the work of Samuel Slater, a man who was able to construct and operate Arkwright's machine in America and thus lay the foundation for the domestic cotton textile industry. Actually, Moses' activities in promoting the cloth manufacturing industry began two years before he met Slater and were indispensable to his later achievement. By the time Slater arrived in Providence in January 1790, Moses knew everything there was to know about cloth manufacturing in

America. He not only had a thorough knowledge of the
technology of the business but had mastered every process
from cleaning the raw material to weaving, fulling, and dye-
ing the cloth. Moreover, Moses and his partners had recruited machinists, carpenters, and other artisans who were
of great assistance to Slater as he struggled to build his
machines in Pawtucket.

It was in the spring of 1787 that Moses began to show
more than an ordinary interest in cloth manufacturing. He
had heard of new spinning machines on display in East
Bridgewater, Massachusetts, and he asked his friend, John
Bailey, a clockmaker formerly of Providence but now living
in Hanover, Massachusetts, to examine them and report to
him.[6] The machines, called the "State Models" because the
Massachusetts legislature had subsidized their construction,
were reported to be authentic reproductions of the Arkwright
machines that produced fine, inexpensive cotton cloth in
England. Their construction had been a co-operative undertaking. Thomas Somers, a native of Scotland who had settled in Baltimore, supplied the plans for the machine. In
1785 he had gone to England to learn about Arkwright's
carding and spinning machines and had returned with a
description of them. Failing to find financial backing in
Baltimore to construct the machines, Somers went to Boston
and was subsequently employed by Colonel Hugh Orr, who
had been encouraged by the Massachusetts legislature to
"construct at his works in East Bridgewater machinery for
carding, roving, and spinning cotton."[7] Assisted by two
brothers, Robert and Alexander Barr, Somers constructed

6. John Bailey, Jr., to Moses Brown, May 18, 1788, Moses Brown Papers,
VI, 26. For much of what follows, see George S. White, *Memoir of Samuel
Slater, The Father of American Manufactures . . . With Remarks on the
Moral Influence of Manufactories in the United States*, 2d ed. (Phila., 1836),
84-85, and William R. Bagnall, *The Textile Industries of the United
States . . . in the Colonial Period* (Cambridge, Mass., 1893), I, 150-51.

7. Samuel Batchelder, *Introduction and Early Progress of the Cotton
Manufacture in the United States* (Boston, 1863), 23-24.

an Arkwright waterframe of sixty spindles, designed to spin cotton and wool, and a carding machine with rollers three feet in diameter. After several attempts to operate the machines had failed, they were put on display to induce others to perfect them.

Bailey examined the machinery and reported to Moses, who then began to correspond with people already engaged in the textile industry. In the fall he made a trip to East Bridgewater to examine the "State Models" himself, before visiting Beverly, Worcester, and Hartford to observe the woolen mills there.[8] The Beverly Cotton Manufactory, which had begun operation in the fall of 1787, was owned jointly by several of the Cabots, a Moses Brown (no relation to the Providence clan), and other investors of Beverly and Boston. Moses formed a fast friendship with his namesake, and with Thomas Somers, who had built the "State Models," and James Leonard, a mechanic who was to be of service to him when he began to manufacture cloth in Providence. Moses also toured the plant of the Hartford Woolen Manufactory, owned largely by Jeremiah Wadsworth, Jesse Root, Thomas Seymour, Oliver Ellsworth, and Oliver Wolcott, who had been given encouragement and financial assistance by the Connecticut legislature. The mill was operated primarily by English mechanics and factory overseers, and one of them, Joseph Ashton, was very helpful with information and suggestions about the business. Ashton, who had learned the various operations of wool manufacturing as a youth in his father's shop in England, carried on a lengthy correspondence with Moses and supplied him with information about the management of the woolen mill and the technology of cloth manufacturing. He also sent Moses samples of the cloth manufactured at the Hartford mill "as a specimen of

8. Bagnall, *Textile Industries,* I, 150-51. For accounts of the early efforts at textile manufacturing in Beverly, Worcester, and Hartford, see pp. 88-109, 127-31.

American Industry," and said that "we are now making
cloths far superior to those but they are not finished as yet
or I would have sent some patterns of them."[9] Ashton's
optimism about the prospects for a woolen mill in Rhode
Island spurred Moses' continued interest in cloth manufacturing.

Shortly after Moses' trip, Daniel Anthony, a Providence
merchant, and John Reynolds, who made homespun in East
Greenwich, visited East Bridgewater and made drawings of
the "State Models" of the Arkwright machines; soon thereafter they began to construct the machines. In November
Reynolds, a Quaker and an intimate friend of Moses, wrote
that the trials of the spinning frame and the carding machine
had been unsuccessful. Discouraged by this failure and
preoccupied with his woolen business, Reynolds offered to
sell his white elephants to Moses who had made frequent
visits to Reynolds' shop and had discussed the machinery
with him many times.[10]

Moses was not yet ready to engage in cloth manufacturing, however, although he continued to collect information
throughout the winter months. In the spring of 1789, he
finally decided to go into business. The immediate cause
for his decision was the announcement by his daughter Sarah
and William Almy of their intentions to marry, "a circum-
stance," he wrote, "which brings on me some exercise to have
him settled in some satisfactory way and as William inclines
to go into the woolen or cotton manufactures or both, which
being new and what we have not been acquainted with seems

9. For the correspondence between Moses and Ashton, see Moses Brown
Papers, VI, 53, 56, and Misc. MSS., B-814, Box 6.

10. John Reynolds to Moses Brown, Nov. 19, 1788, Dec. 22, 1788, Nov. 8,
1789; John Bailey to Moses Brown, Nov. 20, 1788; William Wilson to Moses
Brown, July 1, 1789, Moses Brown Papers, VI, 46-49, 75; Moses Brown to
William Wilson, Jan. 13, 1789, *ibid.*, Misc. MSS., B-814, Box 6; Moses Brown's
notes, Dec. 1788, Moses Brown Papers, Austin MSS., XII, "Personal," Moses
Brown School Lib. See also Smith Brown's advertisement in the *Providence
Gazette; and Country Journal,* Dec. 6, 1788.

to require more of my thoughts than I should chuse at present."[11]

Although reluctant to devote his time to business, Moses plunged into the task with energy, thoroughness, and an attention to detail that were characteristic of everything he did.   The most pressing problems, he well knew, were the lack of skilled workmen and efficient machinery.   Writing to Thomas Ashton at the Hartford Woolen Manufactory, Moses requested information "respecting the scribbling mill [a crude carding machine], its construction probable cost. Also a draught of your Twisting Mill, 'tho I think I could make one."   He added significantly: "It is the machinery in the business that will help us to carry it on to advantage."[12]

Throughout the spring months Moses sought information about the availability of skilled operators; he made inquiries about spinners, weavers, finishers, dyers, fullers, and a sheep shearer.   He also requested data on the construction and operation of the numerous machines employed in the manufacture of wool and cotton cloth and took another trip to Beverly and Worcester to see what progress had been made there.   Generally, owners and operators were reluctant to share their knowledge of the business with anyone else, particularly a competitor.   Moses did not share this attitude. Replying to the Worcester mill operators, he opposed secrecy and advocated a free exchange of industrial information:

I think it will be for the advantage of the manufactory to hold an open correspondence and communicate freely what may tend to perfect the business and promote it in our country, under these views I should wish to hold a friendly correspondence with you, and in case you should think of getting a workman to finnish any of your cloths, might not the same be allso imployed by us and the expence to each thereby lessoned till we have our own workmen.[13]

11. May 9, 1789, Misc. MSS., B-814, Box 6.
12. Apr. 30, 1789; Joseph Ashton to Moses Brown, May 12, 1789, *ibid.*, VI, 66, 68.
13. Apr. 28, 1789, *ibid.*, Misc. MSS., B-814, Box 3.

Moses realized that if American producers hoped to compete
with English manufacturers they would have to pool their
resources and talents. His desire for a free exchange of
information also reflected his habit of becoming as fully
informed about a subject as possible before acting, whether
it was in business, politics, or community affairs. He did
not do this because he was an imitator and lacked imagination, but because he wanted to increase his chances of success. His capacity for careful planning, followed by deliberate action, was a trait shared to a certain extent by all the
Browns and accounts for their long list of achievements.
He also possessed rare talents for organization and leadership,
combined with perseverance, patience, and a desire to serve
the public, without which the founding of the cotton textile
industry in America would certainly not have occurred when
and where it did.

Methodically, Moses moved to put the new undertaking
on a sound financial basis.[14] He called on the town government of Newport to repay a loan he had made in 1776, when
the people were suffering from effects of the war; he drew
on Champion and Dickason, his London agents, for funds;
he wrote to Alexander Hodgdon, the Massachusetts treasurer, and asked that the state repay the loans he had made
during the war, amounting to over fourteen hundred pounds
in silver and gold. He wrote Isaac Kelly, a farmer to whom
he had advanced goods on credit, asking for payment of a
loan "as I find it difficult to raise property to setle my children in business." In addition to the rather large amounts
of money out on loan and the numerous book debts, some
of which could be safely collected despite the legal tender
laws, Moses held substantial amounts of Continental and
Rhode Island Loan Office certificates. Some of these he sold;

14. Moses Brown to Edmund Townsend, May 2, 1789; Townsend to Moses
Brown, May 11, 1789; William Burgess to Moses Brown, May 16, 1789; Moses
Brown to Alexander Hodgdon, Massachusetts treasurer, May 18, 1789; Moses
Brown to Isaac Kelley, Sept. 17, 1789, *ibid.*, VI, 66, 68, 70, 69, 84.

on others he collected interest. He could also count on the profits from the sale of produce from his Elmgrove farm and other properties in southern New England. And his store on Towne Street was a dependable source of profit. None of his business interests demanded frequent investment of large amounts of capital; therefore he could invest all his ready cash in the cloth manufacturing business.

The capital which Moses had accumulated in the 1760's and early 1770's from the spermaceti works, the Hope Furnace, the shipping trade, and the funds he later invested in land and in state and Continental securities were now used to finance the cloth industry. Rhode Island had no banks where Moses could have floated a loan, even had he wanted to, and unlike his predecessors at Beverly, Worcester, Hartford, New York, and Philadelphia, he did not ask the government to subsidize him.[15] All other early textile manufacturers had received government subsidies and special privileges, a practice that owed its origin to the feeling that the development of the industry was in the public interest and therefore entitled to public support. Indeed, the private financing of the textile industry in Providence and vicinity was unique, and Moses was clearly aware of the fact: "no encouragement," he wrote in 1791, "has been given by any laws of the State nor by any donations of any society or individuals but [it was] wholey began carried on and thus far perfected at private expense."

In April, shortly after William Almy and Sarah Brown declared their intentions of marriage, Moses and his future son-in-law entered into a partnership under the name of Brown and Almy.[16] Almy appears to have become the man-

15. For the nature of the charters of the early cloth manufacturing corporations, see Joseph Stancliffe Davis, "Eighteenth Century Business Corporations in the United States," *Essays in the Earlier History of American Corporations* (Cambridge, Mass., 1917), II, 255-90.

16. All writers have followed White, *Samuel Slater*, 65, and Bagnall, *Textile Industries*, 151, in assuming that Almy & Brown was the parent company of Almy, Brown & Slater, organized in 1790.

ager of Moses' store, from which the finished cloth goods
were to be sold; he also assisted Moses in planning the cloth
factory, but his role in the formative stages of the cloth
manufacturing enterprise was a minor one.[17]

Moses now pushed rapidly ahead. On May 18 he purchased for forty-five pounds a spinning jenny and carding
machine made by Richard Anthony and Daniel Jackson,
patterned after those at the Beverly mill.[18] Three days later
he hired Seril Dodge, a local mechanic and woodworker of
considerable skill who subsequently laid the foundation for
the silverware industry in Providence, to make some minor
repairs on the jenny. During the summer of 1789 Moses
installed these and similar machines in the Market House
and in the basements of several houses and shops in Providence.

While Dodge was repairing the jenny and Anthony and
Jackson were putting the carding machine in working order,
Moses and Almy laid in a supply of cotton and wool and
recruited pickers, ropers, bobbin winders, and spinners. By
far the most important labor problem was the hiring of an
experienced master spinner and weaver to supervise the factory. After interviewing and rejecting several applicants,
they signed an agreement with Joseph Alexander, a weaver
recently arrived in America from Scotland.[19] Brown and
Almy agreed to give him room and board and fifteen pounds

17. The articles of partnership, if they were drawn up, have not been
found. The likelihood is that Almy and Moses made a verbal agreement
of their partnership. That the company of Brown & Almy existed is shown
by the letters and indenture agreement signed by William Almy before
Smith, Brown, and Almy became partners.

18. For the details of Moses' purchases and the repairs on the machinery,
see bill of sale, "Moses Bot of Dexter and Peck, May 18, 1789, Providence,"
and Moses Brown to Seril Dodge, May 21–June 13, 1789, Moses Brown
Papers, Misc. MSS., I, 43, 44. The account of the sale is reproduced, although
somewhat altered, in White, Samuel Slater, 66-67. The bill was settled on
Sept. 2, 1789.

19. A list of employees is included in "Pay for Spinning, May 26, 1789 to
August 22, 1789," and in Moses Brown to Richard Cornell ("R. Cornals Bill
against factory"), Moses Brown Papers, Misc. MSS., I, 50, 44.

for three months' work, "provided he makes three hundred ninety yards double Jane back corduroy on said terms which he engages to do unless detained by said Brown and Almy." Alexander agreed to find another spinner "that will spin workman like and make the yarns as fine as six skains and upwards to the pound." Skilled workmen were so scarce that the partners agreed to furnish a horse and chaise to fetch the spinner from Boston.

The preliminaries completed, Moses and Almy were ready to begin manufacturing cloth. As if to give encouragement to the new undertaking the *United States Chronicle* reported that President Washington, Vice-President Adams, and several members of both houses of Congress had appeared at the inauguration ceremonies of the new government in New York dressed in complete suits of homespun clothes.[20] On May 25, four days after the story appeared, the Brown and Almy cloth factory began operations. For almost two weeks, Moses, Almy, Alexander, and the carders, ropers, and other workmen struggled to prepare the raw material for the jenny operators to spin into yarn. On June 6, Alexander began to weave, and six days later he finished "the first piece of double Jane back," a kind of twilled cotton cloth, twenty-nine and one-half yards long. At intervals of about a week, until August 22, Alexander turned out similar pieces of "double Jane back" corduroy.[21] This cloth was of a coarse variety, with a cotton weft and a linen warp. There is no evidence that Brown and Almy made any attempts during

---

20. May 21, 1789. On Apr. 25, 1789, the following item appeared in the *Providence Gazette; and Country Journal:* "For encouragement of manufacturing in the State of Rhode Island—this day assembled at the State House, in the patriotic and federal town of East-Greenwich, a company of ladies, to the number of 43, where no party principle prevailed, but the greatest cordiality and harmony subsisted through the day; the company being composed of Episcopalians, Presbyterians, Baptists, and Quakers. These ladies spun 173 fifteen knotted skeins of good linen yarn."

21. Joseph Alexander's Account from July 15 to Aug. 24, 1789; "Joseph Alexander Dr. to M. Brown, June 8-22, 1789," Moses Brown Papers, Misc. MSS., I, 44, 47.

their first three-month trial period to spin cotton strong enough to make cotton warps, which would have enabled them to weave a cloth of pure cotton.

While Alexander was working in the Market House, Moses and Almy began expanding their operations. On June 2 Moses bought a shop standing next to his store on Towne Street, and a few days later Brown and Almy secured the services of Thomas Kenworthy, the spinner Alexander had agreed to bring to Providence, and installed him in the shop.[22] The terms of the indenture specified that Kenworthy was to weave or spin "for the space of one year from the date hereof [June 6], and when employed in weaving he is to receive the yarn in skains and compleat a piece of sixty yards of double Jane back corduroy for twelve days work having his bobbins wound for him the same to be wrought close and done in a workman like manner."[23] The new spinner also agreed to supply Brown and Almy with "every information and assistance in his power respecting the business of spinning in jennys either in cotton or wool weaving of every kind." As salary Kenworthy was to receive £120, board and room, and small "necessaries," and "as an encouragement to his faithful services," the company agreed to furnish materials for him to weave fustian sufficient for a suit of clothes. This last provision was one that became common practice during the early years of the company.

During the first two or three weeks of operation, the jennies and carding machines broke down repeatedly: bobbins needed repairing, cards had to be replaced, and other repairs made. Alexander and Kenworthy were competent spinners and weavers, but they were of little use in repairing or perfecting the machinery. Moses therefore hired James Leonard as a sort of consulting engineer. Leonard was one of

22. Moses Brown's deed for house, June 2, 1789, *ibid.*, 46.
23. Indenture between Moses Brown and William Almy on the one hand and Thomas Kenworthy on the other, June 6, 1789, *ibid.*, 45.

the mechanics who had helped construct the "State Models" at East Bridgewater and who had also been one of the promoters of the Beverly Cotton Manufactory. Thinking that perhaps Leonard would be able to learn advanced techniques in New York, Moses engaged him to investigate the factory of the New York manufactory on Vesey Street. Leonard was also able to supply Moses with some Beverly cutting knives and other tools not available in Providence. The scarcity of important finishing tools and the lack of knowledge of their proper use continued to obstruct the progress of the business, but with experimentation and practice, Moses and his associates eventually overcame these difficulties.

By the middle of July the jennies and carding machines were operating satisfactorily and the weavers had acquired sufficient skill to turn out corduroy, jeans, fustians, and other coarse woolens, as well as linen and cotton cloth. As the operations expanded William Almy began to take a more active part in the manufacturing end of the business, and Moses' son Obadiah took over some of Almy's duties in the store.

Having no real desire to continue in a business that could be managed by his son-in-law, Moses now turned his attention to the promotion and perfection of the Arkwright method of manufacturing cotton cloth. He bought Reynolds' waterframe and carding machines, hauled them to Providence, and set them up in his barn on the farm. These machines had been designed to be operated by a hand crank, but Moses preferred to employ water power, as was done in England. His idea was to set up the machinery in an old grist mill on the brook running through his property, which would supply it with water for about eight months of the year. For the remaining months he planned to use a steam engine to supply the power.

Steam power had not yet been applied to the textile industry, not even in England. Where Moses got the idea is

not certain. He may have remembered the engine his
brother Joseph had constructed to operate the machinery at
the Hope Furnace before the war; he may have gotten the
idea from reading accounts of Watt's reciprocal engine; and
he almost certainly had read about James Rumsay's improvements on the steam engine and his efforts to use it in grist
mills. In any event, Moses asked James Manning, president
of Rhode Island College, to obtain additional information
while he was in Philadelphia on a special mission to Congress for the colony: "As I want some manufacturing machines carried by water," he wrote Manning, "I desire to
know the cost of Rumsay's machine for raising water sufficient to carry a grist mill by an overshot wheel of 25 feet
diameter, so far as respects the raising the water, but not
to include the cistern or wheel." Moses asked detailed
questions about the construction, cost, and operating ex-
penses of such a machine, and requested "any other information respecting the matter that may appear necessary."[24]
President Manning ferreted out an engine of the kind Moses
wanted, owned by Dr. Joseph Barnes, who had successfully
experimented with running mill machinery by steam power.
Although Barnes gave Manning complete information, Moses
was unable to buy the steam engine because of the difficulties
that the inventor encountered in getting patent rights in
various states. (The United States patent law would not be
enacted for a year.) Had Moses been able to buy Barnes'
improved engine, the textile industry might have been started
on Prospect Hill in Providence rather than in Pawtucket,
and the application of steam power to textile machinery
might not have been delayed for over two decades.[25]

Still determined to operate the frame and carding machine by water power, Moses bought a building on the banks

24. May 8, 1789; Joseph Barnes to James Mannine, Aug. 26, 1789, *ibid.*, 47.
25. For James Rumsay's steam engine, see Victor S. Clark, *History of
Manufactures in the United States, 1607-1860* (Wash., 1916), 49.

of the Pawtucket River near the bridge on the Boston road and installed his machinery in it. Next he recruited workmen and material, obtaining raw cotton from brother John, who imported a quantity from Trinidad in one of his brigs. The short staple domestic cotton was little used, for it was considered inferior in quality to long staple West Indian cotton, and it was usually dirty and carelessly packed.

Securing an adequate supply of good raw material was a serious problem, but it was a greater problem to find skilled operators. Of the numerous managers hired, all turned out to be inexperienced and unskilled. Moses finally visited New York and Philadelphia in search of the right man, but without success. Nevertheless he had two Arkwright spinning frames ready to go by fall, one with thirty-two spindles, the other with twenty-four. They were put to work and a little cotton yarn was spun, but the machines broke down frequently and the inexperienced mechanics could not repair or perfect them.[26] Reluctantly, Moses gave up his experiments and suspended operations until he "could procure a person who had wrought or seen them wrought in Europe."[27]

Following the failure of the experiments at Pawtucket, attempts were made to spin cotton warps on the jennies in Providence, but the soft yarn could not be made strong enough. This project was given up also, and Moses decided to withdraw from partnership with his son-in-law—he was not interested in the routine business activity of the established factory. The company of Brown and Almy gave way to that of Almy and Brown, with Smith Brown, Moses'

26. Moses Brown to Samuel Slater, Dec. 10, 1789, Moses Brown Papers, Misc. MSS., B-814. This letter has been printed many times: see, for example, White, *Samuel Slater*, 72-73; and Arthur Harrison Cole, ed., *Industrial and Commercial Correspondence of Alexander Hamilton, Anticipating His Report on Manufactures* (Chicago, 1928), 71-79. In the latter, the Stuart portrait of Moses Brown facing p. 72 is not Moses Brown of Providence, but Moses Brown of Newburyport, Mass.

27. Moses Brown to John Dexter, Oct. 15, 1791, Moses Brown Papers, Misc. MSS., B-814, Box 2.

cousin, becoming Almy's partner.[28]   Smith Brown operated
a small dry goods and general merchandise shop but he was
attracted to cloth manufacturing by the experiments in
Providence.   About the same time that Reynolds' spinning
frame and carding machine were nearing completion, he
borrowed money from Moses in order to add stocking weaving to his business.   Moses set up the operation: he bought
two stocking frames from John Reynolds, hired one of
Reynolds' workmen, an Irish immigrant named John Ful-
ham, to operate them, advanced the money, and gave advice
about the details of the business, had John Bailey, a clockmaker, build two more stocking frames, and wrote to his
friend William Wilson in Philadelphia asking whether good
looms were made there, how long the workmen took to construct them, and how much they cost.   Wilson, only too
happy to repay Moses for past services, shipped a secondhand
stocking frame.   When Smith Brown became William Almy's
partner, his stocking weaving business became a part of Almy
and Brown and an important source of investment capital
for the cloth manufacturing business.

During the fall of 1789 the young partners concentrated
on the production of woolens, cottons, and stockings, but
they were plagued with labor shortages and mechanical
breakdowns.   Moses, who still conducted most of the correspondence for Almy and Brown, was continually on the
lookout for skilled workers, especially those who claimed to
have had experience in English or European factories, for
he realized that technological improvements depended upon
the transfer of such knowledge from the old world.   He also
outlined the company's plans for the management of the
business.   Whereas the owners of the mills in Philadelphia

28. The origin of Almy & Brown probably dated from Sept. 16, 1789, or
shortly before, for there is a notation in a ledger of the company preserved
in the R. I. Hist. Soc. which reads: "Almy & Brown's Day Book—commencing
with the Manufacturing Business 9th mo '89 but afterwards made use of as
a Comman Day Book No. 3. 1 mo 1793." "Almy & Brown Day Book No. 3.
Commenced 1st month 1793," Almy & Brown Papers.

and Beverly did not assume personal direction of their plants, but left supervision to hired managers, Moses and his associates participated actively as owner-managers, directed operations personally, and learned the technical processes in order to be able to train others.[29]

While Moses was conducting experiments with the imperfect Arkwright waterframe in Pawtucket, Samuel Slater, a young man in Belper, Derbyshire, England, mounted his horse, turned its head in the direction of London, and without a word to his parents, began the first leg of a long journey which finally ended in Providence, Rhode Island. Samuel was only twenty-one in 1789, but he had already served several years as clerk to the cotton manufacturer, Jedediah Strutt, onetime partner of Richard Arkwright and inventor of the Derbyribbed stocking machine. Before his term of apprenticeship expired, Samuel had advanced to the responsible position of general overseer of the mill at Milford, near Belper. During seven years he had learned all there was to know about the machinery and technology of cotton manufacturing.

In the summer of 1789 young Slater heard that American states were giving bounties to people for the introduction of cotton manufacturing machinery. In England he was merely one of many mechanics who stood slight chance of rising above his station, for the cotton industry had already reached a point where further expansion was unlikely, or so Jedediah Strutt informed him. But in America, Slater apparently reasoned, an experienced, hard-working mechanic stood a good chance to make a fortune in a rising industry. Therefore, in defiance of the law that forbade mechanics and technicians to leave England, Samuel decided to go to America. Dressed in the clothes of a country clod and armed only with the knowledge acquired during seven years of experience,

29. Agreement between Almy & Brown to Moses Brown, Oct. 11, 1789, Moses Brown Papers, VI, 87.

he hid his article of apprenticeship in his clothes, left his luggage at home, escaped the notice of the sharp-eyed customs officers in London, and boarded a ship for the new world on September 1, 1789.

After a rough passage of sixty-six days, he arrived in New York early in November; in less than a week he landed a job as a mechanic in the New York Manufacturing Company on Vesey Street. Samuel found that the company's method of intermittent spinning of the jennies could not compare with the continuous process of the Arkwright waterframe, and he saw little chance of profit or fame in New York. Disappointed with prospects in New York, he decided to seek employment in Philadelphia. But a few days before he planned to leave he heard that a Moses Brown in Providence, Rhode Island, had made some experiments with perpetual spinning machines. His interest aroused, Slater immediately wrote his famous letter of December 2 and sent it in the care of Captain Brown of the Providence packet:

Sir,—A few days ago I was informed that you wanted a manager of cotton spinning, etc. in which business I flatter myself that I can give the greatest satisfaction, in making machinery, making good yarn, either for stockings or twist, as any that is made in England; as I have had an opportunity, and an oversight, of Sir Richard Arkwright's works, and in Mr. Strutt's mill upwards of eight years. If you are not provided for, should be glad to serve you; though I am in the New York manufactory, and have been for three weeks since I arrived from England. But we have but one card, two machines, two spinning jennies, which I think are not worth using. My encouragement is pretty good, but should much rather have the care of the perpetual carding and spinning. My intention is to erect a perpetual card and spinning [meaning the Arkwright patents]. If you please to drop a line respecting the amount of encouragement you wish to give, by favor of Captain Brown, you will much oblige, sir, your most obedient humble servant,

Samuel Slater.[30]

30. The details of Samuel Slater's trip to America and his first year here

Thus Moses' adherence to the principle of the free exchange of information paid rich dividends, for Slater possessed the knowledge and experience that he had been seeking for almost a year. Slater was not the first man to claim that he possessed the skills and knowledge of perpetual spinning, and Moses' reply was unenthusiastic, almost discouraging; certainly Moses can not be charged with misrepresenting the progress he and Almy had made, nor of enticing Slater away from his New York employers by painting a rosy picture of prospects in Providence.

Friend,—I received thine of 2d instant and observe its contents. I, or rather Almy & Brown, who has the business in the cotton line, which I began, one being my son-in-law, and the other a kinsman, want the assistance of a person skilled in the frame and water spinning. An experiment has been made, which has failed, no person being acquainted with the business, and the frames being imperfect.

We are destitute of a person acquainted with water-frame spinning; thy being already engaged in a factory with many able proprietors, we can hardly suppose we can give the encouragement adequate to leaving thy present employ. As the frame we have is the first attempt of the kind that has been made in America, it is too imperfect to afford much encouragement; we hardly know what to say to thee, but if thou thought thou couldst perfect and conduct them to profit, if thou wilt come and do it, thou shalt have all the profits made of them over and above the interest of the money they cost, and the wear and tear of them. We will find stock and be repaid in yarn as we may agree, for six months. And this we do for the information thou can give, if fully acquainted with the business. After this, if we find the business profitable, we can enlarge it, or before if sufficient proof of it be had on trial, and can make any further agreement that may appear best or agreeable on all sides. We have secured only a temporary water convenience. If thy prospects should be better, and thou should know of any other person unengaged, should be obliged to thee to mention us to him. In

are taken chiefly from White, *Samuel Slater*, 35-46, 71 ff. Slater's letter is on p. 72, and Moses' reply on pp. 72-73. White's work is extremely eulogistic, but his account checks with the information in Moses' correspondence.

the mean time, shall be glad to be informed whether thou come or not. If thy present situation does not come up to what thou wishest, and, from thy knowledge of the business, can be ascertained of the advantages of the mills, so as to induce thee to come and work ours, and have the credit as well as advantage of perfecting the first water-mill in America, we should be glad to engage thy care so long as they can be made profitable to both, and we can agree. I am, for myself and Almy & Brown, thy friend,

Moses Brown.

Slater accepted Moses' offer, boarded the Providence packet and arrived in Providence about January 17, 1790. Moses drove Slater to the home of Sylvanus Brown (no relation to Moses), a millwright with a shop near the old fulling mill in Pawtucket in which the idle cotton machinery was collecting dust. "I have brought to thee a young man who says he knows how to spin cotton," he told Sylvanus. "I want thee to keep him tonight, and talk to him, and see what he can do." Bright and early the next day, Moses, in company with William Almy, Smith Brown, and young Obadiah, drove out to Pawtucket to pick up Slater and show him the machinery. Sylvanus Brown told Moses that the young Englishman seemed to understand cotton spinning and was confident of his abilities in that business. No time was wasted; the small group immediately walked over to the fulling mill a short distance away. "When Samuel saw the old machinery," Moses related to Slater's biographer many years later, "he felt down-hearted, with disappointment, and shook his head, and said, 'these will not do; they are good for nothing in their present condition, nor can they be made to answer.' " Moses then reminded Slater that "thee said thee could make the machinery; why not do it?"[31]

Moses was a keen judge of men and their abilities. As a result of his wide experience and his recent study of cloth manufacturing, he saw immediately what the managers of the

31. Batchelder, *Cotton Manufacture*, 29.

New York factory had overlooked: Slater was not just an ordinary young man representing himself as a master mechanic like so many others before him; he was a talented and able man who could do what he claimed.   Recognizing this, Moses did not hesitate to follow Slater's suggestion to scrap the old machines and build new ones.   Moses was a cautious businessman and up to this point he had not invested a large amount of money in the experiment.   To subsidize a total stranger in a project, which he knew would take much time and money to complete, he must have possessed a considerable amount of self-assurance as well as confidence in Slater.

After some discussion Slater agreed to reproduce the machinery to carry on perpetual spinning.   He agreed to work for Almy and Brown at a dollar a day for his labor while he was constructing the machinery: Sylvanus Brown was to do the woodwork and assist him in assembling the machines.   Almy and Brown—using Uncle Moses' money— would finance the work.   "Under my proposals," Slater told his new associates, "if I do not make as good yarn as they do in England, I will have nothing for my services, but will throw the whole of what I have attempted over the bridge"— a promise he did not have to keep.[32]

The shop in Pawtucket where Slater began his work was located just off Quaker Lane, now East Avenue, overlooking the Pawtucket River, near the bridge and the road leading to Boston, and is no longer standing.   At Slater's insistence precautions were taken to keep the nature of his work secret; Sylvanus Brown was put under bond "neither to steal the patterns, nor to reveal the nature of the work," the doors to the building were kept locked, and blinds were put on all windows.

Once Slater had decided to remain in Rhode Island Moses introduced him to his Quaker friend Oziel Wilkinson, whose house, not far from the Pawtucket shop, would be a good

32. White, *Samuel Slater,* 74.

place for him to live during his stay. Slater not only found board and lodging in Wilkinson's home, he also found a wife. Slater's biographer tells the story that when Slater entered Wilkinson's home, the two daughters shyly withdrew, but Hannah was curious about the young Englishman and lingered to get a look at him. As in many improbable romances, the two fell in love at first sight. Because they were Quakers, Hannah's parents at first refused to allow their daughter to marry out of the Society, but the two were so obviously in love and Slater so persistent that they finally relented.[33] Perhaps this love affair was a fortunate thing for America, for Slater, while he was struggling to reconstruct Arkwright's machines, was frequently discouraged and might have left Pawtucket had he not been bound by his marriage to Hannah.

Very little is known of Slater's work during his first year in America. Although it proved impossible to keep his project secret, the details were not discussed in the newspapers and Moses mentioned them only once in his correspondence. So many attempts had been made to reproduce perpetual spinning machines in America that one more effort could hardly have aroused much curiosity. Moses frequently drove out to the old fulling mill in Pawtucket to observe Slater's progress, to consult with him about men and materials, to offer suggestions and encouragement, and to advance money as it was needed to finance the project. His extensive knowledge of the industrial resources in New England must have been invaluable to Slater, for Moses could advise him about the best furnaces for casting tools and parts, and recommend the most expert and reliable ironmongers, machinists, and woodworkers in the area. Moses also knew men in Boston, New York, and Philadelphia who would gladly send him parts, tools, and information. The year of successful development of the spinning jennies and the

33. *Ibid.*, 102-3.

months of experimentation with Arkwright's waterframe had paved the way for Slater, making his progress smoother and more rapid than it would otherwise have been.

William Almy and Smith Brown undoubtedly took an active interest in Slater's work and progress, but they are shadowy figures. Their immediate concern was with their store and the cloth manufacturing business in Providence, which they continued during the period when Slater was working on the machines in Pawtucket. They bought more jennies and carding machines, enlarged the store on Towne Street, and extended their business to include every operation involved in turning raw wool and cotton into cloth.[34]

By April 1790 Slater had, with some difficulty, built two perpetual spinning mills, using the parts of the imperfect ones where they would serve, and he was busy on the carding machines. Although barely of legal age, he was a blunt, self-possessed individual, wise in the ways of the world and men, and possessed of a sharp eye for his own interest. He had no intention of remaining a mere mechanic while others grew rich from his endeavors—he had seen too much of that sort of thing in England. Anxious to seek a more permanent and advantageous arrangement than the one originally made, he decided to press for better terms before his work was finished. After watching Slater for three months, Moses, Almy, and Smith Brown were apparently convinced of the young Englishman's capabilities. Anticipating the completion of the perpetual spinning machines, they too saw the desirability of a new agreement that would provide for the necessary reorganization and extension of the business. His partners' thinking on the subject was reflected in a memorandum William Almy drew up in March.

34. Moses Brown to "Robinson Cotton finisher in Philadelphia," May 15, 1790; James Welch to Moses Brown, June 21, 1790, Moses Brown Papers, VII, 15, 20. Welch, who had been superintendent of the factory in Philadelphia that had burned, recommended Robinson to Moses.

As the procuring of the preparatory machinery for water spinning [the carding machines] is likely to be attending with considerable expence, I propose that we (in addition to contracting with Saml [Slater] to receive a part of the profits as a compensation for his services) get some person or persons, if any there may be so disposed to be concerned in one half of that business. That we mark the goods of our own manufacture at moderate advance, in order to encourage the sale of them, and enable us to carry the business to a greater extent, without which, there is not a probability of our getting a living by it, and that we divide the care of the business, to the end that each one may know to which part his attention is to be particularly devoted.[35]

Almy's suggestions of a division of responsibility, specialization in the production and sale of cloth, and quantity production of goods to be sold at a moderate price reflects the competitive nature of the textile industry, even at this early date. Of course, Almy knew that their greatest competitor was the English manufacturer, and he felt that they would have to depend on quantity production of high quality goods and a low margin of profit in order to meet that competition.

On April 5, 1790, William Almy and Smith Brown entered into a partnership with Samuel Slater, following closely the general terms offered to Slater by Moses in his letter of December 10 and embodying the ideas outlined by Almy in his memorandum.[36] Almy and Brown were to finance the construction of the carding machines—a breaker and a finisher and a drawing and roving frame; and Slater was to extend the spinning mills or frames already built, to one hundred spindles. Samuel also agreed "to devote his whole time and service, and to exert his skill according to the best of his abilities, and have the same effected in a workman like manner, similar to those used in England, for the like purpose." The remainder of the document spelled out in

35. Moses Brown Papers, VII, 32.
36. The agreement is printed in White, *Samuel Slater*, 74-75. It was witnessed by Oziel and Abraham Wilkinson.

detail the rights and responsibilities of the partners. Stated briefly, Slater was to build and operate the machinery, and manage the factory in Pawtucket when it was ready to manufacture cotton cloth; William Almy and Smith Brown were to purchase the stock and dispose of the yarn through their company. They would receive half the profits and Slater would receive the other half "as a full and adequate compensation for his whole time and services, both whilst in constructing and making the machinery, and conducting and executing the spinning, and preparing to spin upon the same."

Almy, Brown and Slater was a partnership differing not at all from the many other business partnerships that existed in Rhode Island at the time. It did differ, however, from most of the other cloth manufacturing companies in other states. The practice in Massachusetts, Connecticut, New York, Pennsylvania, and Maryland was for the interested parties to seek a charter of incorporation from the legislature that in some cases involved a grant of money and tax favors.[37] The most reasonable explanation of why Moses and his partners did not seek a charter from the General Assembly is that they wanted to avoid publicity, and that they needed neither money nor assistance from the legislature.

Of the various machines that Slater constructed during 1790, he experienced most difficulty with the carding machine.[38] Without it the waterframe was of no value, for it was the carding machine that prepared the cotton for the waterframe. Slater had no blueprints, patterns, or models

37. In an interesting discussion of the "Origins of the American Business Corporation" in the *Journal of Economic History*, 5 (1945), 22, Oscar and Mary F. Handlin conclude that "at its origin in Massachusetts the corporation was conceived as an agency of government, endowed with public attributes, exclusive privileges, and political power, and designed to serve a social function for the state." The principle that guided the Rhode Island General Assembly, in so far as it was guided by any principle, seems to be similar to that which guided the legislature in Massachusetts.

38. Moses Brown to John Dexter, July 22, 1791, in Cole, ed., *Correspondence of Alexander Hamilton*, 72.

from which Sylvanus Brown could fashion the various parts,
so he drew their outlines on wood in chalk, and after Brown
had cut them out worked with them until they fit smoothly.
The metalwork was performed by Oziel Wilkinson, Slater's
father-in-law, assisted by his sons at their machine shop not
far from the fulling mill. Moses brought another Friend,
Pliny Earle from Leicester, Massachusetts, into the enterprise
to supply the cards, and other artisans and machinists were
utilized when the occasion demanded.

Thus the construction and perfection of the set of
machines for perpetual cotton spinning became a co-operative undertaking, drawing on the skill of woodworkers, machinists, ironworkers, and numerous other craftsmen, but
all under the direction of Samuel Slater. And throughout
the entire period, which lasted for almost a year, Moses contributed not only his money, but his time, knowledge, and
encouragement.

In the late fall Slater at last finished the carding machine,
and experiments were conducted to perfect the operation
of the various machines and master the technology of perpetual spinning. A freed Negro, Samuel Brunius Jenkes,
turned a crank to power the machines; by early winter, however, the machines were hooked to a water wheel, which,
in order to be utilized, had to be broken free from the ice
each morning. Slater performed this disagreeable task himself for a time, and his friends claimed that his health was
permanently affected by the exposure. As the testing of the
machines neared completion in early December and the
owners made plans to begin operations, Moses became ill.
There was some doubt whether he would be able to be
present when the momentous day arrived. By the middle of
the month, however, he had recovered. When Slater put
the big water wheel in motion on December 20, 1790, Moses
was there to witness the culmination of the project he had
started two years before.

It was in the fulling mill on the Pawtucket River that the modern textile industry in America began and with it the industrial revolution. The establishment of the preparatory machines and the waterframe in one building, operated by water power and tended by unskilled labor, became a characteristic of American textile manufacturing, so much so that it was often referred to as the Rhode Island system. Clearly, the credit for the construction of the Arkwright machinery and the introduction of the English factory system into America belongs to Samuel Slater. Without his technical skill the revolution in cloth manufacturing would have been delayed many years. But, without Moses' previous experience in the business, his humanitarian concern for the welfare of Friends, his deep-seated desire to perform a public service as well as make a profit, and the money, faith, and confidence he invested in Slater, it is unlikely that Slater would have succeeded.

The firm of Almy, Brown and Slater was a success from the very beginning. The experience in business organization, management, and marketing, all gained before Slater started the mill in Pawtucket, contributed greatly to its success. From Moses' point of view, it was also a success in promoting the welfare of unemployed Friends. The owners, the mechanics, the workers, and the first employees—indeed, all the principals, with the exception of Slater—were Friends or children of Friends. This is not to say that the project was a success because the people were Friends (most of the unskilled labor was performed by children from eight to fourteen years). From the outset, however, Moses had hoped to assist the members of the Society, and when he later said that the development of the cotton industry would provide employment for idle children, he was thinking primarily of Quaker children.

Clearly, Moses did not understand fully the social implications of what he was doing: he did not anticipate the life

of near servitude that children of future generations were doomed to endure in the sweatshops of the nation. As a humanitarian and Quaker, he could never have countenanced child labor under the conditions it assumed in the textile industry in the early nineteenth century. But if he lacked foresight in this instance, so did most of his contemporaries, for they too looked upon the child population in America as a labor force to be utilized in developing domestic manufactures. In still another respect Moses was unable to see broader ramifications of his actions: he did not realize that the demand for cotton created by the early development of the textile industry in New England would help to perpetuate a labor system based on slavery at a time when that institution was thought to be dying out in America. Moses fought slavery most of his life, and had he known of the contribution he was making toward its continuation, there is little doubt that he would have drawn back.

Although Moses' successful promotion of the cotton manufacturing industry is an important chapter in the economic development of America, its significance lies more in its promise than in its immediate achievement. Slater's success in Pawtucket did not make America independent of English cloth manufactures; it did not usher into America the industrial revolution. The American economy in 1790 was still primarily agricultural, and it remained so for decades. Yet the tiny mill in Pawtucket was the seed from which the textile industry of the early nineteenth century grew. When President Jefferson's Embargo in 1808 and the war with England in 1812 turned New Englanders from commerce to manufacturing, the transition was made easier by the success of Moses and Slater in 1789-90.

Moses had entered the cloth manufacturing business reluctantly, and although he continued to supply money and advice, and maintained a financial interest in Almy, Brown and Slater for many years, his active participation in the firm

ceased when its success was assured.   In 1791, Smith Brown withdrew from the company and moved to the home of his wife in Pembroke, Massachusetts.   His place was taken by Moses' son, Obadiah.   The name of the company remained unchanged.

Moses' course of action in this instance set a pattern for his business and public activities for the remainder of his life.   It is the solution he finally found, perhaps unconsciously, to a problem with which he had struggled ever since he became a Quaker before the Revolution.   At that time, as a fresh convert eager to convince his friends and himself that he was worthy to become a Quaker, he believed that active participation in business or public affairs was incompatible with the principles of the Society.   Like numerous other members he felt that the snares and pitfalls in the outside world were so plentiful that the only way to avoid them was to withdraw to the protection of the Society.   Militating against the achievement of this goal was Moses' strong sense of public responsibility, developed before conversion to Quakerism, that drew him into the profane life of the community.   For years Moses had been unable to reconcile these two desires in his mind, but after 1790 he seems to have given up trying to attain the goal of complete retirement.   He had concluded, apparently, that limited participation in business and public affairs was not inconsistent with the social doctrines of the Society of Friends as long as the motive was not excessive profit or glorification of self, and as long as its ultimate goal was the moral reformation of the community.   For the rest of his life, he was guided by this rule.

II

Working for the Community
1790-1797

EVER SINCE the death of his first wife in 1773 and his conversion to Quakerism the following year, Moses had looked forward to the time when he would be able to retire from business and devote his time to religious work and the cultivation of his own interests. For almost twenty years each step he took towards his goal seemed to be followed by a step backwards, and it was not until 1790, after his son and his son-in-law were safely established in the textile manufacturing business, that Moses, now fifty-two, realized his ambition. During the remaining years of his long life he lived in semi-retirement in his Elmgrove mansion on Prospect Hill. His attitude towards the momentous events of the decade of the 1790's—the political conflict between the Federalists and the Jeffersonian Republicans, the French Revolution, the national elections—resembled his attitude at the time of the Revolution two decades earlier: he remained silent.

Moses' estate, comprising about three hundred acres of "very light poor land," was managed by a resident overseer, leaving him free to indulge his interest in crop rotation,

fertilizer experimentation, improved methods of crop harvesting, and schemes for the advancement of agriculture
promoted by the local agricultural society, which listed him
as a leading member.[1] He studied carefully articles on farming in the newspapers and read the latest magazines and
books on the subject.

His later life may best be described as that of a gentleman
farmer. An ideal retreat from the noisy, dirty business district of South Main Street, his spacious estate was a place
where life varied from season to season, but changed very
little from year to year. The tranquillity and constancy of
this environment were what Moses enjoyed most. Not even
death, which visited his household from time to time, could
destroy the serene atmosphere.

In 1790 Moses' family was not large. Besides his wife
Mary, who was rapidly losing her eyesight and was almost
continually ill, there were his mother, who was ninety and
had only two years to live, his sister, Mary Vanderlight, a
widow since 1755, his son Obadiah, who was nineteen, and
two or three servants. His daughter, Sarah, and her husband,
William Almy, lived in town during the winter months,
although they usually spent summers at the farm.[2] The
overseer and his family occupied a building to the rear of
the big house, as did other workers hired for the planting or
harvesting seasons. From time to time relatives or friends
lived with Moses, and frequently he took into his family
orphans or children of destitute Friends, providing them

1. For Moses' agricultural activities, see the numerous tax estimates, account books, and notes in Moses Brown Papers, Misc. MSS., K-AB, and the
letters and notes scattered through vols. IX-XIV of his papers. In particular
see Moses Brown to Secretary of the Agricultural Society in Boston, Oct. 20,
1800, for a picture of Moses' work for the Rhode Island Agricultural Society,
ibid., X, 18.

2. Moses Brown to Edmund Prior, May 16, 1791, Thomas Rogerson to
Moses Brown, Jan. 9, 1794, *ibid.*, VII, 82, VIII, 41; Moses Brown to wife
[Mary], Jan. 10, 1793, *ibid.*, Misc. MSS., I, 61.

with food and suitable positions in business.[3]   After the
Fugitive Slave Law was enacted by Congress in 1793, his
home became a way-station for Negroes traveling on the
Underground Railroad.   Although Moses, like most Friends,
practiced simplicity in dress, food, and furnishings, he was
a gracious host, and visitors were impressed by his good
table and comfortable home.[4]   When Moses became a
Quaker, and for a number of years thereafter, he had frequently expressed the opinion that his affluence was a "cross
to bear"; after 1790 his apologies became less and less
frequent.

The last decade of the eighteenth century saw the generation of Browns, of which Moses was the youngest member, almost disappear.   In 1791 Moses' oldest living brother,
Nicholas, died at the age of sixty-two.   Moses had great respect for his brother, who had treated him like a son during
his boyhood.   Nicholas, like Moses, had become very religious about the time of the Revolution, although, unlike
Moses, he remained firm in the Baptist faith.   Following his
one misadventure in the slave trade in 1765-66, Nicholas had
come to believe that slavery was unchristian, and during
Moses' anti-slavery crusade in 1784 and 1787 he had given
unqualified support.

Long before he died Nicholas was a wealthy man.   His investments in securities alone totaled over $200,000.   He had
also accumulated extensive holdings in ships, real estate, and
farm land.   When he died, Moses was appointed to administer
his estate until the children could assume the responsibilities.[5]   Nicholas Brown, Jr., who inherited a large part of

3. For example, see Moses Brown to [Daniel or William] Peck, Aug. 25,
1792, to Nathaniel Aldrich, Apr. 15, 1793, and D[orcas] Earl to Moses Brown,
May 3, 1793, *ibid.*, VIII, 5, 25, 26.

4. For an amusing story of Moses' hospitality, see Kelsey, *History of Moses
Brown School*, 36 n.

5. The complete story of Nicholas Brown's fortune is told by Hedges in
The Browns, chap. 15.   For a detailed list of Nicholas' holdings at the time

his father's wealth and took control of the business, gladly accepted assistance and advice from Moses. Young Nicholas possessed many of the characteristics so distinctive in his uncle, particularly his humanitarianism. As a boy, he was Moses' favorite nephew, and although he did not follow his uncle into the Society of Friends, he respected the members and agreed with many of their principles, particularly their abhorrence of slavery and the slave trade.

A few years after Nicholas' death, Moses' sister Mary died, leaving Moses and John the surviving members of Captain James Brown's family. And in 1798 Moses' wife finally succumbed. Characteristically, Moses said little about these events. Mary Brown had been ill off and on since her marriage to Moses in 1779; thus her death was not a surprise, and Moses, good Quaker that he was, considered it the act of a merciful God.

Following Mary's death, Moses withdrew more and more into himself, spending his time in his library among his books and scientific apparatus. Like many of his contemporaries, he was fascinated by the natural world and made the study of it his avocation. He charted the temperature, rainfall, and winds, measured the thickness of the ice on the river, and kept a record of unusual natural occurrences. He also spent long hours at his microscope studying plant and animal life. Excessively sensitive about his lack of formal education and literary abilities, he was reluctant to publish his findings (occasionally he submitted an anonymous piece to the *Providence Gazette* or *United States Chronicle*), although he often passed them on to those he felt were better qualified to use them.[6]

Moses spent his happiest hours with his books. His large library contained one of the most complete collections on

of his death, see his will in Probate Court Records, Wills, No. 7, 248-55, City Hall, Providence, and the inventory of his estate, *ibid.*, 258-69.

6. The references are too numerous to list, but see Moses Brown Papers, Misc. MSS., B-814, Box 2.

Quakerism in America, and it was strong in other religions.[7]
From time to time he ordered books from London or from
American publishers to add to it. He also bought all
the books attacking the Society, reading them carefully
and writing lengthy refutations that he occasionally sent
to the newspapers or to friends in New York, Philadelphia, or England. Scientific and historical works were included in his book orders, and the extensive notes in his
papers show that they did not collect dust on the bookshelf.
He took particular interest in the writings of Priestley,
Lavoisier, and Maclean on chemistry and those of Pringle,
Hillary, Short, Howard, and Jackson on diseases. He was
generous with his books and lent them freely to friends and
strangers alike,[8] keeping an account of the transactions in
small, neatly sewn notebooks.

In Quaker affairs Moses continued to play an active, if
circumscribed, role. He seemed to consider himself an elder
statesman—an adviser to younger Friends and a reconciler
of petty conflicts within the New England Yearly Meeting.
Although by nature inclined to prefer such a position, his
conduct was partly dictated by circumstances within the
Society. In 1790 the Society of Friends was a somewhat
different organization from what it had been when Moses
became a convert in 1774. At that time the Society had been
on the threshold of an internal reformation, the character
of which was not yet entirely clear. What would have happened to the reform movement had the American Revolution not occurred is impossible to say; but in New England,
at least, the war caused Friends to isolate themselves from
the world by retreating within the confines of the Society.
The doctrine of passivity in war was at the same time ex-

7. Many of these books have been preserved in the libraries of the Moses
Brown School, the Rhode Island Historical Society, and the John Hay Library
of Brown University.

8. Moses' notes on the writings of these and numerous other authors are
in Moses Brown Papers, Misc. MSS., I-III; B-814; and K-AB.

tended to almost every aspect of life by many Friends and persisted after the war. Friends refused to participate in political affairs, declined to accept offices in state and local government, and in many instances did not even bother to vote. At one time Friends had been of great importance in Rhode Island politics, but after the Revolution, except in isolated instances, they exerted only an indirect influence. Many Friends also followed Moses' example and retired from business, or at least reduced their activities.

Moses' participation in civic affairs after 1790 was sporadic, though extensive. He served on numerous town committees and state commissions dealing with subjects of general interest;[9] he would not, however, take part in partisan politics. Despite the fact that his support was frequently sought by Federalists and Republicans alike, he maintained political neutrality.[10]

Nevertheless, he could not remain indifferent to the predicament in which the state found itself in the spring of 1790 as a result of its failure to ratify the Constitution.[11] Formerly, because of his strong feelings against slavery and the slave trade, he had reluctantly refused to support the Constitution, since certain sections of it condoned those practices. But Moses loved his state; he could not sit idly by and see it destroyed. And by 1790 he had come to agree with Bennett Wheeler, editor of the *United States Chronicle,* who warned that rejection of the Constitution would result in "anarchy and confusion," whereas adoption of it would bring "peace, liberty and safety."[12]

9. See for example Moses Brown to [unknown] Sullivan by Olney Winsor (Cashier of the Providence Bank), Feb. 16, 1796, *ibid.,* IX, 1; "Report of Committee on Machinery by J. Updike in case of Fire, August 17, 1790," in Providence Town Papers, XIII, No. 5706, 116, R. I. Hist. Soc.

10. George Champlin to Moses Brown, Aug. 15, 1792; Nicholas Brown, Jr., to Moses Brown, Jan. 27, 1794; [David Howell] to Moses Brown, Jan. 27, 1794, Moses Brown Papers, VIII, 4, 42.

11. Frank Greene Bates, *Rhode Island and the Formation of the Union* (N. Y., 1898), 170-71.

12. Jan. 21, 1790.

Moses was interested, therefore, when Henry Marchant, member of the Rhode Island General Assembly from Newport and firm supporter of the new Constitution, rose in the upper chamber of the Providence State House on January 16 and with grim determination moved that the Constitution "be submitted to the people of this state, represented in a state convention, for their full and free investigation and decision." Moses was only too well aware of the divisions within the Assembly and the state. He had watched the freemen reject the Constitution in 1788—as recently as January 15 the assistants and deputies had been unable to agree on a motion for another ratifying convention[13]—and he had little reason to believe that another try would produce different results. Yet another attempt had to be made. North Carolina, which had joined Rhode Island in rejecting the Constitution, had finally accepted it; now Rhode Island stood isolated.

Marchant's motion roused vigorous debate in the state legislature, and the close margin by which it was finally adopted foreshadowed the struggle that took place in the following months. Although Marchant's bill passed the lower house by a comfortable majority of twenty-one votes,[14] it barely escaped defeat in the upper chamber, where the assistants were evenly divided. There the fate of the bill was determined by the vote of the governor, John Collins, who reluctantly broke a four-to-four deadlock to vote for the convention. The narrow margin of victory in the upper house was a much more accurate gauge of the temper of the people than the vote in the lower house.

At this stage Moses decided that he could no longer afford to subordinate the welfare of the state to adherence to

13. *Providence Gazette; and Country Journal*, Jan. 16, 1790.
14. *Rhode Island Acts and Resolves, 1789-91*, Jan. sess., 1790, 16. The actions of Congress may be followed in *Debates and Proceedings in the Congress of the United States, 1789-1824*, 42 vols. (Washington, 1834-56), I, 890, 941, 966; II, 1616, 1629.

Quaker religious principles. After the January session of the General Assembly adopted Marchant's bill for a convention, and before the second Monday in February, when the town meetings were to elect their delegates to the convention, Moses made a tour of the state with Isaac Mott of Portsmouth, talking with Friends in the various monthly meetings about the approaching election.[15] In Portsmouth, a town with a large population of Friends, he heard that there was a move on foot to elect Anti-Federalist delegates. At East Greenwich he discussed the matter with Daniel Howland, another influential Friend, and they agreed that, although the Constitution would have to be amended before it would be entirely acceptable to Friends, it would have to be adopted first. Indeed, Moses and Howland thought that the amendments already proposed by Congress—the Bill of Rights—were so important that, if they were adopted, the government would "be the best and most peaceably founded, perhaps, of any in the world." Many Friends were convinced that slavery was on the way out and that acceptance of the Constitution would not perpetuate it.

Having decided to support the Constitution, Moses, on his return home from his tour, sat down at his big desk and wrote a long, thoughtful letter to the leaders of the Rhode Island Monthly Meeting in Portsmouth. He observed that the time had come when the people must decide whether the state was to enter the Union or not. "I thought," he wrote, "it would be well for our Friends to mannifest their desire of uniting with our sister states in the adoption of the constitution." He suggested that those who had opposed some parts of the document should now

do themselves and the public the justice to show in town meeting or otherwise, that the amendments proposed and the distressed

15. For what follows, see Moses Brown to "Isaac Lawton, Jacob Mott, Sampson Sherman or any other Friends to whom they may think proper to communicate," Feb. 4, 1790, Moses Brown Papers, Austin MSS., XII, "Personal," Moses Brown School Lib.

situation of this state (should we long continue separate) require that we manifest our opinion as a people of some influence in the state among our neighbours and that we think the time is come when our acceptance of the new government will be better for us than to any longer stand out being alone and there can be no possibility, in my view, of any advantageous alteration in our favor.

Moses pointed out that the nature of the new government would depend more upon the caliber of the men who were sent to administer it than on the Constitution. If Friends used their influence to elect men of wisdom and integrity they had every "reason to hope and expect as much happiness under the form agreed upon as under any form whatever." He advised Friends to consider the matter seriously—they might not have another chance—and to elect delegates friendly to the Constitution. With characteristic delicacy he noted that his letter was not designed to serve any political party, but was in the interests of order and good government. Friends had a right and a duty, he insisted, to speak out under such circumstances.

There is no way of measuring the effectiveness of Moses' appeal to Friends in Portsmouth. His influence among members of the Society, however, was such that his advice was not likely to be ignored. He was an elder in the Society, a leader in the Providence Monthly, the Rhode Island Quarterly, and the New England Yearly Meetings, treasurer of the Meeting for Sufferings and the yearly meeting school committee; and he possessed a reputation as a man of principle, particularly on the slavery issue. If an important man like Moses thought that support for the Constitution was not incompatible with Friends' testimony against slavery, then Friends might feel easy in taking his advice. In theory members of the Society were free to follow the dictates of their own consciences; in practice they usually followed the suggestions of their leaders. At any rate, when Portsmouth

voters elected their delegates to the convention they instructed them to vote in favor of ratification. Friends participated in the election; in fact, a copy of the voters' instructions to their delegates was delivered to the president of the
convention by Samuel Elam, a Friend.

Throughout the sessions of the convention in March, and
later in May, the Portsmouth delegates refused to be bound
by their instructions, but on May 29, after having again received strong and explicit directions, which left no doubt as
to the wishes of the voters, two of the four delegates cast
their votes in favor of ratification, while one member voted
against it and one member was absent. When votes for the
motion to ratify were counted, the friends to the Constitution had won by two votes.[16] Rhode Island was now one of
the United States of America.

The first census of the United States, completed a few
months after the ratification convention at Newport finished
its work, showed that Rhode Island had a population of
68,825.[17] Newport was still the largest urban community in
the state with 6,716 people, but Providence, with 6,380, was
pressing hard to overtake her. Newport's leadership in population was the last vestige of her colonial predominance; her
initiative in business and politics had long since passed to
Providence and the northern part of the state.

The basis for the rapid development of Providence had
been its transformation in the last decades of the colonial
period from an agricultural village to a commercial port of
first importance in New England. Among the more visible
signs of the changes in Providence were the expansion of the

16. The debate in the convention may be followed in Papers Relating to
the Adoption of the Constitution of the United States, and Journals and
Minutes Constitutional Convention of Rhode Island etc., 1790, R. I. Archives.
Hillman M. Bishop in his articles on "Why Rhode Island Opposed the
Federal Constitution," R. I. Hist., 8 (1949), 1-10, 33-34, 85-95, 115-26, under-
estimates the importance of slavery as an issue in the ratification struggle.
17. W. S. Rossiter, A Century of Population Growth, From the First Census
of the United States to the Twelfth, 1790-1900 (Wash., 1909), 163.

business section southward towards Fox Point and westward
across the Providence River to Weybossett Neck, and the
erection of a number of public buildings, churches, and private homes. The paving of Providence streets, the project
that launched Moses in his career of public service in 1760,
had continued sporadically; by 1790, most of the main thor-
oughfares had been paved, several streets widened, footways
pitched with pebbles, and gutters dug to carry off the water
to the Great Salt Cove.

Despite expansion and changes, Providence was still a
small town compared to Boston, New York, or Philadelphia,
or even Charleston or Baltimore. But the inhabitants were
not without hope that their town would some day become
a large and prosperous city. The spirit of enterprise that
had led them to challenge Newport's supremacy in the colonial period still prevailed; there were men who hoped the
town would become one of the leading ports in America, for
the future of Providence seemed bound to commerce. In
1790 Moses tabulated the number of vessels belonging to
the port and found that there were 129—among them snows,
brigs, sloops, schooners, and even one polacre—totaling
11,942 tons, a figure that placed Providence in a category
with New York.[18]

With Rhode Island in the Union, businessmen expected
the number of ships to increase, particularly if efforts were
made to encourage commercial enterprise. One deterrent
to the commercial growth of the town was the acute shortage
of wharf facilities along the east bank of the cove. The
channel in the Great Salt Cove, the basin at the foot of the
hill, was beginning to silt up as a result of the ebb and flow
of the tide, rendering it unsuitable for new ships of greater

18. Moses Brown's note: "List of Vessels, belonging to the Port of Providence, June, 1791," Moses Brown Papers, Misc. MSS., B-814, Box 1. See the
Providence Gazette; and Country Journal, Mar. 6, 1790, for a less complete
list; it counted 110 ships, amounting to 10,590 tons, "exclusive of River
Packets, Boats and Shallops."

tonnage and turning the development of the town south towards the confluence of the Providence and Seekonk rivers at Fox point.

Although not engaged in commerce personally, Moses seized the initiative to rectify the situation, organizing a movement to build a "mud machine" to clear and deepen the river channel.[19] He was joined in this enterprise by forty of the most influential and prosperous leaders of the town's commercial houses. Together they petitioned the General Assembly for an act of incorporation as the River Machine Corporation and received a charter granting them all the powers of a "Body corporate and politic." To finance the construction of the dredger, the petitioners subscribed one thousand Spanish milled dollars, divided into forty equal shares. At the company's request, the General Assembly levied a duty on all vessels of sixty tons or over arriving in the port, the money to be turned over to the company to finance the operation of the dredger.

Throughout the formative period of the River Machine Corporation, Moses maintained a keen interest in its activities. As soon as the charter had been granted, however, and its financial future secured by receipts from the tonnage duty, he ceased to have much to do with its operations. Started with enthusiasm and great expectations, the corporation soon ceased to perform any worthwhile service; the dredging was sporadic and without much effect in making the channel suitable for large ships. In 1794 the General Assembly suspended the act of incorporation. One of the reasons for the company's failure may have been that most of the owners finally realized that the narrow, shallow Providence River

19. For what follows, see the original petition, signed on Jan. 2, 1790, in Petitions to the Rhode Island General Assembly, 1789-91, XXV, 24, R. I. Archives; Charters, 1790-1800, 1, *ibid.*; *R. I. Acts and Resolves, 1789-91*, Jan. sess., 1790, 3; R. I. MSS., XIV, 139, R. I. Hist. Soc. The act of incorporation was suspended twice, once in 1794, and again in 1796. *R. I. Acts and Resolves, 1792-96*, June sess., 1796, 23.

channel could never again compete with the deeper, more
spacious waters off Fox Point where the owners of the larger
ships—the East Indiamen and the European trading vessels—
had large investments in wharves and warehouses. Or perhaps it was that the one man who had the time and capacity to make it a success failed to follow through with the
project. Characteristically, Moses had already turned his
attention to another, more important enterprise: the founding of a bank.

Sometime in the summer of 1791, Moses wrote to his
brother John suggesting that the town should have a bank.[20]
When Moses made his proposal, there were four commercial
banks in the United States: the Bank of North America,
established in Philadelphia in 1781; the Bank of New York,
founded in 1784; the Massachusetts Bank of Boston, founded
the same year; and the Bank of Maryland in Baltimore, which
received its charter in November 1790. In December 1790,
Alexander Hamilton had submitted his report to the Congress urging that a Bank of the United States be established.
A charter bill had passed Congress in February 1791, author-
izing the directors of the bank to establish branch offices of
discount and deposit anywhere in the United States. In
November the Board of Directors had decided on the policy
of creating a small number of branches, to be located in
cities that already had banks.[21]

There is no evidence to suggest that there was any connection between Moses' proposals for a local bank and the
establishment of a national bank with local branches.
Whether there was a connection or not, the trading house of
Brown and Francis (John Brown and John Francis) acted
on Moses' suggestion, calling a public meeting at the courthouse to discuss the possibility of founding a local commer-

20. John Brown to Moses Brown, Aug. 14, 1791, Moses Brown Papers, VII,
53.
21. Davis, *Essays*, II, 35-50, 53.

cial bank. They were motivated, the partners remarked, by "an anxious desire to promote the commercial, mechanical and manufacturing interests of this town by the establishment of a bank which experiment has taught (where this establishment has taken place) promotes industry and a rigid punctuality in the performance of contracts."[22] After the meeting, John Brown visited Philadelphia on business where his friends advised him to seek one of the branches of the national bank; he was told that it would be of great benefit to the town and to his own interests.[23] When he returned home, John corresponded with merchants in other parts of America on the subject of banks and banking.[24]

In August the *Providence Gazette* carried an announcement of a second public meeting "to consult and determine on the most eligible method of obtaining a Branch of the National, or of establishing an industrial State Bank," which was made urgent by the sudden rise of bank stock and the scarcity of specie needed to carry on trade and commerce.[25] The day after this meeting, held on August 15, John sent Moses the results of his summer researches into banks and banking: the act of incorporation of the bank of the United States, the charter of the Boston bank, his correspondence with the directors of the Bank of Baltimore, and the original proposals for a bank in Providence.[26] If Moses would sketch out a plan for the bank constitution and charter, he was confident that the charter would be granted by the General Assembly in the October session, since he had already approached several deputies on the matter.

22. Public Notice, Brown & Francis to Colonel Zephaniah Andrews, June 3, 1791, Moses Brown Papers, 47. See also announcement in *Providence Gazette; and Country Journal,* June 18, 1791.

23. Howard Kemble Stokes, *Chartered Banking in Rhode Island, 1791-1900* (Providence, 1902), 2.

24. For example, see Thayer, Bartlett & Co., Charleston, S. C., to B[rown] & B[enson], July 1, 1791, Brown Papers, P-T45, II.

25. Aug. 13, 1791.

26. Moses Brown Papers, VII, 53.

John also enclosed a revision of his plan for a bank. Consistent with his habit of doing things in a big way, he planned on a much grander scale than the proposals printed in the *Providence Gazette* on June 18. Instead of capitalizing the bank at $40,000, he now wanted a capital of $120,000, half to be in specie, the remainder in 6 per cent bonds of the funded debt of the United States. The specie payment was to be made in quarterly installments, the first of which was to be due in October. The entire payment in bonds was to be made fifteen days after the bank began operations, which John thought should be immediately after the first specie payment, amounting to fifteen thousand dollars. The increase in capital, John explained, would make it possible to attract money from outside the state; it would also give the bank's notes wider circulation, by no means an unimportant consideration to a businessman with accounts in most American ports. John wanted to make the bank as "near simmuler to the National Bank as possible, it will be more poppeler than aney other plan." And he did not neglect to point out that Providence stood a much better chance of getting a branch of the National Bank, if there was a bank already in existence. "If we remain slouthfull," he warned, "and therby induce their directors to think this town of no suffitient consequence to intitell us to a branch, or an office of discount and deposit," Providence would not get a bank. And without one, "all our welth, I mean the welth as fast as acquired in this state must be transferred to those other states who by their banks promotes all the valuable arts of mankind." He agreed with Moses that as far as wealth and population were concerned, Providence could not compare with the other towns that had private banks, but he predicted that "by our exurtions and forming a good and substantial foundation for the commercial, manufactural, and mecanical riseing generation it may in time become no inconsiderable cappital."

In conformity with John's request, Moses drew up a plan for a bank and John promised that nothing final would be decided until Moses, who was visiting Friends' meetings in Massachusetts, could meet with him. After suggesting the idea of a bank and helping draft the proposals for its constitution, however, Moses tried to avoid further involvement. As a Quaker, his major justification for being concerned with the bank was to improve the moral tone of the business community. Perhaps a bank, Moses thought, would "promote integrity and punctuality in dealing" between debtors and creditors, and he had bent his efforts to promoting it, but he had always intended to withdraw at the earliest possible moment.[27]

The success of the bank still depended, however, upon the endorsement of men who had the public's confidence, and Moses' reputation for disinterested public service, second to none in the state, made his support essential. John was well aware of the importance of his brother's continued participation, and on September 1 he reminded Moses that "the bank . . . ought to be soone in motion."[28] Failure to establish a bank immediately, John feared, would deprive the state of a branch of the National Bank; unless the Providence group moved speedily, the businessmen in Newport might take advantage of the delay to found a bank which would draw business away from northern Rhode Island.

Finally, on October 3, after numerous private meetings at which the bank constitution was revised several times, another public meeting was held at the courthouse.[29] Now the capitalization envisaged had grown to $250,000, represented by 625 shares of $400 each, 125 of which were to be reserved for the United States and 50 for the state, should

27. Moses Brown to James Pemberton, Nov. 2, 1791, *ibid.*, 61.
28. John Brown to Moses Brown, *ibid.*, 55.
29. See *Providence Gazette; and Country Journal*, Sept. 3, 10, 1791, for detailed proposals for a bank.

the legislature decide to become an investor. During the meeting, however, the shares reserved for government sub-scription were eliminated, leaving 450 shares for private in-vestors who capitalized the bank at $180,000. For the board of directors, the subscribers chose Moses along with others who had been most active in the planning for the bank: Wel-come Arnold, Jabez Bowen, John Brown, Nicholas Brown, Jr., Samuel Butler, John Innis Clarke, Andrew Dexter, and Thomas L. Halsey. The next day his fellow directors offered the presidency to Moses, but he declined. John Brown was then elected president and Olney Winsor cashier. The first payment of specie was completed on Wednesday, October 5, and John announced that the bank would receive proposals for discount at the bank on October 10, 1791.[30]

On the same day the bank constitution was adopted in Providence, the General Assembly incorporated the proprie-tors as the Providence Bank, granting them full corporate powers.[31] A unique feature of the Providence charter was the bank process: when a note fell due, the president or three directors gave notice to the debtor and took an oath before the clerk of the court as to the truth of the notice. The clerk was then required to enter judgment against the debtor and order payment without trial, allowing the debtor ten days to raise the money. If he denied that he actually owed the debt, then he could demand a trial. This was a device that enabled the bank, speedily and with a minimum of difficulty, to collect its debts. Since Moses was concerned with enforcing "punctuality in payment of debts," he may have suggested the bank process, although the likelihood is that it was the product of many minds. The promoters of the bank were creditors who wanted to devise some method

30. *Ibid.*, Oct. 8, 1791.
31. Charters, 1790 to 1800, 6, R. I. Archives. Moses signed the petition for a constitution, and added: "I recommend the substance of the foregoing petition."

that would enable them to collect debts without resort to the courts; they found it in the bank process.[32]

As usual, Moses seemed trapped between the ways of the world and the ways of the spirit. And as usual he rationalized his dealings with the world in moralistic terms. His duties would have to be light, he kept telling himself and anyone else who would listen; he would resign as soon as the bank was firmly established and had earned the public's confidence. He was especially careful to keep in the good graces of Quaker leaders, explaining his decision in great detail to such men as James Pemberton "by way of apology for my name being mentioned among the Directors of the Bank lately established here which probably thou may have seen least friends may misapprehend my prospects there in and the example induce others in like status to go into that business."[33] Ethical considerations, he assured the Philadelphia Quaker, had prompted him to take part in organizing a bank, and although he had refused the offer to become its president, he had reluctantly accepted a place on the Board of Directors, "finding my name was wanted to give some credit to the institution which I really thought would or might if well managed prove useful even in a moral light." Economic factors were not mentioned directly, although he stressed the desirability of raising the ethical standards of the business community. An added personal consideration was the fact that the bank project had brought him and his brother closer than they had been in months, and he did not want to alienate him by remaining aloof. These and other factors, he continued in a sorrowful vein, prevented "a refusal which would have been more to my mind." Friends, he protested, had more useful things to do than to enter "the place of the money changers."

32. The bank process is discussed in Stokes, *Chartered Banking*, 8-11. See also Moses Brown to [William Rotch, Jr.], Feb. 16, 1797, Moses Brown Papers, IX, 26.

33. Nov. 2, 1791, *ibid.*, VII, 61.

For all his pledges to resign, Moses remained among the money changers.[34] Caught in the snares of business, he was not able to extricate himself from the bank's affairs; he continued to serve as a director until 1809 and for years afterward he kept a watchful eye on its management. His willingness to come to the aid of the bank when it was in difficulty and his cautious financial views, which served to check the more impetuous and reckless conduct of some of the other directors, particularly that of his brother John, were important assets to the bank during its early years; his integrity helped inspire public confidence and helped assure success.[35]

The promoters of the bank, particularly John Brown, still hoped that the Bank of the United States would establish a branch in Providence; in that event the local bank might be merged with it. He therefore urged Congressman Benjamin Bourne to use his influence with the national bank directors to obtain a branch. While awaiting a decision from the National Bank, John initiated a plan to sustain the bank, himself, and his friends. Through Benjamin Bourne he managed to persuade the Secretary of the Treasury to order the collectors of the customs in the state to deposit all customs receipts in the bank at Providence, and to accept the notes of the local bank in payment of duties, the bank to be subject to the payment of government drafts on sight. The importance of this additional source of assets for the businessmen of Providence during the first year of the bank's existence, when the total subscription had not yet been paid in and deposits had not yet accumulated, can scarcely be exaggerated.[36] The mere fact that Alexander Hamilton, the idol of the businessmen in Rhode Island, had

34. Moses advised a friend, Edmund Prior, a New York Quaker, not to serve as a member of the Board of Directors of the New York Branch of the Bank of the United States. Prior took Moses' advice. Edmund Prior to Moses Brown, Mar. 29, 1791, *ibid.*, Misc. MSS., K-AB.
35. Moses Brown to Uncle [John] Hunt, Nov. 2, 1791, *ibid.*, VII, 61.
36. *Providence Gazette; and Country Journal*, Nov. 26, 1791.

given his blessing to the bank contributed significantly to its success.

One of the reasons Moses continued to serve as a director of the bank, a reason he did not mention in his apologetic letter to James Pemberton, was his feeling that the president and other directors needed someone to check on their activities—someone not engaged in business who would represent the public interest. Not that he feared actual dishonesty, but he knew that the opportunities and incentives for speculation and mismanagement were tempting, and men, being what they were, could not always resist temptation. Moreover, and this was perhaps of more importance, Moses wanted to make certain that the funds of the bank were not used to finance the activities of the Rhode Island slave traders.

The bank was scarcely a year old when a crisis developed in its affairs that demonstrated the need for a watchdog. In October 1792 the Secretary of the Treasury heard a rumor, whether maliciously circulated or not, that the public funds in the Providence Bank were not secure. Hamilton immediately ordered the customs officers to investigate and to remove the customs receipts, if the rumor were true. The federal officers—Colonel Christopher Olney, Benjamin Bourne, William Channing, and John Dexter—came to Providence and requested permission from John Brown to examine the bank's books. Since they would not permit him to read Hamilton's order, however, he indignantly refused, and wrote to Moses for advice. The request, he added, "of course gave me a little alarm."[37]

John was more than a "little" alarmed. His refusal to give the customs officers any satisfaction and the tone of his letter to Moses suggests that the bank's books could not stand examination. If that had been the case the examiners would probably have recommended that the customs receipts be withdrawn, thereby creating public distrust of the bank's

37. Nov. 1, 1791, Moses Brown Papers, VIII, 13.

soundness. The consequences of such action were not pleasant to contemplate. Fortunately, after prolonged argument, Hamilton's examiners told John that they would be content to deal with Moses, in whose impartiality and honesty they apparently had the utmost confidence—he was the only member of the Board to whom they would show Hamilton's letter ordering the examination. What passed between Moses and the customs officers is not known but he apparently convinced them that the bank was sound, for later Hamilton wrote to Providence saying that he had been misinformed about the bank's condition.

During the early years of its existence, Moses frequently came to the bank's assistance in other ways. He lent money to John, Nicholas Brown, Jr., Welcome and Thomas Arnold, and other businessmen when they could not pay off their short-term notes, and to the bank when depositors' withdrawals threatened to deplete its specie reserves.[38] He urged a cautious policy on loans, and opposed the purchase of bills of exchange, stocks, debts, or estates for merely speculative purposes; the bank should be an institution of discount and deposit only.

Consistent with Moses' efforts to enhance the commercial prosperity of the town were his attempts to improve the approaches to Providence in order to attract business from the northern and eastern sections of the state and from southeastern Massachusetts. Although ferries had long been in operation on the Seekonk River, he thought that a bridge connecting Warren, Bristol, and Aquidneck Island to Providence would more nearly fill the need for an inexpensive, easily accessible, and safe passage into the town. There were two likely sites for such a bridge, one at the lower ferry at Fox Point, another at the upper ferry, near the present loca-

38. Brown & Francis [by John Brown] to Moses Brown, Nov. 19, 1792, *ibid.*, 14.

tion of the Red Bridge.   After a careful survey of the locations and measurement of the distances from the two sites
to the center of the downtown business section, he concluded
that "the upper place is the place for the bridge if there is
but one."[39]   A bridge there would connect up with roads
leading to the lower end of town; a road could be built
through his farm, connecting the road from the Pawtucket
bridge to the new bridge or to the road leading to the business section of Providence; the distance from the bridge to
the west side and northern parts of the town would be much
shorter than from a bridge built at the lower ferry site.

There were persons, however, who for business reasons
desired the lower ferry site, John Brown among them, and a
heated and lengthy debate developed over the location of the
bridge.[40]   In June 1792, the General Assembly granted two
charters, one to the promoters of the upper bridge, including
Moses, his son Obadiah, Thomas P. Ives, David Howell, and
numerous others, and another to the Providence South
Bridge Society, which included among its members John and
Nicholas Brown, Welcome Arnold, Joseph Nightingale, and
John Innis Clarke.   To protect the interests of the Pawtucket
businessmen up the river, the bridges were to be of the draw
variety, which would permit rafts to pass up and down the
river.

Both bridges were constructed by the fall of 1793 and
helped to solidify Providence's position as the leading commercial town in the state.   The upper bridge, a bright red
wooden structure with a draw in the middle, began carrying
traffic in September 1793.   For years the townspeople re-

39. Moses Brown to W[elcome] Arnold, June 19, 1792, Peck Collection,
VIII, R. I. Hist. Soc., where Moses mentions that he has been appointed by
the bridge proprietors to procure an act of incorporation for the company.
40. William Almy summarized the proceedings and added his own ideas
in a letter to Moses from Newport, June [?], 1792, Moses Brown Papers,
VIII, 2.

ferred to it as Moses Brown's Bridge; in later years it was
generally called the Red Bridge, and has that name today.[41]

Although Moses was a partisan of Providence in its commercial rivalry with Newport, he was entirely capable of
surmounting this narrow allegiance if it conflicted with the
larger interests of the state. For years he had been alarmed
by the number of unemployed people in the state who were
forced to rely for food and clothing on the charity of the
towns in which they lived. This, he thought, was not only
a financial burden for the towns to bear, but it was also degrading to those receiving the charity. Since the situation
was worse in and around Newport than in any other part
of the state, he originated a project in 1791 to manufacture
canvas, a product much in demand in New England for sails
and sailor's clothing. Such a factory in Newport would make
Rhode Island merchants independent of importers and at
the same time provide employment for the poor. Many
people, he wrote to William Ellery in Newport, would thus
be able to "get their bread by the business that may be now
dependent on dayly charities."[42] With his assistance and
encouragement citizens of Newport established a canvas factory, giving employment to the needy and contributing to
the economic progress of the state.

In addition to his community activities, Moses gave advice and encouragement to numerous individuals who came
to him with inventions or new processes for manufacturing.
In 1792 Samuel Dorr, a local mechanic who had invented
a machine for shearing cloth, brought his device to him for
an opinion about its usefulness and to enlist his assistance
in marketing it. Moses called it a "new and curious invention and in its construction calculated for great despatch of
business." Although he considered it too complicated and

41. Anna August and Charles V. Chapin, *A History of Rhode Island
Ferries, 1640-1923* (Providence, 1925).

42. Moses Brown to William Ellery, Nov. 19, 1791, Moses Brown Papers,
VII, 63.

expensive for use in America, he thought it would probably be useful in England where wool growing and cloth manufacturing were more highly developed.[43] Two years later Moses helped his old friend John Bailey, who had made parts for his spinning jenny and carding machine in 1789, to perfect a steam jack, secure a patent, and sell licences to manufacturers in other parts of the country. The next year he performed much the same service for James Davis of New Bedford, a Friend who was experimenting with a new process for tanning leather.[44]

One of the most interesting projects Moses sponsored during the early 1790's was the development of a cheap and efficient method of manufacturing potash. Shortly after the Revolution Moses and Thomas Arnold had tried to perfect a new process for manufacturing pot and pearlash in the hope that it would become a product for export to England in place of whale oil, upon which a prohibitive duty had been laid. For several years the two men conducted experiments in an effort to reduce costs and increase efficiency of production, but they made only slight progress. In 1789 they shared their knowledge of the business with other Friends, among them Samuel Hopkins from New York and William Shotwell from Philadelphia. For two years Shotwell and Hopkins experimented with techniques of producing cheap potash, consulting with Moses on visits or by mail.[45] By the middle of 1790, Hopkins had made enough progress to apply for a patent to the newly created United States Patent Office. On July 30, 1790, he received the patent, the first to be

43. Moses Brown to [unknown] Dorr, July 18, 1792, *ibid.*, VIII, 4.

44. Moses Brown to [John Bailey], Oct. 30, 1794; Moses Brown to Hugh Davids & [unknown] Cox, Oct. 12, 1795; Davids & Cox to Moses Brown, Oct. 22, 1795; Moses' reply, Nov. 30, 1795, *ibid.*, VIII, 53, 75, 80.

45. Moses Brown to [Samuel Hopkins], Dec. 14, 1790; William Shotwell to Moses Brown, Jan. 28, 1791, *ibid.*, VII, 30, 35. Moses also supplied information to Sylvannus Hussey, who had a large potash manufacturing plant at Lynn, Mass. Hussey to Moses Brown, Jan. 1, 1791, *ibid.*, 33.

issued by the United States.[46] Although the process never enjoyed the success hoped for by Hopkins, Moses, or its other promoters, it nevertheless was an improvement upon older methods and a definite contribution to the domestic potash industry.

As a result of his participation in cotton manufacturing, the Providence Bank, the upper bridge company, numerous inventions, and other business ventures, Moses became widely recognized as the foremost authority on the industrial and commercial development of the state. It was only natural then that authors writing books about America, or government officials seeking information about the state of Rhode Island, should turn to him. Even before his retirement he had given information to Hannah Adams about the religious history of the state for use in her book, *An Alphabetical Compendium of the Various Sects which have appeared in the World.* In July 1788 he supplied information to Jedidiah Morse, Massachusetts Congregational minister, destined to become famous as the father of American geography; indeed, the section on Rhode Island in the 1791 edition of Morse's famous work was solidly based on Moses' detailed report.[47]

Moses' reputation as an authority on Rhode Island history spread throughout New England as a result of his contacts with Hannah Adams and Jedidiah Morse. When Miss Adams published a revised edition of her *Alphabetical Compendium* in 1791, she once again called on Moses for assistance, not only in collecting material but in promoting the book; to boost sales she used Moses' commendation of the work.[48] Several years later Moses co-operated with the Rev-

46. John Bach McMaster, *A History of the People of the United States, from the Revolution to the Civil War* (N. Y., 1900), I, 583.

47. Moses Brown to "Woman printing History of all Religions," Aug. 1, 1784; Jedidiah Morse to Moses Brown, Apr. 11, 1789, Moses Brown Papers, V, 7, 63.

48. See the correspondence between Moses Brown and Hannah Adams in *ibid.*, VII, and Misc. MSS., B-814, Box 1.

erend William Bentley, well-known Unitarian minister in
Salem, who was particularly interested in documentary material concerning Roger Williams.[49] Bentley also passed
along Moses' information to Christopher Daniel Ebeling, a
German writer who prepared a monumental geographical
and historical study of the United States.[50] Frequently Moses
copied town or colony records requested by some distant
author, and he served on a committee appointed by the town
or state government to transcribe some of the early records
in order to preserve them.

Moses' historical interests, like so many of his other activities, were more utilitarian than antiquarian, and in 1791 he
had an opportunity to put his vast knowledge of the state's
resources and industries to practical use. When Alexander
Hamilton, at the pinnacle of his popularity and influence
as Secretary of the Treasury, began preparation of his famous
"Report on Manufactures," he and his assistants sent letters
to men all over the country asking for information about
industrial and manufacturing resources of the states, "the
first attempt ever to survey the industrial resources and
activities of the United States." John Dexter, Rhode Island's
customs collector in Newport, forwarded Hamilton's request
to Moses, observing that he knew of no one else better
qualified to supply the information. "I shall cheerfully
give every information in my power," Moses responded.[51]

49. William Bentley to Moses Brown, Dec. 8, 1799, and Jan. 14, 1800, *ibid.*,
Misc. MSS., B-814, Box 1. See also William Alexander Robinson in *DAB* s.v.
"Bentley, William."

50. The full title of Ebeling's work is *Erdbeschreibung und Geschichte
von America. Die Vereinten Staaten von Nord-amerika* (Hamburg, 1793-
1816). This work was a continuation of Busching's *Geography*. Moses was
also visited frequently by travelers from England and Europe who were
gathering information and impressions about America. When the Duke de
Liancourt toured America in 1795, he called on Moses in Providence. William Rotch, Jr., to Moses Brown, Oct. 21, 1795, Moses Brown Papers, VIII, 75.

51. Cole, ed., *Correspondence of Alexander Hamilton*, xvi, 71-79. Moses'
letter to Dexter was based on numerous previous reports he had furnished
William Ellery in Newport. Ellery was also collecting information for
Hamilton. Ellery to Moses Brown, Mar. 26, 1791, Moses Brown Papers, VII,
39, 43.

There are striking parallels between Hamilton's "Report on Manufactures" and the account which Moses forwarded to Dexter, particularly on the subjects of protective duties and bounties to encourage manufactures, and on the use of child labor. In a very real sense Moses had already accomplished on a state level what Hamilton was attempting on a national level: a comprehensive economic survey.

This episode symbolizes in a sense Moses' attitude toward national affairs. He was willing to provide Secretary Hamilton with information and ideas that might assist him in his efforts to encourage manufacturing because he recognized its national importance. But he was primarily interested in community affairs; it was to projects that promised to improve the welfare of his neighboring citizens that he devoted a major part of his time.

12

Yellow Fever Epidemic and Public Health, 1797-1800

IN THE 1790's, Moses began an intensive study of medicine. His interest in disease and illness went back to the days before the Revolution when he had traveled over two hundred miles to be inoculated with smallpox. He had returned to urge repeal of the Rhode Island law prohibiting the practice and to recommend construction of a smallpox inoculation hospital. Failing to arouse public interest, he had assisted his friend, Dr. William Barnett of New Jersey, to set up a hospital at Point Shirley in Massachusetts and advised Rhode Islanders who were not afraid to go there to take the cure. For over thirty years he had performed other worthwhile services in the interest of public health as one of the overseers of the pest house, and as a member of local and state committees to draw up regulations concerning contagious diseases and public sanitation.

Although he received no formal education in medicine, Moses acquired over the years an extensive knowledge of the profession. His interest had been stimulated by frequent deaths in his family and by his own protracted illness. Through independent study he became well grounded in theory; from local physicians he learned the accepted diag-

noses of diseases and illness; and from his brother-in-law,
Dr. Jabez Bowen, Jr., who operated the largest apothecary
shop in Providence, he received instruction in the art of
mixing drugs. In a day when men often began practicing
medicine after only a short apprenticeship with an established practitioner, Moses was probably as well qualified to
practice medicine as many who did. He never considered
himself an expert, although he gladly supplied the medicines
to the poor and gave to his friends remedies for ailments
that had baffled the doctors.[1] Local physicians confronted
with a difficult case frequently consulted him, and together
they pored over his medical books in search of a cure.[2]

Moses' chief interest was in preventive medicine. From
experience he had grown to dislike surgery, which was grue-
some and often fatal, and he had serious misgivings about
the virtues of bloodletting. To avoid illnesses which would
make dangerous cures unnecessary, he advised people to
spend as much time as they could in the country, since the
air was less noxious there. From observation he had learned
that strong liquors broke down one's health; he therefore
advocated total abstinence from alcohol. A moderate diet,
preferably without meat, together with regular exercise
would, he maintained, also contribute to good health and
prolong life.

In 1793, when Philadelphia was decimated by yellow
fever, Moses carefully evaluated the numerous articles and
books written to explain the causes of the disaster.[3] Fearful

1. In Moses Brown Papers, Misc. MSS., K-AB, there are literally hundreds
of prescriptions, cures, or "recipes" for almost every disease or illness imagi-
nable. Moses must also have had a large assortment of drugs, for local
physicians frequently called on him for supplies.

2. Moses' closest friends among the medical profession were Drs. Jabez
Bowen, Sr., Thomas Dyer, Levi Wheaton, William and Pardon Bowen,
Reverend Stephen Ganne, Ephraim Comestock (who died of yellow fever in
1797), all of Providence, and Jonathan Easton, Charles F. Bartlett, and Isaac
Senter, of Newport.

3. Moses made inquiries of his friends in Philadelphia about the epidemic
and received several extended accounts. William Wilson to Moses Brown,

that the epidemic might invade Providence, he made an extensive study of the causes of the plague, and kept a close eye on local conditions, visiting Dr. William Bowen frequently to inquire about the state of health in the town. His concern was justified; four years later the disease became a reality.

The dark day in Providence was August 18, 1797, when news circulated through the shops and homes on both sides of the river that three people had died, and several more were sick from a bilious fever resembling the type that had threatened to destroy Philadelphia in 1793. Actually, the epidemic had started at least as early as the twelfth, when Benjamin Carr, a twelve-year-old boy, came down with what Dr. Thomas Greene, who had never seen a yellow fever case, diagnosed as an "inflamatory billious fever."[4]   The next day Dr. Thomas Dyer visited a patient on the West Side, who, he said, was a "worm case."   Dr. Dyer prescribed a potion of powdered pink root for the boy and, since he was not one of his regular patients, did not attend him again for several days.   Undoubtedly these two boys had mild cases of yellow fever, but it was not until the fourteenth that the physicians became alarmed.   On that day Robert Fuller, a blacksmith who worked in Lemuel Pitcher's shop on the wharf, came down with a high fever and delirium.   When he developed severe pains in his head and back, vomited a black substance, and started to turn yellow, Dr. William Bowen, the attending physician, diagnosed his case as malignant yellow fever.

Oct. 9, 1793; James Pemberton to Moses Brown, Dec. 18, 1793, Moses Brown Papers, VIII, 35, 38.

4. The following account of the yellow fever epidemic in Providence in 1797, unless otherwise noted, is based on Moses' unpublished account of the epidemic during the winter following the disaster.   The title of the manuscript is, "An Account of the Malignant Remitting Billious or Yellow fever in Providence from 1791 to 1797 Inclusive with Misselanious Notes and Observations of its Origin whether Domestic or Foreign and Shewing that our Climate has originated Disseases highly Malignant by Moses Brown with an Apendix"; it is deposited at the R. I. Hist. Soc.

Not all the doctors were convinced that Dr. Bowen's diagnosis was correct. The seriousness of the affair, however, caused several physicians hurriedly to re-examine some of their patients whose symptoms, although less marked, were similar to Fuller's. Two of Dr. Bowen's patients—Elizabeth Mitchell and Hannah Goss—had become ill on the thirteenth and upon re-examination were said to have yellow fever. During the next three days there were several new cases with the telltale symptoms. On the evening of the seventeenth Elizabeth Mitchell died, to be followed the next day by Robert Fuller and Hannah Goss. The most skeptical physicians were now convinced—malignant yellow fever was in Providence.

The news produced near panic in the town. Believing that the fever was highly contagious, some citizens packed a few belongings and fled to the country; others closed their shops and retired to the supposed safety of their homes, venturing into the streets only when absolutely necessary. Moses later remarked that the public panic was even worse in 1797 than it had been during the disastrous smallpox epidemic in 1764. Members of the town council noted that the situation was not as serious as reports indicated, but they betrayed their uneasiness by advising the people to remain calm and to take precautions. Moses, summoned to the meetings of the council with the physicians, participated in the discussions and supported the orders that all coffins for yellow fever victims be "made tight, the corpses put in tarred sheets and immediately buryed, to cause the dwellings of the deceased to be cleansed[,] beading and apparel to be buryed—to remove all nuisances that might tend to generate or propagate Disease." The council also recommended that attendance at funerals be restricted to those needed to perform the service and that corpses be taken to the burial ground through back alleys.[5]

5. Town Council Meeting, Aug. 18, 1797, Providence Town Papers, XXVII,

The coffinmakers had difficulty keeping up with the demand. On the twentieth William Tillinghast, well-known merchant and public-minded citizen, and Mary Arnold, member of one of the oldest Providence families, died, to be followed on the twenty-first by Mary Northrup; the next day the Arnold family was struck twice, and on the twenty-fifth, the fever claimed its tenth victim, Reuben Potter. After a temporary respite at the end of August, when the town council optimistically predicted the end of the emergency, the fever returned with renewed vigor. Almost every day throughout September and the first week in October, at least one person died.

During the first few days of the epidemic the citizens seemed to be paralyzed by fear. The fear was not so much of what had happened—death was not a rare occurrence in Providence in the eighteenth century; frequently more than three people died in one day from smallpox or dysentery—but a fear of what could happen. As a result of frequent outbreaks of disease, some of which reached epidemic proportions, people had learned what to expect and seldom became alarmed. But yellow fever was another matter. Over four thousand people had died in Philadelphia in 1793; Providence, with a population of only seven thousand, might easily be wiped out.

With this disease the people of Providence were little acquainted. In recent memory there had been few recognized cases of yellow fever in Rhode Island, and the number of people who had actually seen a case and could recognize its symptoms was small. The true origin of yellow fever was, of course, unknown—that yellow fever was transmitted from one person to another by a species of mosquito, *aëdes aegypti,* which once infected was capable of spreading the

---

147, R. I. Hist. Soc. The course of the epidemic may be followed in Town Council Records, No. 7, 1794-1800, and Town Meeting Records, No. 7, 1783-1804, and in the Providence Town Papers, XXVII-XXVIII, *ibid.*

disease until it died. Nor did the people of Providence have any well-formulated theories about how to treat the patients or to eliminate the pestilence. At the beginning of the epidemic the measures adopted to fight it were about the same as those employed against smallpox or any other disease.

One of the first steps taken by the town council was to appoint Captain Christopher Sheldon on August 19 to supervise the funerals of victims of the fever.[6] The next day, operating on the theory that the disease was contagious, the council issued an order that all deceased victims were to be buried immediately, that the streets in the infected area were to be cleaned, and that other "nuisances pernicious to the health of the town" were to be removed. About this time someone remembered that the schooner *Betsey*, from the West Indies, had tied up a few days previously at Joseph Tillinghast's wharf at the foot of Transit Street, and that several of the crew had been sick with fever on the voyage. Although all had recovered, a chest of clothes had been taken on shore by one of the late victims, and many people now insisted that the disease had been imported from the West Indies by the *Betsey* and had been spread in the town by the chest of clothes.[7] Within a few days this explanation of the origin and spread of the disease was universally accepted. Provisions were immediately made to have the vessel towed down the river where it could be thoroughly cleaned and fumigated.

Moses was too busy to pay much attention to the discussion of the origin of the disease. He spent most of his time with Dr. Bowen in numerous visits to new victims, offering

6. Town Council Records, No. 7, 158, *ibid.*

7. The *Betsey* had stopped at Warren for a few days before proceeding to Providence. On Aug. 22, the council sent Dr. James Mason there to obtain the "most sattisfactory account in his power concerning the introducing the yellow fever into this town"; *ibid.*, 160-61. Apparently Dr. Mason confirmed the rumors of importation. The council ordered Captain Isaiah Cahoone to cleanse the *Betsey; Providence Town Papers*, XXVII, 149, *ibid.*

suggestions gleaned from medical books in his library, comforting the patients and, when they died, the surviving members of the family. During the early days of the epidemic he had, like everyone else, accepted the importation theory without question. Yet within a short time he began to doubt the theory and finally to reject it almost entirely.

From the first appearance of the disease, Moses realized that the doctors would be too busy to keep a complete and accurate account of the epidemic, and he set that as his task. He soon discovered cases that, contrary to the existing theories of contagion, could not possibly have been the result of contact with the *Betsey*, its crew, or the trunk of clothes. He was himself a living example of the fallacious theory of contagion, for he had been at the bedside of numerous patients and had suffered no ill effects. Moses had had extensive experience dealing with contagious diseases, especially smallpox. Yellow fever, he concluded, was not the same kind at all. If the fever was not contagious, perhaps the idea that it had been imported was equally erroneous. Investigating this possibility, Moses found that there had been at least seven cases of yellow fever in Providence before the *Betsey* ever reached port, a fact confirmed by several physicians; indeed, further inquiries revealed that yellow fever had been endemic in Providence since 1791. In the face of this information he was at a loss to explain the causes of the disease, but he tended toward the theory of domestic origin advanced by Drs. Valentine Seaman and Elihu H. Smith of New York in *The Medical Repository*. These physicians claimed that the disease was neither imported nor contagious; rather, they concluded that it was caused by putrifying effluvia from marshy and swampy lands and from pools of stagnant water. No evidence had been produced, they asserted, to prove that the disease could be transmitted from one person to another, either by personal contact or by the

clothing of a sick person.[8]   Moses came to a similar conclusion.   Throughout the epidemic, he "endeavoured to suspend decision" until he had completed his study, although he acknowledged that it was difficult "to stand single in the cause of my enquiries," since his mind "vibrated as the weight of evidence has appeared."

In the fall of 1797 an incident convinced him that yellow fever was of domestic origin. Writing about the causes that contributed to the sudden termination of the epidemic, he observed that "about 8 o-clock this evening [October 8] it rained hard with such a tornado, high wind or whirl wind as I do not recollect to have happened within my memory, about 50 years."   Two chimneys were blown down in the north end of town, a building to the east of the college was demolished, a west window in the tower of the Baptist Church was blown in, the tops of sturdy buttonwood trees were carried away, and board fences, their posts lifted clean out of the ground, were scattered over the countryside. Moses speculated that this wind "removed and changed the atmosphere so materially that no new case of yellow fever seems to have afterwards appeared among us."   He added that "the Lord had his way in the whirlwind and in the storm and the clouds are the dust of his feet and delivered us from the noisome pestilence that walketh in darkness."

Although Moses believed in the efficacy of Divine Providence, he did not think men should rely solely on it for de-

8. Moses' "Notes from and on Reading Sundry Authors on the Yellow Fever, etc"; and his "Notes from Doctors Seamens, Websters Collection, Medical Repository, Macleans Disertation on Epidemics and Doctors Hillary and Jackson on Yellow Fever," Moses Brown Papers, Misc. MSS., B-814, Box 1. This is one of several notebooks in Moses' papers containing observations concerning yellow fever. There were few writers, ancient or modern, whose works Moses had not consulted. He was an original subscriber to the *Medical Repository* and was greatly influenced by the articles on yellow fever that appeared in it during the epidemic of 1797.   There were only five other subscribers in Rhode Island: Drs. William Bowen, Levi Wheaton, and Reverend Stephen Ganne of Providence, and Jabez Benison, bookseller, and Dr. Isaac Senter of Newport.

liverance from an evil like yellow fever, but should do every-thing in their power to determine its causes and cure. People were too prone to overlook physical causes and "to Resolve all in to Providential Events." He too was inclined to regard the Deity as the disposer of events but he thought it "con-sistent with Divine wisdom to work by what we call Natural Causes, and it becomes us as Rational Creatures to attend to these under a just Subordination, and therein to do our parts toward Rectifying such causes of malady affecting the Human System as may be in our power, by way of preventive, as well as by way of Remedy after we are affected with Disease." At the outset, therefore, he adopted the broad general prin-ciple that yellow fever, as well as all other diseases, was brought on by men and that it could be eradicated by men.

There were numerous influential people in Providence who were unconvinced. They saw no connection between the epidemic and the unsanitary conditions of the town, for example, and were consequently reluctant to spend public money to clean up the town. Moses feared that if their views prevailed the good start the town council had made in that direction during the epidemic would not be continued. During the winter he worked diligently to write a persuasive account of the domestic origin of the yellow fever and to point out ways of preventing a recurrence of the disease. The result of his efforts was an "account of the Malignant Remitting, Billious or Yellow Fever in Providence from 1791 to 1797 Inclusive with Misselanious Notes and Observations of its Origin whether Domestic or Foreign and Shewing that our Climate has originated Diseases highly Malignant." He explained that his first object was to inquire into the cause of the disease, and secondly, he wanted to preserve the history of the epidemic for posterity. With a modesty and humility that few early writers on epidemic diseases exhibited, Moses noted that he did not expect "to add much if any new matter to the stock of those who have read the authors on and con-

sidered the subject." He admitted that he was not a physician, but hoped that this would not prejudice his readers since those physicians who had written on the subject were divided, "both as to the origin of the disease, whether generated among us in this country, or imported from foriegn or hotter countries; and whether it is contagious or not, as well as to the treatment of it." If his account should in any degree help to decide any of these questions, he would consider his time well spent.

Moses' account of the yellow fever epidemic was never published, although its importance and influence should not be underestimated for that reason. Two excerpts from it found their way into the New York *Medical Repository*,[9] the first American journal devoted to medicine, and in Rhode Island it was read by almost every physician and by many influential citizens. Dr. Levi Wheaton took it to New York and Philadelphia and circulated it among physicians there.[10] Moses heard that Noah Webster, editor of *A Collection of Papers on the Subject of Bilious Fevers,* was gathering material for an extensive work on epidemics; he had his manuscript copied and sent to Webster, along with permission to use any or all of his material.[11] A comparison of Moses' *Account* with Webster's *History of Epidemic and Pestilential Diseases,* which was published in December 1799, shows that Webster used much of the illustrative material in Moses'

9. "Brief Remarks on the Origin of the Yellow-Fever in some Parts of the State of Rhode Island, drawn up by Moses Brown, Esq. of Providence," in the *Medical Repository*, 3 (1799), 267-70.

10. Moses Brown to Enos Hitchock, Nov. 21, 1798; Caleb Wheaton to Moses Brown, Aug. 8, 1800, Moses Brown Papers, Misc. MSS., B-814, Box 1.

11. Moses heard of Webster's work when the Reverend Enos Hitchock sent him a letter from Webster requesting material relative to the 1797 epidemic in Providence, Noah Webster, Jr., to Reverend Enos Hitchock, Nov. 12, 1798, *ibid.,* IX, 66. See also Moses' letters to Enos Hitchock, Nov. 20, 21, 1798, *ibid.* For an extended account of Webster's work, see these works by C. E. A. Winslow: "The Epidemiology of Noah Webster," in Connecticut Academy of Arts and Sciences, *Transactions*, 32 (1934), 21-109; *The Conquest of Epidemic Disease: A Chapter in the History of Ideas* (Princeton, 1943), 210-34; and *The History of American Epidemiology* (St. Louis, 1952), 11-51.

manuscript and chances are that he found some of Moses' ideas useful.[12] Indeed, when Webster returned the *Account* to Moses he remarked, "You have collected a great number of useful facts, and you have fallen into the right tracks as to the causes. Your principles are unquestionably just, on the subject of the origin and contagion of the disease called yellow fever, and the facts you have furnished, will be of essential service to me."[13]

More importantly, Moses' work on yellow fever served as the basis for the sanitation program subsequently carried out by the Providence town council, which for several years after the 1797 epidemic performed all the functions of a board of health. Although his influence was chiefly local and his efforts to put his program into effect were obscured by his modesty and distaste for publicity, Moses may rightly be considered as the main force behind the efforts to improve the health of Rhode Island citizens and thus a pioneer in public sanitation and health in the United States.[14]

Moses' "Account" is not simply an attempt to destroy the current theories of importation and contagion or to prove other writers "wrong on the subject"; nor is it an attempt to reduce the "phenomena of pestilence into some order and system." It is an accurate and detailed description of existing conditions in Providence and the outlying areas, followed by a correlation of these conditions with the incidence of disease and mortality. His investigation convinced him that

12. Winslow, speaking of Webster's skill in disproving the validity of the importation theory, states that in the case of Providence Webster "is particularly effective"; *The Conquest of Epidemic Disease*, 220-21.

13. Dec. 20, 1798, Moses Brown Papers, IX, 68. Moses later in the month sent Webster the second half of his "Account," and added "some Notes I had made of facts this year, some account of the fever in Bristol in 1797, their Bills of Mortality and the Doctors' Idea of the general State of Diseases in our Town in 1796." Moses warned Webster not to make too much of this information, for "Facts however multiplied when arranged and compared may prove confirming to a just system or destructive of a false one."

14. The movement to clean up Providence got under way about the middle of September; Providence Town Papers, XXVII, 148, 149, 151, XXVIII, 20-27, 31, 37.

where there was filth and a lack of sanitation, there would be disease. Rejecting the ordinary theory of contagion, Moses constructed one of his own.[15] He explained:

It is . . . most probably that the infectious particles which cause the yellow fever is in the air, and primarily produced in a manner and by a composition of certain poisonous particles or by those of a specific nature whether from vegetable, animal, or mixed exhalations or affluvia with which we are not acquainted, but we find by experiment that heat and moisture are necessary to putrefaction, and by observation appears also necessary to raise and retain the contagious miasma or poison in all countries in its most concentrated and active state, and that this heat and moisture may cause local exhalations and affluvia as well as a more general state of atmosphere . . . and that such local atmosphere or places which abound with noxious exhalations from filth or any kind which destroys or lessons the proposition of vital air is most likely to generate the disease.

In his concern for mortality instead of morality, Moses shifted his emphasis from godliness to cleanliness. To prevent disease, he concluded, there was great "necessity for cleanliness." Cities were less healthy than the country because of the filth to be found in them; therefore their inhabitants were more likely to get yellow fever.

After having demonstrated—at least to his own satisfaction—that disease flourished successfully in an unsanitary environment, which was susceptible to change by human action, he outlined a comprehensive program that in many respects anticipated the sanitation reforms of the nineteenth century. He put great stress on the importance of wide, well-ventilated streets. "A free currant of air for ventila-

15. Moses had been intrigued by an article in the *Medical Repository*, 1 (1797), 165-71, on "Observations upon the Yellow Fever, and its Approximate Cause. In a letter from Dr. George Davidson, dated Fort-Royal, Martinique, Sept. 20, 1796, to James Mease, M.D. Resident Physician of the Port of Philadelphia." Moses seemed to agree with Dr. Davidson's suggestion that "hydrogene gas is the exciting or proximate cause of fever, modified possibly by numberless external and accidental causes." See Moses' extended discussion of the subject in his "Account of the Malignant . . . or Yellow Fever."

tion," he insisted, "ought to be the care of all who build or lay streets—for what is a fine house, without a free access of air to it, or a narrow street that cannot be passed in times of fire." He pointed out that a narrow street seemed to promote infectious diseases whereas wide ones were scarcely ever touched. He recòmmended that the narrow alleys and streets in the "contagious ground" be cleaned out and, when possible, widened, and that a wide street be built through Fox Hill to permit the circulation of air in that highly contagious area. Moses had little respect for the traditional methods of treating yellow fever and little confidence that a cure would very soon be found. This attitude helps to explain his promotion of public sanitation and general health laws.

Moses' interest in laws establishing quarantine and inspection stations was intensified by an increase, in 1797-98, of the number of smallpox cases in the state. Everyone recognized that smallpox was contagious and that it could be imported. In the winter of 1797, following the yellow fever epidemic, Moses was appointed to a state committee to draft legislation to control smallpox inoculation. Considering his general interest in public health and his direct involvement in drafting smallpox legislation, it was inevitable that he should be fascinated by Dr. Benjamin Waterhouse's experiments with Dr. Edward Jenner's new method of immunization against smallpox—vaccination with cowpox matter. When he read Dr. Waterhouse's article—"Something Curious in the Medical Line"—in the *Columbian Centinel* for March 16, 1799, and heard of Dr. Waterhouse's experiments with his own children, he saw immediately the importance of this remarkable achievement and called it to the attention of two Providence physicians, Thomas Dyer and Levi Wheaton.[16] Since Moses was a friend of Dr. Water-

16. A good account of Jenner's work is in Louis H. Roddis, *Edward Jenner and the Discovery of Smallpox Vaccination* (Menasha, Wisc., 1930). Mr.

house, he easily secured from him some of the precious cowpox vaccine and, assisted by Drs. Wheaton and Dyer, he introduced the revolutionary practice of vaccination into Providence. By the fall of 1800 the two physicians had acquired an independent source of supply of the vaccine— from their own patients—and had developed an extensive vaccination practice in Rhode Island.

Characteristically, Moses now turned his attention to spreading the new method into other towns and states. He wrote to friends in Rhode Island, Connecticut, New York, and Massachusetts, informing them of the progress in Providence and offering to send instructions and vaccine if they were interested in trying the new method.[17] He distributed both information and vaccine without charge, thus contributing to the breaking of the monopoly that some physicians had attempted to establish. Moses sent vaccine about the country in two ways: he inserted pieces of string impregnated with cowpox matter into small wooden tubes and sealed them with a cork or with wax; or he deposited the matter between two pieces of clean glass and sealed them around the edges with beeswax from the hives on his farm. The second method proved to be the more satisfactory.

Although all of his friends eagerly accepted his offer of vaccine and instructions, they reported considerable resistance to vaccination among the people generally. Shadrach Ricketson, a Quaker schoolmaster in Nine Partners, New York, reported that the practice was spreading, although he noted ruefully that "scepticism and incredulity which have attended the introduction of it, still possess the minds of many, and tend greatly to retard the spread and utility of a practice, which, if it is prosecuted, bids fair to save, or give

Roddis includes an excellent bibliography and prints much of the correspondence between Jenner and Waterhouse, and the latter's article in the *Columbian Centinel* (Boston), Mar. 16, 1799.

17. Charles F. Bartlett to Moses Brown, Sept. 5, 1800, and numerous other letters in Moses Brown Papers, X, 12 ff.

Life to Thousands yet unborn."[18] The reaction was similar almost everywhere.

There was reason for skepticism. Many inexperienced and careless people attempted vaccination, frequently with no results, but occasionally with disastrous consequences. In November 1800, Dr. Waterhouse informed Moses that more than three thousand people in Marblehead, Massachusetts, had the smallpox, "and all arising from a gross inattention to the article of matter, which was smallpox instead of Kine-pox."[19] Dr. Waterhouse discouraged inexperienced people from vaccinating and urged qualified practitioners to take the utmost care. He refused to supply physicians who wanted to vaccinate during the winter months, and advised them to wait until spring, "being firmly persuaded that the winter season is not the most favourable for conveying the infection and conducting the disease to the greatest advantage." He was likewise reluctant to accept claims that American cows were capable of producing cowpox matter, and for a year at least he relied on shipments from Dr. Lettsom in England.

Moses was not convinced by Dr. Waterhouse's arguments of the impossibility or undesirability of vaccinating in cold weather. Thus he encouraged Dr. Charles F. Bartlett of Newport to conduct experiments to determine the validity of Dr. Waterhouse's objections. In December Dr. Bartlett reported to Moses that he had inoculated his youngest daughter, "and having done it in the hardest frosty weather, . . . it notwithstanding took effect; and she had got easily over all the urgent symptoms—and nothing but the sore arm remains tedious, she being an Infant." Dr. Bartlett's success did not immediately gain public recognition. Prejudice against vaccination persisted, and Dr. Waterhouse's criticism of winter vaccination retarded its acceptance.

Moses was not convinced by Dr. Waterhouse's claim that

18. June 6, 1802, *ibid.*, 45.
19. *Ibid.*, 22.

American cows were immune to cowpox, and he conducted experiments to test the assertion, vaccinating cows to see if they would get the disease. Although he did not record the outcome of these experiments, they must have been successful, for he wrote Dr. Waterhouse that he was convinced that cowpox was not peculiar to English cows. He also enclosed evidence which the doctor considered "as clearer and of more importance than most of the accounts that I have seen on that doubtful subject." Dr. Waterhouse thought enough of Moses' report to send it to his friends in England.

Moses' attitude towards smallpox vaccination and his efforts to make its benefits available to everyone are typical of his humanitarianism. Generally his activities were in response to a public need; he seldom promoted utopian or fantastic schemes, preferring to work toward goals that could be attained in the foreseeable future.

13

The Lingering Twilight
1800-1836

MOSES' GIFT for practicality was not confined to public affairs; it also extended to his personal life. The death of his wife in 1798 had left him without a companion and his house without a mistress. In May 1799, he married Phebe Lockwood, a widow with several children, from South County. The two had apparently known each other for years, for they both attended the quarterly and yearly meetings in Rhode Island, and corresponded briefly about religious matters during the 1790's. To say any more about the event would be mere speculation. It is sufficient to note that the match was a success, lasting for nine pleasant years before Phebe died in 1809 at the age of sixty-one.

Shortly after Moses acquired a wife, he lost his brother John. Moses had a fondness for his brother which their numerous differences through the years had failed to diminish. The feeling was mutual, and when John was in Washington as a Congressman, he wrote chatty letters to Moses about national politics and life among the great men of the nation. John's last two years were spent in his comfortable mansion on Power's Lane in Providence where, despite a general deterioration of his health, he continued to pursue

his extensive business interests. He was a mountainous man,
so huge that he filled the entire seat of his chaise, requiring
his grandchildren, who usually rode with him, to sit between
his legs on the floorboards. He refused to heed his brother's
suggestions about diet and exercise, and in his weakened
condition he could not throw off the effects of a mild cold.
He died on September 20, 1803, at the age of sixty-six,
leaving Moses the last survivor of the four brothers.

Moses, always a pessimistic fatalist about death, did not
expect to live long after his brother died. He had made out
his will in 1781 and had frequently brought it up to date
when he was ill. In December 1800, he sustained a serious
injury when he fell from his horse in front of Stephen
Ganno's house where he had gone to pay his respects to the
minister whose wife Mary (Moses' cousin) had died.[1] The
injury was aggravated by exposure, for the accident occurred
late at night, and he lay unconscious in the cold for several
hours before he was discovered. Although confined to the
house for the remainder of the winter, he made a remarkable—and to him, surprising—recovery within a year.

Indeed, the following January when a fire broke out
at the foot of Planet Street, Moses' response to the alarm
was immediate and vigorous for a man of sixty-three
years. A few years earlier he had constructed a fire fighting apparatus for use on his estate. Quickly loading it
into a carriage, he drove hurriedly down the hill to the fire,
which by the time he arrived had consumed his store and
nearly all of Welcome Arnold's.[2] Many other business
establishments and warehouses were lost on the west side of
South Main Street, and when the wind shifted from north
to west the "whole range along the North side of Power's
Lane" was threatened, including John Brown's mansion.

1. Moses Brown to John Brown, Dec. 17, 1800, and John's reply, Dec. 29,
Moses Brown Papers, X, 24, 25.
2. For what follows, see the manuscripts published in *R. I. Hist.*, 4 (1945),
80-83, and comments by Robert Morton Hazelton.

As a precautionary measure, Moses stationed a man on the roof of his brother's house to beat out sparks from the nearby blaze. He then spurred his horse up and down the street, the wide brim of his big black hat flapping like the wings of a crow in flight, shouting instructions to the fire fighters through his trumpet, directing that old houses be pulled down on Power's Lane, that Clark and Nightingale's store be blown up along with several other buildings in the path of the flames, and that the fire engines be brought into play at strategic points. Every able-bodied man and boy turned out to fight the blaze. Women and children carried merchandise and household goods out of the threatened buildings. Finally, Moses, recorded, "we were happy to see the devouring flames stayed."

It was the "greatest and most calamitous fire" the town of Providence had ever experienced, the value of the burned stores and wharves totaling nearly $200,000—an enormous sum for that day. Moses observed that the fire had raged at precisely the spot where the yellow fever had been most severe the previous fall, although he quickly added that "no analogy can be traced." For years Moses had been urging the town council to provide better fire-fighting equipment and a more dependable source of water. As usual, action was taken only after the damage had been done. Moses, with Samuel Jackson, was appointed to investigate a showering system developed by Solomon Thayer. Experiments of the apparatus were conducted at Moses' estate and at his expense. At first, despite several improvements in the pump and pipes designed to spray water on the roof of a building, Moses and Jackson found the equipment too expensive and inefficient to recommend to the council; later, after he had continued the experiments and suggested valuable improvements to Thayer, Moses advised the town to buy some of the equipment and the town followed his recommendation.

Moses' main improvement in the fire-fighting equipment

had to do with the piping. He thought perforated tin pipes would be better than the commonly used wooden pipes. An incidental virtue of metal pipes was that they could also serve as lightning rods, which would encourage installation on buildings. With Moses' improvements Solomon Thayer's sprinkling system was a forerunner of the modern systems that came into use in the 1830's.

Throughout his last years Moses remained active in public affairs, and even though he did not occupy the center of the stage, he had considerable influence on the course of events. Unlike many men who cling to positions of influence and power long after they have ceased to fulfill their responsibilities, Moses resigned his offices when he felt that he could no longer be useful. He gave to Obadiah and to William Almy the stock he owned in Almy, Brown and Slater, and brought to a close his business relationship with Samuel Slater, who was now a prosperous entrepreneur. In 1809 he resigned as a director of the Providence Bank, and a few years later he relinquished his post as secretary-treasurer of the Central Bridge Company.

His interest and activities in the agricultural society continued unabated, however, and in the two decades after the turn of the century, his farm assumed the character of an agricultural experiment station. Because much of his land was of poor quality and not suitable for cultivation, Moses turned it into a sheep pasture. Sometime before 1810 he acquired a number of Merino sheep and began systematically to improve the breed of his sizable flock.[3] Just prior to the war with England, when America was flooded with Merino sheep and the price of these fine wool producers dropped so low that most owners could not afford to feed them, he took several of his friends' rams into his pasture to save them from the butchers. When the price of wool rose

3. Moses Brown to Levi McKeen, Aug. 10, 1811, Moses Brown Papers, XII, 18, and numerous other letters in this volume.

and Merino sheep were again in demand, he returned them to their owners.

Moses acquired a reputation as an agricultural reformer in many parts of the United States. People wrote him for advice about beekeeping, fertilizers, growing crops in sandy soil, and methods of grinding corn for feed. These requests Moses gladly fulfilled, frequently sending books or magazines along with his remarks. In 1815, Jethro Wood, the inventor of the cast-iron plow with interchangeable parts, called on Moses and solicited aid in introducing his invention into Rhode Island.[4] The two men found much to talk about, not only Wood's plow but the "Theory of the operation of gypsum on Vegetation" and other technical subjects. Wood thought Moses was a good farmer and told David Thomas, the author of a successful travel book, that Moses had used gypsum "successfully in situations where others had totally failed."

For several years the most serious thing that bothered Moses was a growth on his nose that increased in size until, in 1812, it was "as large as a small sized cherry."[5] Moses wrote to Dr. Shadrach Ricketson of New York that "it has grown larger the last year yet is not very troublesome, it often aches, but seldom smarts [and] is not open."[6] Because of his aversion to surgery and his advanced age—he was over seventy-four—Moses thought "it would be as well to let it alone." His children and the town doctors, however, advised him to have it removed. Although Moses said he would, a sketch made of him in 1823 shows that he did not, after all, submit to the knife.

From Moses' correspondence for the period of the embargo and the War of 1812 it is clear that he abhorred both.

4. John Earl to Moses Brown, 1815; David Thomas to Moses Brown, Jan. 21, 1817, ibid., XII, 63, XIII, 6.
5. Quoted from a letter by Stephen Gould to Thomas Thompson, Apr. 4, 1823, in Kelsey, History of Moses Brown School, 367.
6. Nov. 12, 1812, Moses Brown Papers, XII, 36.

Although he did not engage in the public debate, he discussed the events in his private letters.[7] He admitted that both France and England had given the United States "Legal cause or National affront" sufficient for war, but he doubted if anything would be gained by fighting. Instead of going to war and involving the country in all kinds of difficulties, he suggested that the administration take off all restrictions on importations, double the duties on English goods, and "promote our manufactures by which means the present debt for preparations will be paid by impost, [and] our country remain in peace."

Once fighting started Moses threw his weight behind the peace movement that was gaining headway in America and England. He became acquainted with men like David L. Dodge, the New York Presbyterian merchant who published *The Mediator's Kingdom Not of This World* in 1809, James Romeyn, president of the American Bible Society and peace advocate, and Noah Worcester, the Massachusetts minister, editor of the journal *Friend of Peace,* and leader of the Massachusetts Peace Society. During the war and for several years thereafter Moses and Worcester carried on a friendly correspondence, in which they discussed not only the activities of the peace societies but subjects such as temperance, capital punishment, slavery, and the Bible Society movement. Moses himself was one of the founders of the Rhode Island and Providence Plantations Bible Society and was elected a vice-president of the American Bible Society in 1816. Two years later, with the help of Thomas Arnold and George Benson, he provided the leadership in establishing the Rhode Island Peace Society, and he helped to finance the printing and distribution of thousands of pamphlets in the cause of peace.[8]

7. Moses Brown to J. B. Howell, Apr. 27, 1812, *ibid.,* 27.
8. Moses Brown Papers, Austin MSS., VII, "Peace," Moses Brown School Lib. Moses reluctantly accepted the office of treasurer of the Rhode Island Peace Society after his son Obadiah died in 1822; *Sixth Annual Report of the*

Among Moses' numerous humanitarian activities in his declining years was his support of the Connecticut Asylum for the Deaf and Dumb at Hartford, which was established in 1817.[9] He had always shown great compassion for the physically disabled—his son had a lame leg—and he made generous contributions to support students in the Hartford institution. He contributed funds and a lot for a schoolhouse to the "Female Society for the Education of Colored Children on the Lancastrian plan" and frequently attended the examinations of the scholars in the tiny schoolroom on Middle Street.[10] He was also one of the founders of the Providence Athenaeum and of the Rhode Island Historical Society, and he donated money and "a large number of books, pamphlets, and newspapers" to the American Antiquarian Society in Worcester.[11]

The most lasting and, to Moses, his greatest achievement in the field of education, however, was the re-establishment of the yearly meeting school which had closed years before for a "vacation," and had stayed closed. Moses, who had remained treasurer of the school committee, had invested the small fund carefully; by 1813 the few hundred dollars had grown to over $9,000. Still, this amount was inadequate to buy land and to build and support a school. Repeated

Rhode-Island and Providence Plantations Peace Society, June 24, 1823 . . . (Providence, 1826).

9. "Subscription to send George Comstock to the Assylum for the Deaf and Dumb at Hartford," Feb. 18, 1818, Moses Brown Papers, Misc. MSS., K-AB.

10. Subscription list, Dec. 27, 1805, Moses Brown Papers, Austin MSS., IV, "Education," Moses Brown School Lib.; Harriat T. Chase to Moses Brown, Oct. 17, 1818, Moses Brown Papers, XIII, 26. The lot Moses gave to the school he purchased from a Negro, George McCarty, for $200. Moses Brown to "George Mccarty and others concerned," Jan. 20, 1819; and Nicholas Brown, Jr., to Moses Brown, Apr. 17, 1819, *ibid.*, 32, 33. See a *Short History of the African Union Meeting and School House, Erected in Providence (R. I.) in the years 1819, '20, '21, with Rules for its future government* (Providence, 1821). Moses' deed for the lot is printed here. He stipulated that the school should be open to all denominations of Christians.

11. J. B. Romeyn to Moses Brown, Jan. 3, 1817, Moses Brown Papers, XIII, 5.

appeals for additional pledges had been ignored by Friends and the project lay dormant.

During his convalescence from a serious illness in the winter of 1813, Moses concluded that he must make one last effort to reopen the Portsmouth Meeting School. Looking back on the Portsmouth school, the seventy-six-year-old patriarch could now see that an important reason for its failure had been its location. In a small town, isolated from those most anxious for its success, the school had been neglected by the country Friends, to whom education was suspect. Moses naturally concluded that Providence was the logical place for the school. Here materials and labor could be easily and cheaply obtained, and interested Friends could supervise the construction and operation of the school. Moses had often thought that the ideal site was on Prospect Hill back of the college. He owned much of the land there, and if the school committee would agree to support his efforts to revive the school, he conceived of donating a plot of ground—43 acres—suitable for the purpose. There was some need for speed; the state was about to carry out a land re-evaluation scheme, and if the donation were delayed, Moses would have to pay higher taxes on the property. The money, he thought, could be better used to support the school.[12]

In May, still infirm from his long illness, Moses submitted his plan to the Meeting for Sufferings, which recommended that the Yearly Meeting accept Moses' offer.[13] Although members of the Yearly Meeting wished to reopen the school, they pointed out that the building fund of $9,300 was inadequate to finance both the building and operation of a school. The success of the project would depend upon

12. During the winter Moses had discussed the school with a number of Friends to test their reaction to his plan; John Osborne to Moses Brown, Apr. 12, 1814, *ibid.*, XII, 54.

13. New England Meeting for Sufferings, 1793-1842, 166-67, Moses Brown School Lib.

Friends' willingness to support it, and in the past that had not been very great. To test the temper of the members the Yearly Meeting authorized the Meeting for Sufferings to circulate new subscriptions, urging Friends to contribute according to their ability, reminding them that they were "only stewards of the goods we possess, that we hold them by a very uncertain tenure, and that a righteous and benevolent disposition of a part of them may call down a blessing upon the remainder."[14]

The response to the appeal was more enthusiastic than at any previous time. During the year Friends in New England pledged nearly $10,000 to the school fund.[15] At the Yearly Meeting in 1815, a committee was appointed to draw up plans for separate school buildings for male and female students, but it eventually decided on a single building.[16] In the fall of 1815 the contract was let to the firm of Almy and Brown,[17] but construction did not begin until the next spring.[18]

The building plan called for an "H"-shaped structure, with the center section three stories high; the costs were estimated at approximately $20,000.[19] As the building progressed, Moses' health rapidly improved, and he drove down to the site every day in his chaise to supervise the project. When subscriptions were slow in coming in, he frequently advanced money out of his own pocket and from time to time made generous outright contributions. Before the

14. June 14, 1814, New England Yearly Meeting Records, 1788-1819, 371-72, Moses Brown School Lib.
15. Ibid., 388-89.
16. New England Meeting for Sufferings, 1793-1842, 175-76, Moses Brown School Lib.
17. Ibid., 176-77, 186-87, 188, 200.
18. Ibid., Dec. 6, 1815, Jan. 31, May 1, 1816, 176-86.
19. Ibid., 175-76. The estimate turned out to be too conservative. Rising costs of material and labor brought the total expenditures to over $24,000. Moses, as treasurer of the school committee and of the Meeting for Sufferings, was never able to collect the subscriptions as fast as the money was needed.

building was completed, the school committee decided to
add a story to the center part of the building for a meeting
room and to finish the house "in a better manner than was
contemplated."[20] The cost of these additions, estimated at
$7,000, was met by further subscriptions, half of which came
from Obadiah and Almy.

By the time of the Yearly Meeting in 1818 the building
was almost ready for use, and the school committee expected
to begin classes sometime during the winter. The task of
procuring superintendents and instructors, hiring a housekeeper staff, and handling administrative details was en-
trusted to a joint committee composed of members from the
Meeting for Sufferings, the school committee, and the Yearly
Meeting of Women Friends.[21] Moses did most of this work,
however, and on important decisions the committee deferred
to his judgment. He carried on a heavy correspondence with
Friends about school management, seeking advice on subjects
ranging from the best cooking stoves to the "general bill of
fare as to dayly or weekly breakfasts dinner and supper" and
general rules and regulations for Friends' schools.[22]

Finally, on the first Monday of the new year, 1819, the
New England Yearly Meeting Boarding School opened its
doors and resumed its task of providing a guarded education
for Friends' children. Now in his eighty-first year, Moses
nevertheless derived greater satisfaction from the reopening
of the school than from the numerous public services he had
performed throughout his long life. The financial position
of the institution was precarious for the first few years, but
that problem was solved in 1822 when, on the death of
Obadiah Brown, the school acquired the grand sum of

20. *Ibid.*, 178; New England Yearly Meeting Records, 1788-1819, 413-14,
Moses Brown School Lib.
21. New England Yearly Meeting Records, 427 ff., Moses Brown School Lib.
22. Moses Brown to M[icajah] Collins, Aug. 10, 1818, and Collins' reply,
Aug. 25; Thomas Willis to Moses Brown, Sept. 27, 1818; Moses Brown to
Collins, Oct. 15, Nov. 23, 1818, to Matthew and Betsy Purinton, Oct. 23, 1818,
to Sophrinia Foster, Nov. 23, 1818, Moses Brown Papers, XIII, 25-28.

$100,000, the largest single contribution made to an American educational institution up to that time.[23] Moses continued to make contributions of money and books to the school, and he served as treasurer of the school fund until near his death. He had an office in the new building and spent much of his time there talking with teachers, students, and visitors.

The students enjoyed his company immensely. One of the early pupils, Mary E. Nicholas from North Kingston, kept a diary that reflects the attention he devoted to students. She related one episode in which seventeen girls visited Moses' farm.[24] "We had a royal time," she recorded, "went into the house, we had some excellent wine with water then went out to the mulberries. I realy injoyed myself well, we ate as many as we wished. Then they asked us to go to the garden and get some currents. The bushes were loaded with them. Time to go. Very pleasant walk hom." Until he died, Moses always made the students feel at home in his Elmgrove mansion. He frequently brought vegetables and fruit from his farm to the school kitchen and regularly attended the religious services held in the school meetinghouse. He gave a large part of his valuable library to the school and presented students with books, maps, and scientific equipment. His generosity and kindness were emulated by many other Friends for years to come.

The nature and tone of the school was in certain fundamental ways determined by the influence Moses exerted during the remaining years of his life. As far as he was concerned, the three principles by which the school officials

23. Obadiah had made out his will in 1814, and added a codicil on Oct. 14, 1822, the day before he died; *ibid.*, XIV, 70. For official copies see Probate Court Records, Wills, No. 14, 132-39, City Court House, Providence. The inventory of his estate is in Probate Court Records, Inventory, No. 1, 518-23, City Court House, Providence. Obadiah gave most of his library to the school.

24. Diary of Mary E. Nicholas, Moses Brown Papers, Austin MSS., XIX, "Yearly Meeting School," Moses Brown School Lib.

should be guided had been laid down thirty-one years earlier
when the school had opened at Portsmouth: first, the school
must provide an education for poor children; second, it must
be open to children not members of the Society—it must
serve not only the Society of Friends but the entire New
England community; and third, it must provide a course of
advanced studies for students of unusual qualifications. Not
all these goals were achieved at once, but before Moses' death
they had been generally accepted and put into practice, and
in his will he provided the funds to perpetuate them. The
crowning tribute to Moses' role in founding the yearly meeting school was paid in 1904. In recognition of "his generous
charity and far vision, his practical statesmanship joined to
high spiritual ideals, his sterling character and great soul,"
the New England Yearly Meeting Boarding School was
named the "Moses Brown School."[25]

Moses often commented on his advanced age in letters
to friends, and each year he thought would be his last. But
the years passed until he was in his nineties.[26] He continued
to attend the monthly, quarterly, and yearly meetings as well
as the meetings of the elders and ministers, the Meeting for
Sufferings, and sessions of the school committee. Although
his correspondence did not cease, it dropped off sharply after
his ninetieth birthday in 1828. A rheumatic condition made
writing difficult, and he stopped making copies of many of
his letters, merely noting on those he received that he had
replied.

There are two oil portraits of Moses late in life, both of
them made during the years he was involved in the reopening
of the school. The most famous is that by John Wesley
Jarvis from a pencil sketch surreptitiously drawn by a

25. Kelsey, *History of Moses Brown School*, 126-27.
26. See particularly the touching letter Moses wrote to Noah Webster in
which he gives a clinical description of Obadiah's illness and death, remarking at the end, "It has often passed as a Query in my own mind, what am I
continued so long here for?" Oct. 30, 1822, Moses Brown Papers, XIV, 9.

FRIENDS' BOARDING SCHOOL, PROVIDENCE, RHODE ISLAND

The New England Yearly Meeting Boarding School, which opened in Providence in January 1819, was built through the efforts of Moses Brown on land he donated. In 1904 its name was changed to the Moses Brown School. This lithograph was made by Pendleton's Lithography in Boston, Mass., and was published by Pliny Earle, Jr., in 1831.

nephew, William J. Harris, in 1823, when Moses was eighty-five.[27] Like many Quakers, Moses had an antipathy to having his portrait painted, and he had withstood the constant urgings of his family and friends. Tradition has it that the subject came up one day when young Harris was at Moses' house and Moses, becoming annoyed with the conversation, went into the library to read. Later, young Harris was sketching in the garden and noticed Moses seated in full view at the window. Hiding behind a nearby shrub, Harris quickly made a sketch of him, and the next year Jarvis executed the oil painting that hangs in Sayles Hall on the Brown University campus. The Jarvis portrait is a profile view showing a venerable old man, rather stout, with a long, sharp nose, and small bright eyes shaded by a wide-brimmed hat. He had apparently lost most of his teeth, for his lips recede and his chin protrudes noticeably. The steel-rimmed spectacles and the wool stocking cap he always wore are also shown.

The second oil portrait was copied by Henry E. Kinney from a watercolor painted by Joseph Partridge, a Providence artist, sometime in the 1820's.[28] The copy bears slight resemblance to the original, which is a clumsy, amateurish effort; the wart on Moses' nose, clearly evident in Partridge's watercolor, is absent in the oil painting. The Ann Mary Brown Memorial Library in Providence has the original oil painting, and copies of it hang in the Rhode Island Historical Society and the Moses Brown School.

The two subjects that had attracted Moses' attention when he first became a Friend—war and slavery—continued to interest him. He had long thought that in the United States the two evils were inextricably bound together. He

27. James Greene to Augustine Jones, Sept. 17, 1887, and Jones to R. W. Kelsey, June 20, 1888, Moses Brown Papers, Austin MSS., XX, "General," Moses Brown School Lib.

28. See frontispiece. Partridge's watercolor is in the John Carter Brown Lib.

was convinced that unless slavery was abolished the North would either separate from the South or resort to force to abolish it. While he vigorously supported those who called for federal action under the Constitution to abolish slavery, he also made generous contributions to the various peace societies in New York, Connecticut, and Rhode Island to educate the public to reject war as a solution to the problem. The separation, if it came, should be a peaceful one. In 1833 he wrote a long letter to John Quincy Adams concerning the argument in Congress over the anti-slavery petitions that were flooding the capital. Adams had voted against allowing the petitions to be received by the House of Representatives and Moses wanted to know why. Written in his ninety-fifth year, the letter was lucid and coherent, reflecting Moses' mental alertness and his continued interest in national affairs.

In May 1834 Moses made out his will and testament for the last time and in June the next year added a codicil.[29] The following winter he was ill for several months, but revived sufficiently in the spring of 1836 to visit the school and attend meetings. In May at the "advanced age of 97 years and eight months," he composed a short poem for one of the students and presented it to her. The poem, entitled "Remedy for Injuries," reads:

Have any wounded you with injurys
Meet them with patience.
Hasty words rankle the wound
Soft language dresses it.
Forgiveness cures it
And oblivion takes away the scar.[30]

29. Moses' final will was made out on May 12, 1834, and a codicil added on June 25, 1835. Probate Court Records, Wills, No. 14, 23-36, City Court House, Providence. The inventory of his estate is in Probate Court Records, Inventory, No. 4, 357-61, City Court House, Providence. By the time of his death Moses had given away most of his library, but he still had over six hundred volumes. See Moses Brown Papers, XIV, 69, for a copy of his will.

30. Printed *Reports of Boarding School Committee and (temporarily) Programs of New England Yearly Meeting*, in Moses Brown School Lib.

When Moses wrote this poem he knew that he did not have long to live; although still mentally alert, he was very tired. In preparation for the end, and in order to leave no business unattended, he presented to the clerk of the New England Yearly Meeting his resignation as treasurer of the school committee, a position he had held for fifty-three years.

I have, through thee, to ask of the Yearly Meeting a release of the care and labour of being the treasurer of the Yearly Meeting's School Fund, which I have sustained from its commencement on Rhode Island, under the care of the Meeting for Sufferings, and since under the School Committee, now about fifty-three years; and though my concern for the propriety of the institution remains, I find my age, debility and often infirmities are such as induces me to ask for release from the necessary cares and labours of that office, and that some suitable person may be appointed in my place; which please to mention on my behalf to the meeting; and thy compliance will oblige.

Thy friend,

Moses Brown.[31]

On September 6, 1836, seventeen days before his ninety-eighth birthday, he died.

31. The letter is in the New England Yearly Meeting Records, 1836-1847, 5, Moses Brown School Lib.; it is quoted in Kelsey, *History of Moses Brown School*, 71.

Epilogue

As I walk'd through the wilderness of this world, I lighted on a certain place, where was a Den, and laid me down in that place to sleep: and as I slept, I dreamed a Dream. I dreamed, and behold *I saw a man clothed with Rags standing in a certain place, with his face from his own House, a book in his hand, and a great burden upon his back.* I looked, and saw him open the Book, and read therein; and as he read, he wept and trembled: and not being able longer to contain, he brake out with a lamentable cry; saying, *what shall I do?*

Christian in John Bunyan's
Pilgrim's Progress.[1]

A**T THE TIME** of his first wife's death Moses, like Christian, felt that his previous life had been a journey through an evil world. Like Christian he felt that he had suddenly become bowed down with an insupportable burden of sin. He too turned his back on his house, sought frantically for the answer to his problem in scriptures, and finally cried out in despair: "What shall I do?"

Moses' journey in search of the answer was no easier,

1. John Bunyan, *The Pilgrim's Progress with Biographical Introduction and New Index. Illustrated with 25 Drawings by George Cruikshank* (London, 1912), 11.

no shorter, than Christian's. At first he thought that his burden was the world itself, thus he attempted complete withdrawal, tried to put an end, immediate and total, to his previous business, political, and social affairs. It was while he was in this state that he fled to the security of the Society of Friends, surrendered himself to God, and resolved to wait for the divine light within to show the way to safety. He was attracted to Quakerism because most of the people he met during the critical months of his emotional crisis were Friends who were withdrawing from the world, particularly the political world. They rejected the idea that politics was a necessary, normal part of man's existence; in fact they subordinated the reality of man's existence in this world to some transcendent mystical reality. They believed that the only way of preventing corruption in politics was refusal to participate in it, ignoring the fact that this merely left the field clear for other men. The temptation for Moses to follow their lead was great, but in the end he did not give in to it completely. In time he emerged from retirement; he found that the answer to the question, "what shall I do?" was involvement in the affairs of the world, although he accepted it reluctantly.

Moses had acquired a sense of social responsibility from association with Uncle Obadiah and his brothers, Governor Stephen Hopkins, Daniel Jenckes, and other friends in Rhode Island, who shared with many other people of the eighteenth century the idea that men had a duty to engage in public affairs and thus contribute to the progress of the world. Moses accepted their view almost without thinking. He believed in the certain advancement of society if men would only accept the responsibility for the welfare of their fellows. Those more richly endowed with talent and wealth had an obligation to help the poor, the afflicted, the unfortunate. They also had a duty to create a world in which human beings could live a decent life and maintain their self-respect.

Before his conversion Moses had on more than one occasion told his brother John that indifference to the public good was immoral. After indulging for a time in self-pity and concern for the salvation of his own soul, Moses realized that if living in an evil world was a weighty burden, withdrawal from it and refusal to do anything to purge the world of its evils was not the way to lighten the load.

His conviction was reinforced and redirected by Quakerism. Although Moses was attracted to Quakerism at first because of its otherworldliness and because he thought it would enable him to achieve salvation, he soon began to embrace its tradition of social responsibility, a tradition as old as Quakerism itself. As the result of an exhaustive study of Quakerism, he learned that in origin it was a religion of social action. He admired the early founders, particularly George Fox, because they labored courageously and humanely to reform an evil and hostile world.

For Moses, rejection of his desire to retire from the world did not come quickly or easily. For years he was a deeply divided man. He participated in public affairs, but he always felt guilty about it and wrote long apologetic explanations to Friends. Eventually he was able to reconcile his desire to isolate himself from the evils of the world with his sense of duty toward society and his fellow man. In so doing he reconciled two strong traditions in Quakerism at a time when most Friends were finding it impossible.

He also reconciled two traditions in the Brown family, the one represented by his grandfather who emphasized the priority of the spiritual side of man's life, and the other, represented by his father and his brothers, who gave greater attention to the secular side of man's activities. Moses passed both these traditions on to other members of the Brown family, particularly to his son Obadiah and to his nephew, Nicholas Brown, Jr.

After his conversion, the event that drew Moses into wel-

fare activity was the American Revolution and its devastating effects on the Society of Friends. During the long years of warfare, he gave full rein to this sympathetic impulse. To Moses the war with England was a tragedy, not because like many Quakers he deplored the severance of ties with England—in this he thought America justified—but because the war caused human suffering and was morally degrading. Throughout the conflict he worked energetically and successfully to soften its effects. Significantly his efforts were not limited to Quakers. Many people deplored the neutralism of the Quakers which they considered merely a cover for loyalist sympathies. Moses' strict neutralism and his selfless efforts to help innocent victims of the war regardless of their religious or political affiliation undercut much of the criticism of the Quakers in New England. The practice of nonpartisan relief established by Moses during the Revolution in time became a fixed principle in the Society of Friends.

Moses' wartime humanitarian activity was an apprenticeship for a lifetime of service to others. From Quakerism he had learned compassion, a virtue that took deep root in his character and grew stronger over the years; infused with his sense of social responsibility, it molded him into one of America's important humanitarians. Few men in America have been involved so closely over such a long period in so many useful and successful humanitarian projects. He was a pioneer in movements to provide education and training for the handicapped, and for orphans and Negroes; he was among the first sponsors of urban renewal and development, sanitation and public health; he was active in prison reform and the promotion of international peace. When the reform movement swept America during the early decades of the nineteenth century, Moses was already a veteran of many causes. It is no wonder that so many people sought his advice and counsel. A visit made by President Andrew Jackson

and Vice-President Martin Van Buren to Moses' Elmgrove estate in 1833 symbolized public recognition of his great services to humanity.

The influence he exerted within the Society of Friends was much greater than is generally recognized. Writers on Quakerism have concentrated so much on Friends in Pennsylvania that they have missed the significance of Quaker activity elsewhere. Moses' contribution to the Quaker tradition of humanitarianism is also obscured by his strict adherence to another tenet—modesty: the habit, Moses' Uncle Elisha once remarked, of hiding one's talents under a bushel. If Moses had possessed less of this virtue, his role would have been more widely recognized.

Of the many humanitarian projects in which Moses participated, his anti-slavery activities deserve special mention. He was an opponent of the slave trade and a crusader for the freedom of the slaves long before most men of his time even recognized the evil of those practices. To champion such reforms when he did was an act of high personal courage that cost him, besides considerable money, many friends of long standing and the frequent estrangement of at least one member of his own family. And he actually accomplished more than any other American anti-slavery leader of the eighteenth century, including such notables as John Woolman, Anthony Benezet, and the Reverend Samuel Hopkins. He spearheaded the movement that culminated in the abolition of the slave trade and of slavery in New England and set an example for other states to follow. Those institutions would undoubtedly have survived longer had Moses not persisted in his efforts to abolish them. Moreover, unlike many of the nineteenth-century reformers who seemed unconcerned about what happened to slaves after they were freed, Moses always recognized that provision must be made for educating them and assisting them to adjust to the responsibilities of free men.

Moses' early attack on slavery illustrates another conspicuous quality—a modern cast of mind. His feet were
planted firmly in his own time, and his face turned toward
the future. Possessed of a strong historical sense, he read
and studied avidly the early Quaker writers, but his purpose
was to learn what they had to teach him about the principles
of conduct, not to find a program of action. The problems
of the seventeenth century and Friends' answers to them were
not, in his opinion, the same as those of his own time. Unlike some people who become conservative in their old age
and close their minds to the changes in the world they are
about to leave, Moses never lost interest in the events going
on about him. He maintained a youthful optimism about
the future. His consistent modernity is all the more remarkable when it is remembered that he lived for almost a
century and was active for most of that period. When he
died in 1836, America was a vastly different country from
the one he entered in 1738—it had passed through several
eras. Yet Moses did not belong more to one than to another.
In his last years his body slowly declined—his eyesight began
to fail, and his once firm hand could no longer guide the
quill—but his mind remained alert. Young people still found
his comments about the problems of the day worth heeding;
for example, shortly before he died, William Lloyd Garrison,
the rising star of the anti-slavery movement, journeyed to
Providence to talk to him about slavery and abolitionism.

He narrowly missed becoming a man of the first rank,
partly because of his conversion to Quakerism, which blunted
his personal ambitions and diverted him from participation
in some of the major political issues of his time—the Revolution, the drafting of the Constitution, and the successful creation of a new nation.

Rather than a great man, he was a good man. But like
all men he had his defects, although they appear as faint
blemishes, mere flyspecks on his character. His greatest sin

was an excess of moral pride. This trait was most apparent during his early life. Before his conversion to Quakerism he let few opportunities pass to demonstrate to himself and to others his moral excellence. His conversion to Quakerism taught him humility. Eventually he was able to curb, but not entirely to eradicate, this early trait.

Moses' great curiosity about the world of man and nature, the variety of his experiences, his ability to sense the direction of events before it was apparent to others, the high moral tone of his life—these were the elements of his character that attracted people to him. In the range of his interests and the intensity with which he pursued them, he was on a par with such giants as Franklin and Jefferson. He shared with them a willingness to consider seriously ideas that challenged long cherished beliefs, and he had a talent for channeling other people's energies as well as his own along constructive lines. He was more practical minded, more utilitarian than either Franklin or Jefferson. Most of the things he did he did with a particular end in mind, but frequently his innate curiosity carried him far beyond that end.

After Moses became a Quaker his qualities of social responsibility, humanitarianism, modernity, curiosity, and practicality figured prominently in almost everything he did. They were brought sharply into focus in economic activity. It is true that following the death of his first wife Moses withdrew from his earlier business enterprises, but he did not cease to engage in business; instead, he became far less concerned about personal profit than about social service. As a Quaker he was involved in a wide range of business affairs— salt manufacturing, foreign trade, book publishing, bridge building, potash production, among others. His involvement in textile manufacturing grew out of a feeling that its development would provide jobs for Quaker children, contribute to the well-being of the community, and promote American economic independence, as well as enable his son-

in-law to make a living. He was well aware that devotion to religious principles depended upon a certain measure of material security. He saw more clearly than many Quakers the interrelatedness of economic and religious life; he most often approached the solution to moral problems by economic means. But for himself he sought profit in business only as capital for humanitarian purposes.

If the desire for fortune was not present in Moses, neither was the desire for fame. There are those rare individuals who can work tirelessly and successfully for no other reasons than a feeling of responsibility to improve the world and a genuine love of mankind. Moses Brown was such a man.

Bibliographical Essay

THE indispensable sources for this study of Moses Brown have been the manuscript collections in the libraries in Providence, Rhode Island. Of greatest value are the Moses Brown Papers in the Rhode Island Historical Society, which contain copies of Moses Brown's outgoing correspondence, as well as the letters he received. Of almost equal importance are papers of the Brown family in the John Carter Brown Library, which have been described in detail by James B. Hedges in "The Brown Papers," Amer. Antiq. Soc., *Proceedings,* 51 (1941), 21-36. Next in importance have been the manuscripts in the Moses Brown School Library vault: the Austin manuscripts, which consist mostly of Moses Brown correspondence and papers, the New England Yearly Meeting records, and numerous other manuscripts related to Quakerism. Although the John Hay Library contains many manuscripts about the founding of Rhode Island College (Brown University), most of them are copies from originals in the Moses Brown Papers in the Rhode Island Historical Society. The Rhode Island Archives in the State House at Providence contain extremely valuable

material throwing light on Moses Brown's political career
and on the history of Providence and the colony.   I have
also used the materials available in the Historical Society of
Pennsylvania, the Haverford College Library, the Arch Street
Library in Philadelphia, and the William L. Clements Library, Ann Arbor, Michigan, although many of these letters
are clear copies of drafts available in the Rhode Island Historical Society.

There has been only one full-length study of Moses
Brown's life, that by Robert Morton Hazelton, *Let Freedom
Ring!* (New York, 1957), but it deals only with his life as a
Quaker.   Very brief appraisals have been made by Augustine
Jones, *Moses Brown: His Life and Services* (Providence,
1892), and by Claude Moore Fuess in the *Dictionary of
American Biography.*

I have, of course, relied heavily on the work of other
scholars in this study.   But I see little point in listing all the
printed books and articles that I have consulted; they are
mentioned in the footnotes at the appropriate places.   I
would, however, like to include here those printed works
that have been of the greatest assistance: Walter C. Bronson,
The History of Brown University (Providence, 1914);
Thomas Edward Drake, *Quakers and Slavery in America*
(New Haven, 1950); William E. Foster, *Stephen Hopkins,
A Rhode Island Statesman: A Study in the Political History
of the Eighteenth Century* (Providence, 1884); Reuben
Aldridge Guild, *History of Brown University, with Illustra-
tive Documents* (Providence, 1867); James B. Hedges, *The
Browns of Providence Plantations: Colonial Years* (Cam-
bridge, Mass., 1952); Rufus M. Jones, *The Quakers in the
American Colonies* (London, 1911); Rayner Wickersham
Kelsey, *Centennial History of Moses Brown School, 1819-
1919* (Providence, 1919); Arnold Lloyd, *Quaker Social History, 1669-1738* (London, 1950); Mary S. Locke, *Anti-Slavery*

in America, from the Introduction of African Slaves to the Prohibition of the Slave Trade, 1619-1808 (Boston, 1901); and George S. White, *Memoir of Samuel Slater, The Father of American Manufactures* . . . *with Remarks on the Moral Influence of Manufactories in the United States* (2d ed.; Philadelphia, 1836).

Index

INDEX

War of 1812, 281-82
Ward-Hopkins Controversy, 29-30, 32
Ward, Gen. Artemas, 122, 123
Ward, Henry, 32, 63-65, 67, 97; and
    Rhode Island College, 58-60
Ward, Samuel, 29, 32, 33, 59, 68
Warren, James, 43, 123
Warren, R. I., 254; and Rhode Island
    College, 55-67, *passim*
Warren Baptist Church, 55, 58
Warwick, R. I., 147
Washington, Gen. George, 120, 121,
    129, 147, 215
Waterhouse, Dr. Benjamin, 173, 273,
    275
Watertown, Mass., 123, 140
Watson, Elkanah, 110
Webster, Noah, 270-71
Wells, Thomas, 178
Wesley, John, 101
West Indies, trade with, 4, 5, 10, 11,
    15, 16, 23, 28, 97, 98, 203-4, 219;
    and slavery, 102; yellow fever im-
    ported from, 266
West, Benjamin, 42, 45
Weybosset Bridge, 31

Weybossett Neck, 244
Whale oil, 18, 203
Wheaton, Dr. Levi, 270, 273, 274
Wheeler, Bennett, 179, 187, 239
Whitefield, George, 146
Wilkinson, Hannah, 226
Wilkinson, Jemima, 146-49
Wilkinson, Jeremiah, 146
Wilkinson, Oziel, 225-26, 230
Williams, Roger, 259
Wilson, William, 74, 79, 86, 88, 125,
    128, 220
Windham, Conn., 16
Winson, Rev. Samuel, 25
Winsor, Olney, 250
Wolcott, Oliver, 209
Wood, Jethro, 281
Woolman, John, 93, 101, 296
Woonsocket, R. I., 90
Worcester, Mass., 209, 211
Worcester, Noah, 282

Yale College, 14, 147
Yearly Meeting of Women Friends,
    286
Yellow fever, 262-73

MOSES BROWN

Reluctant Reformer

by

MACK THOMPSON

Published for the
Institute of Early American History and Culture
at Williamsburg, Virginia

By the University of North Carolina Press   Chapel Hill

MOSES BROWN

This oil portrait was copied by Henry E. Kinney of Worcester, Mass.,
from a watercolor painted by Joseph Partridge of Providence, R. I., in the
1820's. The portrait was given to the Rhode Island Historical Society in
1907 by Obadiah Brown Hadwen. Courtesy of the Rhode Island Historical
Society.

leader in many reform movements—crusades against slavery and war; efforts to provide education for the underprivileged, for orphans, and for Negroes; and programs of what we now would call urban redevelopment and public health. By the end of the Revolution, he had become the most important Quaker in New England.

Yet this man in whom were mirrored so many of the dominant themes of American history became, as well, a pioneer in the development of American manufacturing. Brown sponsored the work of Samuel Slater, who laid the foundation of the domestic textile industry. He carried on a wide range of business activities, seeking profit, but only as capital for humanitarian purposes.

Brown narrowly missed being a great man. His change of heart on the eve of the American Revolution blunted his ambition for worldly power and diverted him from the political issues of his time. He was, however, a good man, and Dr. Mack Thompson, chairman of the division of humanities at the University of California, Riverside, writes with rare fluency and form of Moses Brown's attempts to find the balance between meetinghouse and countinghouse for which Americans are still searching.

The Institute of Early American History and Culture is sponsored jointly by the College of William and Mary and Colonial Williamsburg, Incorporated. Publication of this book has been assisted by a grant from the Lilly Endowment, Inc.

MOSES BROWN